11/24/85

T. W. Phillips Memorial Library.

In memory of "Old Bethany" in whom all "disciples" share a common inseparable heritage.

J. E. Choate

36.6092
726c

DISCARDED

THE CHRISTIAN SCHOLAR:

A Biography of Hall Laurie Calhoun
Protege of John William McGarvey

Adron Doran
and
J. E. Choate

Gospel Advocate Company
Nashville, Tennessee 1985

DEDICATION

To Mignon McClain Doran and Marie Jones Choate, our beloved wives, to express our appreciation for their constant devotion, loyalty, and support in mutual pursuit of our ideals and goals for most of the days of our years.

THE CHRISTIAN SCHOLAR
Copyrighted © 1985 by Gospel Advocate Co.

All rights reserved. No part of this publication may be reproduced, stored in a retrieval system, or transmitted in any form or by any means without the prior permission of the publisher.

Published by Gospel Advocate Co.
P. O. Box 150, Nashville, TN 37202

ISBN 0-89225-279-0

Contents

	Acknowledgment	5
	Foreword	9
	Introduction	19
1.	The American Calhouns	23
2.	Heritage and Education of Hall Laurie Calhoun	33
3.	The Progress of a Preacher	47
4.	Georgia Robertson Christian College	61
5.	The Halls of Ivy	75
6.	From Professor to President	87
7.	A Firestorm in the Bluegrass	103
8.	On Campbell's Mountain	123
9.	Back Home in Tennessee	137
10.	The Crowning Years	159
11.	The Aftermath	175
12.	The Full Turn of the Circle	193
	Epilogue	211
	Endnotes	223
	Bibliography	237
	Index	241

Acknowledgment

HISTORIANS are rarely afforded the opportunity to open the pages of history to the hidden events of an age which emerge suddenly from the shadows of conflicting opinions and nebulous facts that extend back no further than recalled memories of yesterdays. The greatest temptation a historian faces is to arrange and force the facts of the past to correpond to his own personal opinions and prejudices calculated to make history and not simply to record history. Such a person will hardly be pardoned for all his lamentations for this failure at a later date.

This book, in a totally surprising manner, materialized from the research begun by Adron Doran while preparing a lecture on Hall Laurie Calhoun for the 1981 Freed-Hardeman College lectureship. I wish to acknowledge a personal indebtedness to Adron Doran for first recognizing this neglect of Hall Laurie Calhoun in Restoration history, and for his invitation to collaborate with him in researching and writing this volume to determine, in some measure, the rightful place and role of Calhoun in the history of the Restoration movement. Our personal acquaintance goes back some forty-five years. He arranged for my first gospel meeting, and my first preaching appointment with the Knob Creek church of Christ in Graves County. He served as principal of Wingo High School while I was a member of the faculty.

We were both born in Graves County, Kentucky, across the state line from Henry County, Tennessee, about thirty miles from Conyersville, the birthplace of Hall Laurie Calhoun. This region, its people, schools, and churches are a part of our common heritage. Doran's ancestors moved from North Carolina to Henry County in the early 1800's. Doran is one of a diminishing group of people who knew and personally worked with Calhoun. Doran's research in Restoration history has largely centered in Lexington and the Central Kentucky area where the Restoration movement began. My research interests have mainly centered in Tennessee between Nashville and Henderson. We have labored for four arduous years in putting this book together. We have had free access to the archives of the Lexington Theological Seminary, Transylvania University, Bethany College, Freed-Hardeman College, David Lipscomb College, and the Disciples of Christ Historical Society. Our travels have carried us from the July 1981 meeting of the North American Christian Convention in Kansas City, Missouri, to Bethany College in West Virginia.

A great many people know of the distinguished career of Adron Doran and his wife, Mignon Doran, and a great many do not. He is a 1930 alumnus of Freed-Hardeman College and has preached since 1928. He is President Emeritus of Morehead State University where he served for 23 years. In his long public service career, Doran has served on every level of public education in the state of Kentucky. He was elected to the Kentucky House of Representatives for four consecutive terms, and served one term as the Speaker of the House. His honors include the Kentuckian of the Year, the Horatio Alger Award, and the Outstanding Alumnus Award from the joint Alumni Council of Kentucky, and numerous other personal honors.

Mrs. Doran is the equal of her husband serving in positions of high honor in both public and Christian service. She is the founder and director of the Personal Development Institute at Morehead State University, and past president of the Kentucky Federation of Women's Clubs. Throughout the years, Mrs. Doran has conducted workshops for church women in personal Christian development. She has been a never failing presence and support by the side of her husband through the years. We cannot think of one without thinking of the other.

The church of Christ has always been put first in the long and distinguished careers of the Dorans, and continues to be as they advance in years. When they went to Morehead to head up Morehead State University, no church of Christ existed in that city; however, they were instrumental in shortly establishing a church there which thrives today. And today the Dorans are devoting their energies and time in never ending church work and related activities.

And I pay special tribute to the wife of my youth, mother of our children, Jerry and Teresa, for the unfailing and the unflagging support she has given to me and our children, and to Jerry's wife, Dr. Joyce Choate, distinguished author and professor in Northeast Louisiana University, as we have earned eleven college and university degrees including two doctorate degrees, four M.A. degees, and one B.D. degree.

Marie is the daughter of the late Mr. and Mrs. J. S. Jones. Her father was a well-known evangelist of the church of Christ where Kentucky, Tennessee, and Arkansas meet the Mississippi River. And to them and to my deceased mother, Mrs. Emily Margaret Creed Choate, who once described Marie as having more common sense and good judgment than the rest of us put together, I owe to them the substance, quality, and the joys of my days and years. And I am thankful that I have this place and time in my life to say these things.

J.E.C.

5/1/85

Foreword

THIS BOOK proposes to chronicle the life of Hall Laurie Calhoun (1863–1935). No other leader in the Restoration movement was positioned in so many different relationships to the Restoration church. He lived and labored during one of the most significant periods in American Restoration history. Calhoun appeared on the scene when the church was striving to identify itself. It is no easy matter to understand and present Calhoun in his true light. Pomp and circumstance often cloud his real personality. He was one of the most highly educated religious leaders of his day. He shared the most meaningful experiences which both the conservative and liberal elements of the Christian Church had to offer during his heyday. Calhoun was, likewise, hailed and raised to positions of high honor and great prestige in the church of Christ. He is the only man to have labored with such great success with all three of the religious groups which trace their roots back to the eighteenth century Restoration movement. He exerted a far greater influence on each than time will ever be able to record.

The genesis of the Restoration movement is traced back to the late eighteenth century. The story is often related that James O'Kelly generated the largest of the independent Christian movements about 1794 in North Carolina and Virginia. The Restoration movement was a phenomenon indigenous to the American frontier which produced the peculiar "Christian Church." The sole intent of the movement was to create a singular church patterned after the model of the first century church through a reliance of a strict and literal interpretation of the New Testament. The grand design called for a return to the Jerusalem church and the reestablishment of the church. The restorers did not envision a "by pass" of the established protestant denominations to create another sectarian church. The sole intent was to bring about a universal unity in Christendom.

The stirrings of the religious ideal was not a shared enterprise. Independent movements spontaneously emerged in New England, in Virginia and North Carolina, and in Kentucky. One such group centered in the evangelism of Elias Smith (1796) and Abner Jones (1772–1841) in New England. Whatever the religious "stirrings" on the frontier meant, one singular fact established itself. It acclaimed the freedom of the individual to accept the gospel, to read and interpret the New Testament for himself, and to set himself free from sectarian theology and ecclesiastical machinery.

James O'Kelly (1735–1826) of North Carolina who broke with the Methodist church, is credited with the adoption of the name "Christian Church" and declaring the Bible would be their only guide. He is also credited with devising five cardinal principles of the Christian Church: (1) there should be equality among all preachers; (2) there should be no bishops, superintendents, and presiding elders; (3) ministers and lay people alike were to enjoy the fullest liberty in interpreting the Scripture; (4) the principle of a congregational independence was to be applied; (5) conferences would be advisory and every church would "call its own pastor and enjoy the greatest freedom."

Church historians discovered the origin of the Christian Church in the frontier region of Kentucky at Cane Ridge, in Burbon County, Kentucky. The climax of the sensational frontier camp meetings happened in Cane Ridge, Kentucky, east of Lexington where Barton W. Stone was preaching. The Cane Ridge Camp meeting came to a full head on August 7–12, 1801, when a crowd numbering some thirty thousand came together in one place. Every frontier personality was represented. Although Presbyterians sponsored the meeting, Baptist and Methodist preachers mounted their stumps and preached God's love for sinners. Only in the loosest sense may the beginnings of the Restoration movement find its starting in the Cane Ridge revival. One truth forces itself that the revival was a remarkable story of Christian unity "for denominational loyalties melted in the heart of the revival." Any attempt to describe this sensational frontier happening would beggar at the feet of the contemporary narrators and the creators of frontier literature who witnessed and chronicled first hand this indescribable outpouring of ecstatic and unrestrained religious fervor on the Kentucky frontier.

The genius of the Restoration movement is shared between Barton W. Stone, Thomas Campbell, and Alexander Campbell. Their individual contributions to the movement were unique. And the joining of their shared religious beliefs and their respective followers insured the success of the emerging "Christian Church" unlike any protestant church after Martin Luther. There is lacking a common knowledge as to the identity of the Christian Church, the Disciples of Christ, and the Church of Christ on the contemporary scene. But they are in evidence across this broad nation, from the frozen wastes of the northern hemisphere, to the equatorial regions of Africa, across Europe and into Asia, and among the people "down under." History shows the early "restorers" did many things right; and history, likewise, sadly records that the "Christians" caused two major divisions in their ranks in 1906 and 1968, and are now separated into three distinct major fellowships and numerous other related splinter groups.

The subject of this biography was born in Conyersville, Tennessee, during the days of the War Between the States and grew to the age of accountability during the Reconstruction Period in the South. Though the immediate community had been kept free from the ravages of battles, his family found itself in the throes of an economic struggle in the post-Civil War period. Furthermore, the Calhouns were also faced about this time with critical decisions regarding their spiritual welfare.

The post war period was marked by bitter religious controversy and division. Denominationalism had established a secure foothold in West Tennessee as the frontier of civilization moved westward from the seaboard states of North Carolina and Virginia. In the early 1870's, the Calhouns were persuaded to leave the community Methodist Church and to accept the gospel as preached by such men as David Lipscomb and James A. Harding. The oldest daughter, Mattie, had married W. T. Shelton, a preacher identified with the Restoration movement in Kentucky and Tennessee. Under the preaching of Shelton, the parents made the decision to be baptized and to affiliate with the Blood River church of Christ.

At the age of fourteen, while enrolled as a student in the Mayfield (Kentucky) Seminary, young Calhoun was baptized into Christ, a decision he said he "never regretted." He pursued his quest for learning in the most reputable institutions of the country which ultimately culminated in his receiving an earned doctor's degree from the Harvard School of Divinity. Calhoun distinguished himself as a student, teacher, preacher, and administrator for nearly fifty years. He was associated with Georgia Robertson Christian College, the College of the Bible, Bethany College, Freed-Hardeman College, and David Lipscomb College.

Many doors of opportunity opened and many closed to him as a preacher during his chequered career. He experienced phenomenal success as an evangelist from the time that he graduated from Kentucky University in 1892. David Lipscomb and James A. Harding endeavored to persuade Calhoun to withdraw himself from the fellowship of those churches which practiced the use of instrumental music and affiliated with the American Christian Missionary Society. Instead of agreeing to the proposition and accepting a faculty appointment in the Nashville Bible School, he maintained fellowship with the "organ churches" and joined the faculty of the College of the Bible under John W. McGarvey and I. B. Grubbs.

Calhoun was assured that he would become the heir apparent to the presidency of the College of the Bible at the end of McGarvey's tenure. His growth and development within the hierarchy of the Christian Church indicated that he would stand high among its leaders. However, because of extenuating circumstances, the mantle of McGarvey was not to fall upon Calhoun. The pendulum had begun to swing away from the conservatism of the McGarvey era to that of a new liberalism brought to the College of the Bible by President R. H. Crossfield and his faculty appointees following McGarvey's death in 1911.

Calhoun as dean of the College eventually brought charges before the Board of Trustees against Crossfield and his faculty appointees for supporting and teaching destructive criticism in the college classrooms. The Board conducted the famous series of hearings in May 1917, which were referred to by W. C. Bower and other adversaries as the "heresy trial." The fight which suddenly erupted in the College of the Bible in 1917 was the first major "show down" fight among the Disciples. The Disciples had disputed continuously almost from the beginning of the Restoration movement over points of doctrine and practice. Even the separation of the church of Christ in 1906 was accomplished without fanfare, and was actually instigated by S. D. N. North, the Director of the United States Religious Census, who was unable to determine the dividing lines of fellowship separating Disciples.

The controversy in the College of the Bible in 1917 broke out over the teaching of the liberal theology of higher criticism in the college which had been dubbed by John W. McGarvey as "destructive criticism." He led a caustic and relentless attack on the tenets of modernistic theology for the last eighteen years of his life through his special department, "Biblical Criticism," featured in the *Christian Standard*.

Hall Laurie Calhoun did not instigate the "Battle of the Book" that shook the entire Christian Church fellowship through the spring and summer of 1917. However, he was the principal figure in leading the attack against the liberal incumbents in the College of the Bible. This was mainly accomplished through the pages of the *Christian Standard*. Calhoun's allies were the strongest and the most highly respected leaders in the Christian Church. Their primary objective was to save and retrieve the College of the Bible from the destructive critics. Calhoun was their chosen champion, and he was eminently qualified for the role. He was the acknowledged protege and successor of McGarvey, and his avowed mission was to keep the College of the Bible true to the Book.

The Board finally exonerated President Crossfield and the faculty members from the charges, and this resulted in Calhoun's resigning the deanship of the college. However, the summer fight in 1917 on the "Lexington Green" proved to be only the first skirmish between the conservatives and liberals. There would be long and bitter battles ahead which continued for more than sixty years, long after Calhoun departed the Christian Church. The final blow was struck in 1971 when the *Yearbook* of American Churches recognized the emergent separate identities of the (Independent) Christian Church and the opposing separate fellowship of a self-acclaimed denomination, the Disciples of Christ.

In the fall of 1917, Calhoun went to Bethany College as a member of the faculty in the Graduate School. Calhoun remained at Bethany College and preached for the Christian Church until June 1925. With the assistance of N. B. Hardeman, F. W. Smith, and M. C. Kurfees, he departed the Christian Church acknowledging the error of his way which had been pointed out to him by David Lipscomb and James A. Harding thirty years before. He reached the understanding that he believed instrumental music and the missionary society were wrong in doctrine and practice which led to disturbance and division in the church. He decided to resign his teaching position at Bethany College and to notify the Christian Churches for which he was preaching that he would no longer be available for appointments. Whereas, he had defended the use of instruments in worship as aids and the missionary society as an expedient, he then renounced both in the stongest of terms. Calhoun said that evolution and "destructive criticism" were trying to destroy Christianity, and that instrumental music and the missionary societies were divisive and trying to corrupt the church.

In the fall of 1925, Calhoun became Associate President of Freed-Hardeman College and the full-time minister of the church of Christ congregation in Henderson, Tennessee. One year later, he moved his family to Nashville, Tennessee, where he suffered a complete physical and emotional breakdown in the spring of 1926 which continued through the summer months. He later recovered from his illness and spent the latter months of 1926 as minister of the Belmont church of Christ and for a period of time thereafter. By 1928, his usual good health was restored. Calhoun eventually became the full-time pulpit and radio minister for the thriving Central church of Christ in downtown Nashville. Calhoun was among the first pioneer radio evangelists and commanded a vast and appreciative audience over the powerful WLAC radio station. He continued in this capacity until his death September 4, 1935. His funeral service was conducted in the War Memorial Auditorium in Tennessee's capital city which drew the largest crowd that had ever attended a funeral in Nashville. Calhoun was buried in the Woodlawn Memorial Park. His beloved Mary Ettah died on October 30, 1953, and was laid to rest beside the physical remains of her loyal and devoted husband.

This book presents a long and significant chapter in Restoration history in the years between 1888 and 1935 which best explains the two major divisions of the Christian Church in this century. This assertion is made because the role of Hall Laurie Calhoun has been largely ignored or denigrated in the accounts of Restoraton historians. This calculated neglect tends to obscure the disruptive forces which troubled and rent the church of the Restoration twice in a time span of sixty years. And this error of omission becomes flagrantly obvious when the presence and influence of Hall Laurie Calhoun's niche in Restoration history is ignored. He never sought the limelight though his person, genius, and presence merited such a superlative recognition. Calhoun has been hidden behind the veil, but he will not remain in the limbo of a non-entity where both friend and foe seemed to have consigned him for undisclosed reasons.

It is almost impossible to weigh the influence which Calhoun had on the direction in which the conservative wing of the Christian Church would go. It is equally difficult to determine the role which he played in isolating the liberal element of the Disciples and forcing them into denominationalism. Furthermore, it is very difficult to appraise the effect which he had on the churches of Christ while he was still preaching for "organ churches," and after he renounced his affiliation with the "instrumental group of the Christian Church."

The role that Calhoun performed in the Restoration movement has been either reduced or ignored altogether by church historians who could have been better informed had they chosen to be. The recounting of Restoration history in this age must take into account the presence and influence of Calhoun on the course of the history of the Christian Church and the Disciples of Christ. This will tend to clarify facts which have clouded the life and influence of Calhoun and concealed the looming presence and influence of Calhoun in Disciple history. In all fairness, there is no evidence that Restoration historians have intentionally done this.

Calhoun has been the subject of one non-complimentary master's thesis in the Lexington Theological Seminary. One doctoral dissertation is now in an advanced stage of research in Harvard University. Numerous articles and books address Calhoun; however, none award him proper recognition to which he is entitled by all academic standards and church leadership; and history will not favorably record the fact that Hall Laurie Calhoun has been relegated to obscurity. The persons who have done so, and seemingly for personal reasons, will likely in turn be censured for this calculated design to reduce the great stature of Calhoun.

And heretofore all attempts to research the life and times of Hall Laurie Calhoun have ended in impasses because the paucity of information has not encouraged the researcher's pursuit. The writers acknowledge their debt to Margaret Lee Seely and Dorothea Eloise Elder, for their consent and encouragement of us to handle aright the facts of their father's life and works. One of the daughters reflected that "we have been reluctant to revive painful memories long since forgotten." We are indebted to his grandson, Hall Calhoun Crowder, who made available all of the personal papers and memoirs of Hall Laurie Calhoun. We express particular appreciation to another grandson, Orvel Calhoun Crowder, longtime faculty member in Milligan College and now the Chaplain of Phillips University, for his personal contributions and memoirs which provide a personal perspective of Calhoun.

Many individuals have aided and lent encouragement to the writers of this biography. Notably among them are David McQuiddy, Jr., President of the McQuiddy Printing Company, who was the first to listen to our proposal and committed himself to publishing the book; Guy N. Woods, Editor of the *Gospel Advocate,* who has brought the subject to the readers of the *Gospel Advocate;* Neal Anderson, President of the Gospel Advocate Company, who has managed the details for publishing the work; Don Humphey, Vice President of the Gospel Advocate Company who has guided the publication of this book from the art format to final publication; Basil Overton who has published a number of articles we have written regarding the subject in the *World Evangelist;* President Willard Collins, David Lipscomb College; and President E. Claude Gardner, Freed-Hardeman College, who have made available the resources of their staffs and libraries; David McWhirter, Curator of the Disciples of Christ Historical Society and Roscoe Pearson, Librarian of the Lexington Theological Library who have given invaluable assistance in locating original source material.

We also express appreciation to those whom we have contacted at Bethany College and Transylvania University for their intrinsic assistance in locating materials which have proved necessary to us.

We commend this biography of one of the most private individuals and complex personalities connected with the efforts to win the "Battle of the Book" against the trappings of those who would destroy and corrupt to those who desire a more thorough study and insight into the goings on during the first quarter of the twentieth century.

We have set forth our personal appraisal of Hall Laurie Calhoun in this biography, and we urge the reader to do the same in an effort to form his own judgment as we have presented them.

The *Christian Scholar* is not meant "to grind the axe from a different direction," though it may very well prove to do so in some places.

The authors assume errors of fact, and judgment may have crept into the study, but not by design. We have endeavored to present Dr. Hall Laurie Calhoun and his deeds in a fair and unbiased manner. We are not able to see him as he was in his lifetime, but we have tried to see him as he is reflected in what he said and did. His deeds and influence persist to the present day and will follow him to the judgment. We can say concerning him that "He being dead yet speaketh." May this book prove profitable to the readers, and bring a measure of glory to God.

Introduction

BIOGRAPHICAL WRITING and reading require much on the part of those who prepare it and those who perceive it. The writers must collect the details of another's life by retracing paths long since forgotten—save to a cherished few, recreating for themselves and others the longings, hopes, dreams, ambitions, failures, successes, and strivings which combine into the making of any life. Out of the tracing of long since completed hopes and dreams, long forgotten accomplishments, often unrecognized turning points in a life, the writers must catch the essence of the life, reduce it to manageable proportions and weave these strands into the imagery and beauty—and where present the tragedy—which was the life being etched. The individual whose life by such imagery is being retold may not himself have been fully conscious of the totality of events which shaped his destiny and may even at best have only palely understood what it was that he was struggling for and what he ultimately left behind. The later researcher, with determination, with occasionally rude, frequently overly zealous persistence, but with a frequent tear and sigh must delve into not only the events but the forces, both known and latent, which were involved and were simultaneously shaping and limiting the effort and the achievement. These must be gathered, analyzed, and rewoven in miniature so that through the webs and skeins of type the person is made to live, to move, to achieve again.

For the reader there is the requisite effort to open his eyes and heart, with due regard for both acceptance and rejection, to the combination of varying proportions of research and romance with which the writers practice their craft. Not too sympathetic, not too resistant, but with a willingness to be caused to see, to understand, to wonder, to love, even perhaps to hate, he must follow the lines crafted by the writer and through them he must allow the person to emerge in increasing fulness as the gossamer words flow from page to heart.

By means of this process of combining the moods and moves embedded in the prism of the past events with the heart and hand of the writer and the eyes and soul of the reader there comes into being pleasant to thrilling moments of enjoyment and learning. Unfamiliar places, names, events come into new-found awareness. By the magic of the written page there comes more and more into focus in the heart of the reader another person from an earlier but strangely present time. Line by line the story unfolds, the character comes to the center of the mental stage, the mists of the years fade away and one becomes not just a reader; instead he an observer, an interpreter, even a friend—wishing on occasion to sound a caution, to pose a question, to offer encouragement, etc. The work consequently takes on the nature of an encounter with the principal person of the history as it now becomes a not-visible though not unreal drama which casts its imaginative spell upon the reader. The chronicle, now become a bewitching story, moves ever more rapidly to its conclusion. Too soon the story is ended, the drama closes, the spell is broken and the reader, now informed but also deeply touched, moves into his coming night, better for being thus led, wiser perhaps, but also aware that so it is with others and himself; there are hopes one will never achieve, each leaving its sadness; there are victories won, each leaving its exultation; and there is the inevitable leaving of the stage and the closing of the curtain with the observers moving away with their own thoughts and longings.

So it is with all well written biographies . . . so it is indeed with this biography now held in your hand.

This biography may be read on a series of levels or with a series of insights. It may be seen as an indication of one man's genuine achievement—a poor young man rises to achieve the highest of academic training and serves in most influential educational roles. It may be read as a microcosm of the problems faced by many in the turbulent years in the first decades of this century in the restoration movement—the ties of love and relationship were being strained by differing beliefs and practices which could or would not be resolved and had to work their way to whatever conclusion would result. It may be read as a foreshadowing of broad movements which were to emerge out of the swirling, shifting tides which surrounded not only Hall L. Calhoun but many, many others—the forces which produced the shifts and changes in his career were not so much directed at him as they were the context in which he served; their impact was much larger than whatever they produced in him and went on to carry not only individuals but large groups to disagreement, separation, and even estrangement.

At whatever level one reads and reflects on the book, it will be informative about both the man and the movement. One would, as this writer sees it, overstate the case to see Calhoun as causative of the various changes which followed his experiences of 1917, but it is the case that he reflected in his personal experience much of that which culminated in his removal from the College of the Bible and subsequently moved others to a division between the Disciples of Christ and the Independent Christian Churches which still obtains.

The involvement of Calhoun in the internal, embryonic struggle which was eventually to result in the division noted above and his later acceptance and ministry within churches of Christ make Calhoun, as a man and as participant, a figure of significance, one deserving of careful study for insights and understandings of continuing importance.

The writers have portrayed the life and conflicts of the man. They have anticipated and summarized some of the results of the forces at work in his career. In so doing they have produced an interesting, informative and significant biography.

William Woodson
January 10, 1985

Hall Laurie Calhoun

1

The American Calhouns

The American Calhouns are descendants of a distinguished family of Scotland listed among the British aristocracy. The Calhoun family emerged in the late thirteenth century through Umfridus (Humphrey) De Kilpatrick, a Norman knight. Humphrey acquired 1265 acres of the lands of Culchone (Colquhoun) from Maldowin, Earl of Lennox, as a reward for serving in the army of Alexander II of Scotland. Humphrey adopted the name of the lands which he received for his surname which became the ancestral name of his descendants—the Calhouns.

During a period of three-hundred and forty years, the Colquhouns prospered and multiplied. Sir John Colquhoun of Luss received in 1604, from King James I of England (who had reigned as King James VI of Scotland), a land grant of one thousand acres in the North Ireland country of Donegal about twenty miles from Londonderry. Sir John Colquhoun gave the land to a younger son, Robert, who lived on the land and became the forefather of the Donegal Calhouns.[1]

About one-hundred and fifty years later, in 1770, three brothers of the Donegal Calhouns, Patrick, John, and James seeking fame and fortune, migrated to America going first to Philadelphia, Pennsylvania. One of the brothers, John, moved to North Carolina, and the other two settled in western Pennsylvania. In time, the Calhouns of Pennsylvania and North Carolina grew into a large family clan. Many of them were doctors, lawyers, preachers, teachers, businessmen, and farmers. The Calhouns moved with the advancing American frontier, distinguishing themselves in the communities where they settled.[2]

The immediate ancestry of Hall Laurie Calhoun emerges near the close of the eighteenth century. John Samuel Calhoun and Nancy Seely Calhoun, great grandparents of our Hall Laurie, moved from Mecklenburg, North Carolina, and settled in Middle Tennessee shortly before 1800. John Samuel and Nancy Calhoun's children were named John, Thomas, James, Samuel Hanna, Jane and Mary. The son of John Samuel and Nancy, whose name was John, was born August 6, 1779, perhaps in North Carolina. This John Calhoun married a girl in Middle Tennessee whose surname was Shelton. Their children's names were James C., Abagail, and John Shelton. John Shelton Calhoun, who wore his mother's maiden name, became the father of Hall Laurie, the subject of this biography. John Shelton was born September 27, 1819, in Wilson County, Tennessee, near Lebanon.[3]

John Shelton Calhoun married Martha Louisa Hall. Martha Louisa Hall was born February 10, 1827, in Davidson County, Tennessee. Soon after her birth, her father, John Hall, Esq., moved to Wilson County, Tennessee, where the Calhouns and Halls became devoted neighbors. Martha Louisa's childhood was spent in her family home on the banks of the Stone River, five miles from Lebanon.[4] Esquire Hall was of Welch ancestry. He was a man of unflinching courage. Legend has it that John Hall was a liquor distiller in his younger days. And the story is told that once he won a horse in a contest known as a hammer throw. John Hall joined the Cumberland Presbyterian Church a few years after his marriage, and later became a Presbyterian elder.[5]

The mother of Martha Louisa Hall was Temperance Perry, who was the daughter of Burrill and Esther Perry. The Perrys were of English extraction. Burrill and Esther were the parents of five daughters and two sons. One of their daughters, Temperance Perry, married John Hall. John and Temperance Hall were the parents of one son and four daughters. One of their daughters, Martha Louisa, was the wife of John Shelton Calhoun. They were married September 30, 1847, in Wilson County, Tennessee.[6] They probably moved from Wilson County to Henry County shortly after their marriage because the Henry County Deed Book 2, page 19, shows that John Shelton Calhoun bought two-hundred and eighty-five acres of land from John Craig for $750 on May 27, 1848. The land was located two and one-half miles east of Conyersville, Tennessee, in Civil District 14.

Conyersville, located in the northwest part of Henry County in West Tennessee, was established in 1846 on a land site belonging to Pack Conyer, and soon became a flourishing village with about eight stores. The little town was much like the settlements of that period which stretched across the American frontier. Conyersville soon developed into an important trading post. The village was a stopping place for the stage coach traveling between Paris, Tennessee, and Murray, Kentucky. An academy with an excellent reputation, was established in Conyersville about 1850. However, only a small Methodist church and a well kept graveyard remain at the site of the old village today.

The community was isolated from the ravages of the Civil War, though a battle was fought at Fort Henry on the Tennessee River about fifty miles away. Hard times set in which marked the post war period. Conyersville lost its identity in the early 1890's when the Louisville and Nashville Railroad was built connecting Paris, Tennessee, and Paducah, Kentucky. The railroad was built to pass through Puryear, Tennessee, two miles west of Conyersville displacing Conyersville as a trading center. Puryear remains today the center of a fertile agricultural section of the county.[7]

The story of the family of John Shelton and Martha Louisa Calhoun and their children is told in isolated statements and in short biographical poems written by Hall Laurie. John Shelton stood six feet tall with black hair and steel blue eyes during the prime of manhood. He was a man of his word which was marked by his concern for truth and justice. John Shelton was kind and trusted by his neighbors whom he served in the Conyersville community as a justice of the peace for many years. He was a familiar figure as he rode his favorite horse along the countryside.[8]

His wife, Martha Louisa, was loved by her family and admired by her neighbors. Martha Louisa was affectionately remembered by H. A. "Gus" Brown, a neighborhood boy who was a few years younger than her son Hall Laurie. Brown was a student with Hall Laurie in the College of the Bible. He preached the funeral sermon of Martha Louisa Calhoun. Brown remembered her as a kind neighbor who was completely devoted to her family. By her habits of industry, economy, and perseverance, she instilled in her family those traits of character that make noble men and women. She read widely on many subjects and was a close student of the Bible.

The years were fruitful that John Shelton and Martha Lousia Calhoun lived on their farm east of Conyersville and were filled with happiness while they were rearing their children. John Shelton prospered. Their land lay on the banks of Blood River (a large creek) that empties into the Tennessee River. In later years, John Shelton owned and operated a general store in Conyersville. The family built and lived in a comfortable farm house. Their home was a welcomed stopping place for visiting preachers who had appointments in the community, notably among whom were James A. Harding and John R. Williams.[9]

The children of John Shelton and Martha Louisa were: John Hall, who was born October 5, 1848 and died in infancy; Martha L. (Mattie) and Agnes T. who were older than the sons; James Caldwell was born January 2, 1858; Hall Laurie was born December 11, 1863; and the last child, Pleasant Hope was born in 1865 and was nicknamed "Pleaz." Pleaz died in his early boyhood. Agnes was born in 1850 and died in 1928 and was buried in Martin, Tennessee. Mattie and her husband, W. T. Shelton, moved to Fresno, California, around 1880 after Shelton developed a throat problem. They both died in Fresno and were buried there.[10]

Little is known about some of the children of John Shelton Calhoun and his wife during their childhood years. Hall Laurie remembered his older brother, James, with deep affection and wrote in later years that all who knew him in the community said he was the best young man in the neighborhood. W. T. Shelton, his brother-in-law, wrote at the time of the death of James that he was remarkable for unswerving honesty and integrity from childhood. He was graduated from the Ecclectic School of Medicine in Cincinnati, Ohio, in 1884. Dr. A. B. Shelton under whom he read medicine and practiced one year said of him: "If he lives, he will soon be among the very best doctors of the land." Dr. James Calhoun died in Conyersville during a typhoid epidemic that claimed many lives in West Tennessee. He had practiced medicine less than two years. His death was a great blow to the family.[11]

Hall Laurie Calhoun was born, as he said, in Spout Hollow, the location of his father's farm on Blood River. He was named for his maternal grandfather and a Dr. Laurie, the physician who delivered him. Hall relates his mother's story that he suffered what was known as the three month's colic and cried a lot. His mother called him "Hallie," the other children called him "Bawlie." Hall was a lively boy who demanded and received the attention he desired.[12]

At fourteen years of age, Hall was sturdily built with gray-green eyes and jet black hair. His voice was pleasant and sweet in song. Hall was hot tempered but equally tenderhearted. He could excel all of his playmates and was a leader in all of their activities. Hall knew where the wild grapes grew and the sweetest apples could be found. At age fourteen, he whipped a "wild and wooly" seventeen-year-old bully in a fair fist fight. Not everybody loved Hall. Some said one day he would be hanged as they dodged his fists and were stung by his tongue.

Young Hall stood five feet and eight inches tall and weighed one-hundred and forty pounds. He was a leader in every class in all of the schools he attended. Hall described himself as truthful and energetic with a clever brain that saw things "pretty true." He was reared to respect the dignity of the family name. He was loyal to his friends and fair to his foes. He stood firm in his convictions and was deeply religious from early boyhood.[13]

The early settlers of West Tennessee brought with them that mode of "worship in the woods" known as the "camp meetings." The great revival which climaxed in 1801 at Concord and Cane Ridge, Kentucky, swept the Central South. Later campgrounds, usually built by the Methodist or Cumberland Presbyterians, dotted the countryside of the entire region, and continued to do so throughout the nineteenth century. One of the most prominent was Manley's Campground in Henry County, Tennessee. The camp meetings and the religious fervor which characterized them continued on a smaller scale in the form of revivals (protracted meetings) as the region was settled and stabilized by organized schools and churches. This was the kind of religious setting into which Hall Laurie Calhoun was born. The religious extravagances that marked the great "Western Revival" in 1801 were still the order of the summer revivals lasting well into the twentieth century.[14]

"Campbellite" preachers, as many people nicknamed Christian evangelists, went into every community of West Tennessee. The controversial preachers were militant proclaimers of the Word condemning the sectarian practices of all denominations. They were generally unpopular with sectarian preachers; however, they were respected in the communities. The "Campbellites" were opposed because of their theology, but were accepted in the free American society of the frontier. It was not uncommon for the denominations to offer the "Campbellites" the use of their meeting houses for revivals in many instances.

The best insight into the earliest religious life of the family of John Shelton and Martha Louisa Calhoun was written by Hall Laurie in 1930 in the *Gospel Advocate*. He described the circumstances leading to the baptisms of members of the Calhoun family into the church of Christ. John Shelton and his wife were devout sectarian believers. Martha Louisa had been a Presbyterian since childhood and was taught to be deeply religious. A Methodist church was established in the early history of Conyersville. All indications are that the Calhoun family attended and were active members in the Conyersville Methodist Church due to the absence of a Presbyterian church in the community.

Hall tells that his mother taught him to say his prayers at her knees. His parents believed in "getting saved" at the "mourner's bench." On his twelfth birthday, his mother gave him a Bible. He promised her that he would not miss a day reading it. At this time, young Calhoun began to take a personal interest in the church as he understood it to be. He resolved to seek religion as his brother, James had done six years before.

When Hall Laurie was twelve years of age, a revival was in progress at the Conyersville Methodist Church in the early spring of 1875 during the time of planting field crops. On the very first night of the meeting, Hall went forward at the call for mourners, and he related what happened:

> The first night of the meeting, when a call for mourners was made, I was one of the first to go forward. Never in my life have I more sincerely desired to please God than I did then. I was doing exactly what my parents, brothers, sisters, and Sunday school teachers had taught me was the proper way to become a Christian.[15]

Despite his fervent prayers, Hall felt no change while others about him, seemed to have had a religious experience, and were shouting happily. Hall went home disappointed with his feelings. His father told the boy that he should return to the meeting for the daytime service the following day. Though it was a busy season on the farm, his father said he should go to the revival for that was a matter of greater importance. Hall submitted his life to God at the "mourner's bench" during the service that day. However, he was not satisfied with the way he felt since his religious experience was different from the one which he had been led to expect. He went home that day with one of his married sisters, (Agnes) after the service. She encouraged Hall to believe that he had been saved, and she told him his doubts were not unusual and would leave after a while.

During that summer and the winter months of 1875-76, he read the Bible earnestly seeking for an expression by someone who had said: "Here, Lord, I give myself to thee," and at that moment had experienced a mysterious feeling of salvation. The boy was disappointed that his search of the Bible proved to be fruitless:

> I had read the entire New Testament and much of the Old Testament, and some parts a number of times, and I was startled and disappointed that I had not found the promise that it seemed to me should have been so easy to find. I became greatly disturbed over my failure to find this promise.[16]

A year later in mid-June of 1876, Hall began to doubt that his sins were pardoned or ever had been. His brother, James, came home from medical school in Cincinnati to help with the farm work during the summer. Hall awaited the arrival of his beloved brother thinking that James could help him solve his problem. So on the very afternoon of his return, Hall and James were working in the cornfield. Hall told James about his anxieties and that he had been searching for almost a year to find a promise from God that he would save people in the way Hall thought he had been saved and he had failed in the search. He exacted of James the promise that he would not relate the conversation. The response of James startled the twelve-year-old boy. James said he also had something to tell Hall, and exacted the same promise from him. Hall was surprised to hear James say: "I cannot help you for I have been in the same condition . . . two weeks after I professed religion. I have tried all through the six years I have been in my profession to find where God would save me that way, and I cannot find it. I do not know whether I am saved or not."[17]

Hall Laurie was caught up in more serious doubt. He did not think well of the people whom he called "Campbellites." Hall had spent many hours with his mother searching the scriptures with which to refute the "Campbellites." His mother was a good Bible student, and denominational preachers often came to their home to talk with her on Bible subjects.

The following fall, a "Campbellite" preacher, W. T. Shelton, came to Conyersville and conducted a revival in the Methodist meeting house. Shelton had married Martha (Mattie) Calhoun,

Hall's sister, in 1874, and had converted her to the truth. Shelton was a well-known Christian minister who preached in Murray and Mayfield, Kentucky, and in Union City and Franklin, Tennessee. It was in the fall of 1876 that members of the Calhoun family attended the revival conducted by Shelton. Hall was left behind to take care of the home.

Hall was dumbfounded when the family returned from the meeting to hear that his mother had responded when the invitation was extended confessing her faith and requesting baptism. There was considerable excitement and conversation in the community over her decision. Some wondered how her husband would react. Hall described the careful preparation which his father had made to assist in the baptism of his wife. Hall said he stood with his father on the banks of Blood River and both had tears in their eyes because of the solemnity of the occasion. Hall experienced great difficulty in becoming reconciled to his mother's baptism.

Martha Louisa had little to say to the family about her decision to be baptized. Her family knew that only her profound belief in the Bible led her to do what she had done. Hall told his mother that she had gone against all that she had taught him, and he resolved that the "Campbellites would never get him." Soon after his mother's baptism, a letter came from James who had returned to school, saying he had united with the church of Christ in Cincinnati. Shortly afterwards, his sister, Agnes, took the same step.[18] Calhoun himself many years later bapitzed his grandsons, Orvel C. Crowder and Hall C. Crowder. Both became Christian Church preachers.

Hall recalled that his father said nothing about his mother's conversion, but he noticed that his father was reading his Bible more than he had ever seen him. John Shelton was a man of good education and a bright mind. He had been a teacher in Sunday school and a steward of the Methodist church where the family attended. Less than a year later in 1877, Hall saw his father baptized in Blood River into the church of Christ. Hall had not changed his mind, however, about the "Campbellites."

The nearest congregation of "Christians only" to the Calhoun home was the Blood River church of Christ located east of Conyersville. John Shelton and Martha Louisa placed their membership with the Blood River congregation and worshiped there. John Shelton and Martha Louisa moved with dispatch to establish a congregation in Conyersville. John R. Williams wrote an item for the *Gospel Advocate* thirteen years after the baptism of Martha Louisa: "From Paris, I came to Conyersville . . . where we have a good little congregation established mainly, I think, by brother James A. Harding. My home is with brother J. S. Calhoun, a home too, that makes one feel at home."[19]

John Shelton's baptism was in the fourteenth year of Hall Laurie's life. In the winter of that year, John Shelton and his wife went to Mayfield, Kentucky, to enroll Hall in the Mayfield Seminary, one of the best schools in the region. In the fall of 1878, Hall attended revival meetings in the Christian Church in Mayfield, and listened to the preacher deliver forty-two sermons. Hall then obeyed the gospel. He was in his sixteenth year. Hall Calhoun related this story in the *Gospel Advocate* in the sixty-seventh year of his life. He said he never afterwards doubted his salvation.[20]

John Shelton and Martha Louisa Calhoun continued to live on their farm for thirty years following the time of their marriage and reared their family during this quiet and happy period. They may have lived in Mayfield, Kentucky, during the winter months while Hall attended the Mayfield Seminary (1877–79). W. T. Shelton was probably preaching for the Christian Church there during those years.

The details of the education, the marriage, and the first preaching years of Hall Laurie Calhoun will be dealt with in another chapter. The immediate chapter is designed to conclude the end of the Conyersville years of the Calhoun family. Hall had moved back from Lexington to Henry County in 1893 to help look after his aging parents. He built a house across the road from his parents on a plot of ground purchased from a Mr. Littleton. Except for serving as principal for the Conyersville Academy (1893–94), his energies were given to evangelistic efforts. When he took up regular work as the minister with the Tenth Street Christian Church, Paducah, Kentucky, he commuted by train from Puryear, Tennessee, to Paducah. He maintained his Conyersville home.

Mary Ettah, the oldest daughter of Hall Laurie Calhoun, remembered her childhood days in Conyersville. On Sunday, the family would ride to church or to town in a horse-drawn double-seated surrey with "fringe around the top." Trips that Hall and his wife made were in a buggy drawn by a beautiful chestnut horse named "Ruby." John Shelton and Martha Louisa looked after matters around the place for their pleasure.[21] After Calhoun moved to Franklin, John Shelton and his wife agreed to break up housekeeping. They divided their time between living with Agnes in Martin, Tennessee, and their son in Franklin. A highlight in the experiences of the elderly couple in the last years of their life was a trip to visit their daughter Mattie who was living in Fresno, California, where her husband, W. T. Shelton was preaching. The end of Martha Louisa's life was drawing near after Calhoun moved away from Conyersville.

Martha Louisa died on October 5, 1899, and was buried in the Yellow Fever Cemetery in Martin, Tennessee, where she lived with her daughter, Agnes.[22] In the fall of 1878, yellow fever struck Martin, Tennessee, probably brought in by the railroad construction workers. There were four hundred cases among the town's seven hundred and ten residents. Fifty-two deaths resulted. They were buried in a special cemetery located away from the populated community. It was called the Yellow Fever Cemetery and bears the name to the present. Martha's tombstone epitaph reads: "Blessed are the dead who die in the Lord. For they rest from their labors and their works follow them." John Shelton, who had served as an elder in the Martin church of Christ, died on July 13, 1901, and was buried by the side of his beloved Martha Louisa. They had been married fifty-two years at the time of her death. The epitaph of John Shelton reads: "Let me die the death of the righteous and let my last end be like his.—Numbers 23:10."

Hall Laurie continued to live in Conyersville until 1897 when he moved to take up work with the Franklin, Tennessee, church. After Martha Louisa's death, John Shelton divided his time between Hall and Agnes since Mattie was living in Fresno, California. With the death of John Shelton in July of 1901, Hall moved from Tennessee to New Haven, Connecticut, for graduate study in the Yale Divinity School. He left one world to enter another world unlike anything that he had known. Hall Calhoun would not have been able, even in fantasies of imagination, to envision the courses and influence and impact of his life for more than thirty years.

2

Heritage and Education of Hall Laurie Calhoun

It is significant that John Shelton and Martha Louisa Calhoun followed the examples of their families and became members of the Cumberland Presbyterian Church. The Presbyterian immigrants were well-fitted to live in a free America and they easily adapted to the rigors of frontier life.[1] The American Scots and the Scotch-Presbyterian Church were dedicated to religious liberation as indeed had been the fiery reformer, John Knox. They were devoted to their families, churches, and schools. The Presbyterians settled on every trail that led into the West. They came to the new world from England, Scotland, and North Ireland. The Scot-Irish Presbyterians never founded a colony of their own and never enjoyed the privileges of a permanent establishment.[2] The Calhouns were counted among the best families of these early settlers.

The Scotch-Presbyterians gave whole-hearted support to the American Revolution. They produced a well-educated American leadership. The Presbyterians were among the first settlers in Kentucky and came in increasing numbers to Tennessee. They were the chief founders of the Transylvania Seminary (1783), in Lexington, Kentucky, the oldest college west of the Alleghenies. The Presbyterian clergy were the best educated and they organized educational institutions on every level of learning. The clergy established log cabin schools in the most primitive settings to teach the three "R's" and the advanced levels of higher education. The Presbyterians were not adverse to education, and ignorance was no qualification for any pursuit, least of all, to occupy the pulpit.

The schools which the Presbyterians established were "common schools" for all youth. They did more to bring education to the South and West than any other particular group. The early backwoods schools were called academies or seminaries. The advanced academies in the more highly developed frontier sections taught the Classical, Literary, and Mathematical subjects: Latin, Greek, algebra and Euclid. In the nineteenth century, the academies began to offer courses in English grammar, geography, ancient history, natural history, and material philosophy. The colleges of the nineteenth century were designed to train for living as well as to prepare for advanced schooling. Subjects were added later in rhetoric, *belles lettres,* modern languages (French and Italian), ethics, (natural philosophy), surveying, and navigation.[3]

The curricula of such schools and colleges in the nineteenth century established the tradition of a liberal arts education. Such schools were forerunners of high schools and normal colleges which came later. The normal schools were of a superior grade and designed to train elementary teachers for the "common schools."[4]

West Tennessee was settled chiefly by people who had moved from East and Middle Tennessee, and by Carolinians, Virginians, and Kentuckians. Unlike most of the frontier communities, the Western District of Tennessee was not settled by the rude barbarians who were constantly on the move westward. Most settlers came from older permanent districts associated with organized churches which provided strong moral training. The number of immigrants who came into Tennessee from the North was negligible. A class of settlers of considerable size consisted of "squatters." The "manless" land beckoned the "landless" man. Some who were shiftless and uncouth were found in many areas of the frontier. Many men and women were of worth and dignity whose only handicap was penury. These, however, prospered and remained with their families forming the stable middle class, the "golden mean" of the early American society. Indeed there was more than a trace of the aristocratic element on the frontier and a few of them sought by mode of life a pretention to justify such a claim. The Scot, Irish, and English settlers brought with them age-old folk wisdom, customs, and religion, and their children reflected the ideals, values, and mores of their parents.[5] No better description could be given to explain the persons of John Shelton and Martha Louisa Calhoun.

Free schools supported by public funds did not exist in the period of the early pioneers. The first schools were known as subscription schools. The teachers were paid directly by the pupils or by the parents or guardians. As soon as the villages were formed and with a sufficient population to sustain them, academies were organized. The academies were well patronized by the supporting families. There were adequate schools to provide for the education of the white masses and few schools, if any, existed for the black people.[6] Some of the blacks were taught by the children of the Freeholders.

The education of Hall Laurie Calhoun in his early school days was in such a setting. The Conyersville Male and Female Academy provided his earliest academic training. The Conyersville Academy was organized in 1850 or a little earlier. Such semi-public academies were the chief organized centers for education prior to the Civil War. A news item reads in part from the *Paris Tennessee Republic* dated August 11, 1854:

> Conyersville Male and Female Academy
> The undersigned trustees of the above institution take great pleasure in announcing to parents and guardians that they have procured the services of Mr. E. L. Scruggs, his daughter, Miss Harriet Scruggs, an Mill M. Coulter, all renowned for their skill and ability in conducting a school. The session will commence on Monday, September 18, 1854.[7]

Rural communities took great pride in having the best possible schools they could afford. The Calhouns of Conyersville were among the leaders in this respect.

The organization for such academies provided for primary, intermediate, and advanced departments. The advanced department offered some of the art and science courses usually taught in good modern high schools. The Conyersville Academy considering its location and size enjoyed an excellent reputation.

In the fall of 1877, the Calhouns carried Hall Laurie to Mayfield, Kentucky, and enrolled him on September 3, as a student in the Mayfield Seminary. The Mayfield Seminary was one of the more advanced schools in Western Kentucky. It was the only school of its kind in Graves County that was devoted to the interests of higher education. Mayfield was a center of farming and trading boasting of excellent church and Sunday School facilities and advertising a total absence of drinking saloons and gambling dens. Hall studied spelling, writing, geography, first and second parts of mental arithmetic, written arithmetic, Ray's third part of arithmetic, English, grammar, and *Harvey's History of the United States*. Tuition was $3.00 per month.[8]

W. T. Shelton, who was married to Mattie, Hall's sister, was a native of Graves County. The timing of Hall's education in the Mayfield Seminary appears to support the assumption that Shelton was the regular preacher at the time in the Mayfield Christian Church. Shelton and his wife moved in 1879 to Obion County, Tennessee, where he was listed as the preacher for the Christian Church in Union City. Hall Laurie transferred to Union City and enrolled in the high school in 1879. He lived with his sister and her husband until they moved to California some time later because Shelton had developed a "preacher's throat."

The high school in Union City was housed in a brick building located on North First Street, and the headmaster, H. E. Crockett, was an outstanding educator of his day. Calhoun received instruction in algebra, higher mathematics, Latin and Greek, as well as the ordinary subjects. Calhoun mastered the subjects which he studied, graduating in June of 1884 with first honors. An article in a Union City newspaper, published in 1901, giving a history of the Union City High School, listed Hall C. (sic) (L.) Calhoun as one of the 1884 graduates. Hall was an honor student from his earliest school days until his final graduation from Harvard University Divinity School in 1904.[9]

Hall taught in Union City during the school year 1884–85. We assume that he taught on the elementary or intermediate level. He then returned to Conyersville and taught for two years (1885–87), in the Conyersville Academy.[10] During the following year, Hall helped his father with the farm work while engaged in intensive home-study, especially in Latin and mathematics, in preparation for the qualifying examination to enter West Point Academy in the fall of 1888.[11]

A news item appeared in the county paper announcing a Teachers' Institute which was held in Conyersville during the period July 9–13, 1888. At the conclusion of the sessions, a report of the Resolution's Committee stated: "To Professor Calhoun—Hall L. Calhoun (tender of thanks) for his kindness in securing homes for the teachers."[12]

The year of 1888 is passed over in silence by Hall in his memoirs. He wrote sparsely of the events of his personal life. He was then in his twenty-fifth year. What supplementary information that is available comes from the writings of his oldest daughter, Mary Ettah Crowder. She wrote that the United States Congressman from his district obtained an appointment to West Point for her father which he accepted. With little hope of getting an advanced education in such hard times, this appointment seemed to be his only alternative. He hoped that after completing his military training and service he could begin preparation for the ministry. There had not been a time in his early manhood when he had not given the ministry serious and prayerful consideration. The day of his departure to go to New York came. His bags were packed and he had his railroad ticket in his pocket. After an early breakfast, he went out in the field where his father was working to tell him good-bye. John Shelton Calhoun was not given to much talk. He, however, was deeply grieved that his son had decided to go to the army academy at West Point.

When Hall Laurie reached his father in the field, John Shelton finally brought himself to ask his son not to go to the military academy. He promised Hall that they would somehow find the money for him to enter the College of the Bible in Lexington, Kentucky, that fall. Hall chose to honor his father's wishes and began making preparations to enter the Christian ministry. In the fall of 1888, Calhoun enrolled in the College of the Bible; and upon this choice hangs a long and complex tale.[13]

Hall Laurie Calhoun entered the College of the Bible at the zenith of John W. McGarvey's life and career as a preacher and teacher of young aspiring ministers. McGarvey was then fifty-nine. McGarvey had in mind building a college within the framework of Kentucky University to educate preachers. He was elected in 1865 by the Curators to teach Bible in the University while it was still located in Harrodsburg, Kentucky. Although Alexander Campbell had made the Bible the central textbook at Bethany College and gave daily lectures on the Bible and related subjects, McGarvey was convinced that such colleges for preparing preachers were too limited in their role and scope. He shared with his contemporaries a distrust of the theological seminaries in America which had followed the pattern of the ones of the Old World. He insisted that the proper training for preachers must be through a complete reliance on the Bible.

McGarvey accepted the responsibility to develop and organize a curriculum in Kentucky University for the education of ministers. McGarvey's plan divided the course of study for the training of preachers into three categories: (1) knowledge of the Bible;

John William McGarvey

College of the Bible

Isaiah Boone Grubbs

Robert Graham

(2) moral training; (3) the liberal arts. McGarvey believed that such a school could bear only one descriptive name: The College of the Bible. The ideas for the creation of the College were drawn from the combined thinking and experiences of Campbell and the older contemporaries of McGarvey, among whom was Robert Milligan. From 1865, when the College of the Bible was established, until 1911, when McGarvey died, the name of McGarvey was synonymous with the College of the Bible.[14]

That the College of the Bible once flourished in Lexington, Kentucky, is known to a limited number of the members of the churches of Christ, but most certainly is well known among the rank and file members of the Christian Church. The history of the Restoration movement is incomplete without a general knowledge of the history of the College of the Bible. Very few members of the church of Christ are aware today that the name of the College of the Bible was changed to the Lexington Theological Seminary. The change was made August 1, 1965, in the centennial year of the founding of the College of the Bible. The graduate seminary today is financed and controlled by the liberal Christian Church (Disciples of Christ) with splendid buildings and well-kept gounds. The seminary is located in the city of Lexington, across South Limestone Street from the College of Law which is on the sprawling campus of the University of Kentucky.

It is our purpose at this point to set forth a "thumb-nail" sketch of the College of the Bible where Calhoun's vital place in Restoration History is determined. The College of the Bible shares in the common history of Transylvania College, Bacon College, Kentucky University, and the University of Kentucky, as each appeared and disappeared in the movements of Kentucky history. All are thriving today under new and old names—Transylvania University, Lexington Theological Seminary, and the University of Kentucky.

Restoration historians are unwilling to set the beginning of the Restoration movement at the time of the great camp meeting that took place at Cane Ridge meetinghouse, east of Paris, Kentucky, August 7–12 in 1801. However, the basic concept of unity as advocated during the early days as the Restoration movement did emerge from the Cane Ridge revival and is more than a remote concept. The idea of the union of all Christians developed as Barton W. Stone pulled away from Calvinistic theology and he and his followers aligned themselves with the Campbell followers to advance the principles of the Restoration movement.

Religious schools in America began to train new ministers for the increasing American population ever on the move westward. The first attempt to set up a school among the Disciples was made by Alexander Campbell. Campbell opened the Buffalo Seminary in his Bethany home in 1818, primarily to train ministers. Campbell was disappointed that most of the young men who came to his thriving school later chose law and medicine rather than the ministry which caused Campbell to abandon his project.[15]

The oldest institution of higher learning in America, west of the Allegheny Mountains was Transylvania Seminary which was authorized in 1780 by an act of the General Assembly of Virginia.[16] "Old Transylvania" had a long and troubled history under the control of the Presbyterians; but in 1865, Transylvania University was merged with Kentucky University and came under the stable financial support of the Disciples which is maintained to the present.

Bacon College was the first institution of higher learning to be organized by the Disciples in America.[17] The college was founded in Georgetown, Kentucky, in the fall of 1836, with Walter Scott as president, four years before the opening of Bethany College. As long as Bacon College existed, religion had its definite place in the curriculum, but the interest of the new school was primarily scientific. It was named in honor of the great scientist, Roger Bacon. The fortunes of Bacon College rose and fell in a tangled skein of conflicting financial and personality forces.

Bacon College survived during the early period of its existence due to the influence and support of John Bryan Bowman, who was one of the few students to receive degrees from Bacon College. Only twenty-seven degrees were awarded by Bacon College during its existence. Bowman was a son of one of the college trustees and the grand nephew of one of the incorporators of the Transylvania Seminary. Bowman entered the picture at a time when the financial collapse of the college seemed imminent. Even then Bowman envisioned a people's university suited to the American dream and an "auxiliary to the cause of sound morality and pure religion in our state." His attempt to revive Bacon College succeeded. The college, which had failed in Georgetown, Kentucky, was reorganized and reopened in Harrodsburg, Kentucky, on September 21, 1857.[18]

Bacon College was re-chartered by the Kentucky General Assembly on January 15, 1855, and emerged under the new corporate name—Kentucky University.[19] The school's opening was postponed until September 21, 1857, due to a delay in the construction of buildings on a new site in Harrodsburg. Kentucky University survived the Civil War, but emerged scarred and threatened. Bowman was elected by the Board of Curators as Regent of the University. For all practical purposes he was the chief executive officer because the university did not have a president. The main college building burned on February 16, 1864, and the Curators began to develop plans to rebuild the university. The Curators accepted the invitation of the Trustees of Transylvania to move to Lexington and occupy its campus and possess all other assets. The opposition to the move away from Harrodsburg was bitter and feelings ran high. However, Kentucky University took over the plant of the defunct Transylvania University in 1865 and moved to Lexington, Kentucky.

Bowman proposed to the Kentucky Legislature that an Agricultural and Mechanical College in the new university be authorized and financed. Bowman's move seemed to assure the eventual fulfillment of his dream for a great public university to serve the entire citizenry. Transylvania and Kentucky Universities were consolidated under the name of Kentucky University. The Agricultural and Mechanical College was authorized by the Kentucky General Assembly and funds allocated by the congress of the United States under the Smith-Hughes Act. It was organized as one of the colleges in the university.[21]

The College of the Bible had been organized in 1865, as one of the new schools in Kentucky University. Robert Milligan was elected as the first president, and John W. McGarvey and I. B. Grubs became members of the faculty during the first year. A conflict soon developed between Professor McGarvey and Regent Bowman. It was Bowman's ambition and plan to establish a great university supported by state funds, and to organize schools of the Liberal Arts, Law, Medicine, Agriculture, and Religion.

Trouble arose as a result of two radically different philosophies regarding the purpose and function of the university. Regent Bowman advocated a strong university to serve all the people of the state and thought the training of ministers should be made secondary. On the other hand, members of the faculty of the College of the Bible, led by McGarvey, maintained that Kentucky University was founded by Disciples, belonged to the Christian Church, and should be under the control and management of the church. Whether the tax payers of Kentucky should support Kentucky University with their dollars which at the same time would subsidize the Disciples' College of the Bible was apparently of no concern to McGarvey. The controversy between Bowman and McGarvey continued until the Curators, on the recommendation of Bowman, eventually dismissed McGarvey on September 16, 1873. This action by the Board of Curators solved nothing because the Disciples stood with McGarvey and the religious denominations continued opposition to the use of public funds to support the College of the Bible. The College of the Bible, as a school in Kentucky University, would not be able to survive without the full support of the Christian Church and the influence of McGarvey.[22]

The College of the Bible operating within the corporate structure of Kentucky University without McGarvey as a member of the faculty did not succeed. In June of 1874, McGarvey was reinstated as a professor in the College of the Bible along with Robert Graham. McGarvey and Graham, failed to receive the support which they expected from the Board of Curators of Kentucky University. Later Graham was dismissed and McGarvey was placed on half salary of $750 annually. Dissatisfaction among leaders of the Christian Church led to the decision to organize, on July 10, 1877, a new College of the Bible. The new College of the Bible was quartered in the Main Street Church building with McGarvey, Graham, and Grubbs as members of the faculty. Bowman persuaded Moses Easterly Lard to accept the presidency of the College of the Bible in Kentucky University for the 1877-78 school year. Lard accepted the appointment under the impression that Bowman would resign as Regent. However, the enrollment shrank to three students and Lard resigned as president.

The Board of Curators of the University decided that they must submit to the inevitable. The Curators extended to the new College of the Bible, on July 11, 1878, the use of the classrooms in the university buildings and access to other student services. The College returned to the campus during the 1878-79 school year under the management of an independent Board of Trustees. Bowman was dismissed by the Curators as Regent, and Henry H. White was elected President of the university. The College of the Bible that Hall Laurie Calhoun entered in the fall of 1888 changed very little under the influence of McGarvey from that time until his death in 1911.[23]

Heritage and Education of Hall Laurie Calhoun   43

The history of the ventures of the Disciples into ministerial and higher education have been marked by complications. The history, however, has been carefully researched and written by competent scholars of Restoration history. Dwight E. Stevenson's *The Lexington Theological Seminary* is a superb compendium of the history of the College of the Bible told against the broader background of the Disciples history in a time framework. Alonzo W. Fortune's *Kentucky Disciples* is a splendid reference work telling its story by a first-hand observer. The biography of John W. McGarvey written by W. C. Morro titled *Brother McGarvey* is a lovely book written without the encumbering apparatus of scholarship. The story of "Old Transylvania" also is told by competent historians. One especially stands out because of the unfavorable attention given to Hall Laurie Calhoun by John D. Wright, Jr., who is the author of *Transylvania: Tutor to the West.*

An inclination of Restoration historians to cast Calhoun in an unfavorable light in the history of the Disciples is very unfortunate and unfair. The role of Calhoun in the history of the Restoration movement against a background of growth, struggle, and conflict deserves, at least, an unbiased and respectable treatment, however minor his role may seem to some historians. For the time being, suffice it to say that Hall Laurie Calhoun distinguished himself as an honor student in the College of the Bible earning the Classical Diploma and the Baccalaureate Degree from Kentucky University in four years.

In the third year of study in Lexington, Calhoun married Mary Ettah Stacey on December 31, 1890, in Paris, Tennessee, about ten miles south of his birthplace. When Calhoun first saw Mary Ettah, she was in her middle teens. She lived with her mother, Huldah (Peyton) Stacey in Lexington. The ancestry of Mary Ettah Stacey is traced to Miranda E. Walker, who was born on March 10, 1827, in Clay County, near Liberty, Missouri. While in her infancy, Miranda's father moved to Jackson County, near Blue Springs, Missouri, which is close to Independence.

At fifteen years of age, Miranda became a member of the Christian Church but later changed her membership to the Presbyterian church. Her father was engaged in the mercantile business. Miranda was married to Dr. Greenwood Peyton about the year 1848; which was her second marriage. Huldah Peyton was the daughter of Greenwood and Miranda. She was married in 1865 to John Cockerel Stacey in Lexington, Kentucky. It was their daughter, Mary Ettah Stacey, who married Hall Laurie Calhoun. The circumstances of John Cockerel Stacey and Huldah's marriage and settling in Lexington is not known. They were divorced when Mary Ettah was quite young.

Hall Laurie Calhoun saw Mary Ettah Stacey for the first time when she was entering a pew for worship on Sunday morning in the Lexington Broadway Christian Church. Her Sunday School class was taught by Calhoun. He said that he fell in love with her at first sight. Hall made his first courtship call on Mary Ettah in her mother's modest home on Jefferson Street. Mary Ettah was well brought up and Calhoun described the girl as graceful with nut brown ringlets falling along her forehead. During the evening of his visit, she played the piano for Hall.

On a later wintry evening when snow lay on the ground with logs burning brightly in the fireplace, Hall proposed marriage to Mary Ettah. She accepted his proposal. They were married on Wednesday, December 31, 1890, at 12 noon, at the home of a friend, Lafayette Cherry, in Paris, Tennessee. R. W. Dunlap, a minister of the Christian Church, performed the ceremony. Mary Ettah was sixteen years old at the time of her wedding and Hall was twenty-seven.

The marriage took their Lexington friends by complete surprise. Mary Ettah had let it be known that she planned to visit friends and relatives in Texas and would possibly live there with her relatives. However, Hall pressed the suit to his advantage. Mary Ettah boarded the train in Lexington for Paris, Tennessee, on a cold, blustery, and snowy day. Hall was waiting anxiously at the train station in Paris not knowing for certain whether or not she would be on the train. Mary Ettah promised to send a telegram to Hall at the time of her departure from Lexington; however, no message came to the waiting groom. Mary Ettah was indeed on the train; but a sleet storm had downed the telegraph lines in Kentucky. The telegram did not get through to the groom, but the bride arrived safely in Paris as scheduled.

Many guests were present for the Paris wedding and reception. And a short while later, the newlyweds were driven by a horse-pulled rig to Conyersville about ten miles north of Paris. Hall's parents saw Mary Ettah for the first time. The Calhoun neighbors gave the couple a rousing welcome home. They were given the usual boisterous *charivari* by the young men of the community, which was a custom in the South, on the evening of their wedding.

Hall and his young bride returned to Lexington on January 3, and took up residence at Huldah Stacey's home at 347 North Broadway. The mother had agreed to the marriage provided that the couple would live with her in her home. She helped with the home chores and cared for the five Calhoun children who later came along. Hall and Mary Ettah were free to pursue their careers with a freedom that was made possible by "Momsey" whose presence and constant care kept the home in good order. She became and remained a member of their family for as long as she lived.

The love of Hall and Mary Ettah for one another was constant and enduring. Hall was sensitive about their age differential. In the later years of his life, he would not tell his age because people would know how much older he was than his wife. Hall remembered his wife in their early marriage as being as playful as a kitten and she seemed more like a child to him than an adult. She would tease him to the point of aggravation and then win back his good humor with a tear in her eye. But children soon came along and the years matured the sensitive and intelligent young lady.

Mary Ettah (Stacey) Calhoun is remembered by acquaintances and her students as a gentle and refined lady with a superior intelligence befitting such persons who belong by birth and rearing to a natural aristocracy. Mary Ettah attended Hamilton College in Lexington. This was a girl's school managed by the administration of Kentucky University providing opportunity to young women for an education deemed best for girls with strong religious backgrounds. Mary Ettah was enrolled in Hamilton College during the period 1889 to 1891. She studied music and became an accomplished pianist. There is no school record in Hamilton of her after 1891. A while later, their oldest daughter, who was her mother's namesake, was born in Lexington which accounts for her having to drop out of college at the time.

Hall Calhoun graduated from both the College of the Bible and Kentucky University in 1892. Calhoun remained in Lexington for another year, taught in the Kentucky University Preparatory School and served as the assistant principal (1892–93). He had also taught part-time the previous year in the Academy. At the close of the 1893 school year, Hall moved his family back to Conyersville, Tennessee, to help care for his aging parents.

Upon his return to Conyersville in the spring of 1893, he built a home across the road from his parents. Hall served as principal of the Conyersville Academy during 1893–94. And in the following two years, he conducted gospel meetings with great success throughout the surrounding country. Then for a brief time (1896) he was the minister for the Tenth Street Christian Church in Paducah, Kentucky. He continued to live in Conyersville and commuted by train from Puryear to Paducah. In 1897, Calhoun moved to Franklin, Tennessee, and preached for the Christian Church in that city until 1900. The school year 1900–01 marked another critical juncture in Calhoun's life. He moved his family to Henderson, Tennessee, at the invitation of President A. G. Freed to teach in the Georgia Robertson Christian College. And one year later, he would accept an appointment to the faculty of the College of the Bible, move to New Haven, Connecticut, and study one year for an earned Bachelor of Divinity degree in Yale University.

3

The Progress of a Preacher

The College of the Bible was beginning its twenty-third year when Hall Laurie Calhoun enrolled in the fall of 1888. Calhoun went to Lexington to study the Bible with the sole intent to become a gospel preacher. The College of the Bible was not a theological seminary and did not conform to the standards set for one. The College of the Bible, a part of Kentucky University, was a single purpose institution existing to train young men for a useful ministry in the church. John W. McGarvey would not permit women to be in his classes, but did later permit them to enroll.

Charles Loos was president of Kentucky University and Robert Graham served as president of the College of the Bible when Calhoun enrolled as a freshman. Members of the Bible faculty were the celebrated John W. McGarvey, Robert Graham, I. B. Grubbs, Alfred Fairhurst, and Mark Collis. The College of the Bible was a "new and peculiar institution" unique in the history of the Disciples colleges.

The *magna charta* of the College of the Bible was set forth in *Lard's Quarterly* in April of 1865 under the Title of "Ministerial Education." The article appeared five months before the openings of the College of the Bible. The declaration was written by McGarvey and signed with a pen name: "Allan". It was customary for writers to use another name in journals of the period designed to attract interest and to provoke, on occasions, controversy. One of the lines states: "That one who is to preach the gospel, and teach the disciples the whole will of God, should be educated for his work is a maxim of common sense". There is little question that Calhoun, in the estimation of McGarvey, met that standard as set forth in that 1865 article. Hall Laurie Calhoun was an infant of fifteen months of age at the time of this publication of McGarvey's article in the *Quarterly*.

The name of Calhoun appeared for the first time in print in the *Gospel Advocate* in 1887, eleven years after the baptism of his mother, Martha Louisa. And by this time, the Conyersville church of Christ was securely established. John R. Williams, field evangelist for the *Advocate,* wrote of a visit to the Conyersville church and the home of John Shelton Calhoun:

> From Paris I came to Conyersville . . . where we have a good little congregation established mainly by bro. J. A. Harding. My home is with bro. J. S. Calhoun. A home, too, that makes one feel at home. His son, Hall, is a live enthusiastic student of the Bible, and we have enjoyed ourselves well. I had met them all before. Brother and sister Calhoun keep the congregation well worked for the *Gospel Advocate*.[1]

The words of John R. Williams portrays the young Calhoun as an "enthusiastic student of the Bible." It may be safely surmised that Calhoun was deeply involved, at this time, in his studies preparing for the academic challenges awaiting him at West Point Academy. A key statement of Williams is that the Conyersville church had been "established mainly by James A. Harding." This means that Calhoun was acquainted with the major leaders of the Restoration movement from "square one." Harding was the "prince of the preachers" at that time in the South. At least many thought so including David Lipscomb.

Another item appeared in the June 6, 1888, issue of the *Gospel Advocate,* sent in for the Conyersville church by Mattie Shelton, Hall's sister. This would be the summer of decision for young Calhoun who was destined to create a major juncture in the course of the Restoration Movement. The involvement of the Calhoun family in missions and religious debates is revealed in Mattie's comments. The name of Harding appears again. About a decade later, Hall Laurie Calhoun, a young scholar and an outstanding preacher, would find himself at loggerheads with both Harding and Lipscomb over religious issues that would soon thereafter separate Calhoun from their fellowship. That, too is another story, little known, but with far reaching significance.

Mattie (Calhoun) Shelton's item for the *Advocate* stated:

You find enclosed ($5.00) which is sent by the church of Christ in Conyersville to the Indian mission. There will be a debate at this place beginning on the seventeenth of July between brother J. A. Harding and Mr. J. N. Hall of the Baptist church. Subjects to be discussed are the operation of the Holy Spirit and the Design of Baptism. Brethren from a distance will be provided for, and we hope to have a number present.[2]

There are two eyewitness accounts from one who was outside the inner circle of the Calhoun family at an early period and both were written by a life-long family friend, H. A. "Gus" Brown. Brown preached the funeral of Calhoun's mother October 6, 1899, and wrote her obituary which was published in the *Advocate*. At the death of Hall Laurie Calhoun in 1935, Brown's memory carried him back to his boyhood days in Conyersville. He wrote in the *Gospel Advocate:*

Since my childhood, I have known H. L. Calhoun. We were born and reared in the same rural community. He was a few years my senior when he and his father and mother became my benefactors. He made provision for me to enter with him in the College of the Bible in Lexington. I heard him deliver his first sermon. He was a great preacher. I think his greatness was in his simplicity.[3]

Very little is known of Calhoun's personal life during the Lexington, Kentucky, years (1888–93). A great deal, however, can be inferred from an examination of the college catalogs and scattered comments here and there which were made. Especially significant is the fact that Hall worshipped in McGarvey's home church, the Broadway Christian Church.

McGarvey helped to establish the Broadway church and became the regular minister January 1, 1871, and continued as the pulpit minister until 1882. McGarvey resigned as minister, but continued to preach for rural churches. However, he served as an elder of the Broadway church until 1902. On November 2, 1902, the elders of the Broadway Christian Church deemed it wise to submit the organ question to a vote of the church to decide whether or not to bring the organ into the church. McGarvey and his wife decided then to withdraw and to leave the Broadway church and did so on the day the decision was made to submit the matter to a congregational vote. Mark Collis, minister of the Broadway church, gave the McGarvey's their letters which expressed the good will of the entire congregation. The affirmative vote to introduce the organ into the worship services was taken after McGarvey's departure.[4]

What this means to the Calhoun story is clear. McGarvey would not draw the line of fellowship over the organ. He would preach for Christian churches which used the organ but would not "hold membership" in an "organ church". Calhoun adopted McGarvey's position at first; but later, he was preaching for the Providence Christian Church near Lexington, Kentucky, in 1910 when the organ was introduced without opposition from Calhoun. And at this time in Calhoun's preaching life, it should be kept in mind that it was not until 1903 that E. A. Elam and A. G. Freed were willing to make the moves that led to their separation from the Christian Church in Henderson, Tennessee, over the organ and to establish the church of Christ. Whatever doubts Lipscomb may have had in mind to draw the hard line of fellowship over the "organ" and the "missionary society" were completely dispelled at the conclusion of the Newbern, Tennessee, church trial in 1905. Lipscomb was painfully drawn after a decade of study to the position that the church of Christ and the Christian Church were, in fact, two separate fellowships.

The 1890's was the "gray time zone" in the growing "music controversy". Calhoun's position became increasingly apparent. He would both preach and hold membership in Christian Churches using the organ and seemed to be equally at home in churches of Christ where the organ was not used.

Soon after Calhoun graduated from the College of the Bible, he began to be acknowledged as an outstanding gospel preacher. Lipscomb and Harding were attracted to him as were Freed and Hardeman. Calhoun already counted McGarvey, Graham, and Grubbs among his ardent supporters. The remainder of this chapter will trace the meteoric rise of Hall Laurie Calhoun into positions of eminence in the Christian Church and Christian education. The 1890's were indeed the years of the development of the preacher and educator.

One of the first appearances of Calhoun's name in the *Advocate* after his moving back home to Conyersville in 1893, was included among the names of several preachers who had preached in the newly built Huntington, Tennessee church. Calhoun proved his worth in the meeting he conducted for the Huntingdon "organ church" in June of 1894. E. C. McDougle wrote a glowing account of Calhoun's pulpit ability:

> Huntingdon, June 13—Our three week's meeting closed last night. The immediate results of brother Calhoun's preaching were twenty-four confessions and baptisms, five taking membership, and one restored . . . adding thirty new names to the numerical strength of our noble congregation. Of those added, five were formerly Methodist, one a Cumberland Presbyterian, and one a Baptist. Brother Calhoun ingratiated himself in the hearts of our people and those differing essentially from us in doctrine could but regard his fearless plainness of speech and genuine tenderness of feeling with respect and courtesy.[5]

It should be kept in mind that Calhoun was thirty-one years old at this time, endowed with outstanding natural ability, and possessed a splendid education from the best college among the Disciples.

Calhoun's evangelistic efforts were crowned with success in the summer of 1894. He sent in a resume of his summer's work to the *Gospel Advocate* on August 31, dated from Winchester:

> Winchester, August 21—Please report the following meetings which I have held since July 1: Sulphur Well, Henry County, TN, five-day's meeting with twelve additions; Lynnville, Graves County, KY, ten-day's meeting with thirty-two additions; Blood River, Henry County, TN, ten-day's meeting with thirty-eight additions; New Providence, Calloway County, KY, eight-day's meeting with fourteen additions. I am in a meeting now at Forest Grove near Winchester. The meeting has been in progress nine days with eighteen additions so far, making a total of one-hundred and fourteen additions since July 1.[6]

One of Calhoun's meetings for 1894 in the late summer was in Murray, Kentucky, just a short distance north of Conyersville. The remarks of Calhoun about "good music" in the church takes on added significance when it is known that Leonard Daughtery, like Calhoun, was much at home with the organ church:

> Conyersville, September 24—Our meeting at Murray, Kentucky closed on Friday night, September 21, resulting in forty-five additions to the congregation from all sources. The writer did the preaching and brother Leonard Daughtery, of Elizabethtown, Kentucky, conducted the song service. We were all delighted with the singing, and feel that much of the success of the meeting was due to the most excellent help given by brother Daughtery. Good music is essential to the success of a meeting, and any congregation desiring

James A. Harding and David Lipscomb

a first-class singing evangelist could not do better than to secure the services of brother Daughtery. We are all delighted with the meeting. It is the best Murray has had for many years.[7]

Calhoun proved himself to be a powerful proclaimer of the gospel in the first years of his ministry. His reputation grew in this respect until the very end of his life. However, the facts of the life of this remarkable man are little known by those who knew him best, including his surviving children, Margaret Lee and Dorothea Eloise. Hall Laurie Calhoun strove to deserve the respect of his contemporaries, and never sought pity, not even in the midst of the greatest disappointments of his life.

The direction that Calhoun would eventually take in relation to the "society and music innovations" became increasingly apparent over a brief period. Calhoun conducted a meeting for the Tenth Street Christian Church in Paducah, Kentucky, in March of 1895. Leon Daughtery and his wife conducted the music services. The Paducah Church used the organ in the worship at the time. The Tenth Street Christian Church was started from a Sunday School organization in 1890 by L. M. Stetin. Two years later, P. B. Chalk and J. K. Bondurant advanced funds for a building site at the corner of Tenth and Ohio Streets, and the Tenth Street Christian Church was erected. Calhoun served as one of the early "pastors" of this church. Fred Newman wrote in his *The History of Paducah:* "Though young at the time he was the pastor, the Reverend H. L. Calhoun is remembered among the best informed ministers to hold charge!"[8]

Calhoun was engaged to begin preaching for the Tenth Street Christian Church on a regular basis in November of 1865. He conducted a second protracted meeting with the Paducah church soon after his employment with large audiences and great interest. Calhoun's tenure as "pastor" of the Paducah church ended on July 4, 1897. He had continued to live in Conyersville during his Paducah ministry, commuting by train from Puryear to the Kentucky city. Hall Laurie and Mary Ettah would stay over in Paducah when it was necessary to fulfill additional church obligations. Their first child, Mary Ettah, was born in 1891 in Lexington, and John was born in Conyersville, a year and a half her junior.

One of the most critical transactions in the career of Calhoun took place in Nashville, Tennessee, in the spring of 1896, at the time he was preaching in Paducah. Lipscomb wrote a letter to

Calhoun about the possibility of Calhoun teaching in the Nashville Bible School, which had been founded in 1891 by Harding and Lipscomb. Calhoun was very interested and went to Nashville to discuss the matter.

The following information is taken from the depositions of Calhoun given December 19, 1904, in Lexington, Kentucky, during the Newbern, Tennessee, church trial. Calhoun had begun teaching in the College of the Bible in September of 1904 prior to giving his depositions. He had returned from New England with his array of prestigious Yale and Harvard degrees the previous spring. Dr. Calhoun by then was irrevocably committed to the practices of the Christian Church. All connections with Lipscomb, Harding, and his more conservative brethren had been severed. J. C. McQuiddy and M. C. Kurfees were among those who were convinced by 1900 that Calhoun indeed favored both the organ and the missionary society. Calhoun had already resolved these questions at the time of the Newbern trial.

Calhoun's depositions record that his memorable meeting with Lipscomb and Harding took place in the spring of 1896. Calhoun was notified by Lipscomb to make a visit to Nashville in view of joining the faculty of the Nashville Bible School. Calhoun was advised his salary would be insufficient to support his family. Arrangements were made for Calhoun to preach for the Fayetteville, Tennessee, church to see if arrangements could be made for him to preach there regularly to supplement his school salary.

In discussions mainly with Lipscomb and Harding, it became evident that their approval of him was conditioned by Calhoun's position on the use of the organ in worship. The opinion was expressed by Lipscomb and Harding that Calhoun was too free in his associations with those who favored the organ. Lipscomb and Harding thought it best for Calhoun to state in the *Gospel Advocate* his position in opposition to the use of the mechanical instrument of music in worship and to cease preaching for the "organ churches" in the future. The concern was expressed that his presence in the "organ churches" left the impression that he favored the innovations. Calhoun reminded Lipscomb that he too had preached in churches using the organ. Lipscomb responded, "I do, but you stay with them too long."

Calhoun immediately reached an impasse with Lipscomb and Harding over the matter. He was willing to state his position on both the organ and the missionary society. However, he was unwilling to declare such churches which endorsed them "off limits." Lipscomb at that time would preach in meetings for churches which used the organ. Calhoun strongly defended the organ's use as proper as long as the organ was considered to be an aid to the worship like the tuning fork or songbook. Calhoun held the position for a lifetime that to use the organ as a part of the worship was indeed sinful. Calhoun equally condemned the missionary society should it be used to displace the authority and the autonomy of the local church and supplant the mission of the church to proclaim the gospel.

Lipscomb and Harding were inflexible in their opposition to the organ and the missionary society and were no longer willing to fellowship churches of that persuasion. Responding to a direct question put to Lipscomb and Harding by Calhoun if they considered John W. McGarvey worthy of fellowship, and both indicated they could not fellowship McGarvey. Calhoun responded by saying he considered McGarvey to be as good a Christian as they and worthy of fellowship. The conversations lasted from Friday through Saturday. They were unable to find a common ground of agreement. Calhoun raised the question if he should preach in Fayetteville the next day, and he was urged to do so. He went to Fayetteville and returned to Nashville on Monday for further conversation. There was no change, however, on either side.

The *Gospel Advocate* began to pay special attention to the gravitation of Calhoun toward the Christian Church in 1896, before and after Calhoun had discussions with Lipscomb and Harding. J. C. McQuiddy noted that: Brother Hall L. Calhoun was booked to begin a meeting for the "organ church at Union City" last Monday, and also noted that W. H. Sheffer was preaching for the Union City Christian Church to the satisfaction of all. Sheffer wrote about that meeting:

> Union City, July 3—The meeting that has been in progress at the First Christian Church here for nearly four weeks closed last night. This was one of the most successful meetings in the history of this congregation. Brother H. L. Calhoun, of Paducah, Kentucky did the preaching. His sermons were strong, simple and scriptural. I regard him as one of the best men in a meeting that I know of.[9]

Sheffer was a highly respected minister in the Christian Church in Tennessee and belonged by choice to the "organ branch" of the fellowship. Sheffer had been a classmate of Calhoun in the College of the Bible which explains their warm friendship.

J. C. McQuiddy noted in what amounted to a reprimand after receiving the Sheffer report, and he meant for his remarks "to sting" both Calhoun and Sheffer:

> The meeting at Union City, conducted by Hall Calhoun, has resulted in over fifty additions. This is the meeting with the "organ" church. These were no doubt converted by the word of the Lord, as the "law of the Lord is perfect, converting the soul." They can find authority for every step that they have taken but no more authority for the organ in the worship than for infant baptism.[10]

The split between the Christian Church and the church of Christ was near at this time. The lines of separation were already drawn in the use of instrumental music in worship and affiliation with the missionary society. A number of the members of the Union City Christian Church in opposition to the organ had withdrawn in 1891 and began meeting first in the Obion County Court House. They eventually organized the Exchange Street Church of Christ. Lipscomb preached the first sermon for the group. The opposition to the missionary society concept had been unremitting on the part of David Lipscomb. But it is not every day that the missionary society could be observed in action. The use of the organ was another matter. It was both visible and audible and used whenever the church came together. If the organ came, so would the society or *vice versa*. The society had already made its appearance in 1849 and the organ had followed close behind.

Calhoun's summers were given to conducting gospel meetings marked by large crowds and numerous responses. His work with the Tenth Street Christian Church in Paducah prospered. But Calhoun continued to keep up his contacts with the *Gospel Advocate*. J. C. McQuiddy reported: "Brother Calhoun and his wife were visitors last week. We were glad to see them." Calhoun's regular work with the Paducah church ended in July, 1897. At the end of the summer, the *Advocate* reported that Calhoun had gone to Franklin, Tennessee, to work for the noninstrumental music church in that city.[11] The presence of the organ in the Paducah church and its absence in the Franklin church seemed equally acceptable to Calhoun.

About two years after Calhoun had moved to Franklin, he again entered into conversations with Lipscomb in view of his going to the Nashville Bible School. He felt keenly the fact that some of his brethren did not regard him as worthy of fellowship. Calhoun was indeed anxious to teach in the Nashville Bible School. Lipscomb expressed the hope after Calhoun went to Franklin that he would reach the point where he could work for them. Lipscomb was working out a similar matter with J. C. McQuiddy and F. D. Srygley in this same period of time. Their problem was the missionary society which they favored and McQuiddy and Srygley were slow in making up their minds to oppose the society. However, they finally did come around to Lipscomb's expectation.

The presence of Hall Laurie Calhoun in the churches of Tennessee and Kentucky was appreciated. His successes in revival meetings were phenomenal. A. G. Freed honored Calhoun by inviting him to preach the dedication sermon for the New College (Georgia Robertson Christian College) in Henderson. The auspicious occasion took place at 11 a.m. on December 7, 1897, in the auditorium which is standing today on the Freed-Hardeman College campus.[12] McDougle may have influenced Freed to invite Calhoun. McDougle was co-president with Freed.

The year closed on the up-beat for Calhoun. E. A. Elam, who was holding a meeting in Franklin, and Calhoun paid a visit to the *Advocate* office. McQuiddy, the managing editor, said, "We were pleased with such a visit last week from brother H. L. Calhoun and brother E. A. Elam. Both reported that the meeting at Franklin was an interesting one and well-attended by church members.[13]

Calhoun worked for the Franklin Church from 1897 into the year 1900. Reports of his protracted meetings were not reported as fully as in previous years. However, we are indebted to an unidentified church member who summed up a year of activity in the Franklin church as follows:

> Franklin, November 7—Thinking perhaps it would stimulate and encourage others to greater diligence in the work, not for the purpose of boasting, I write that the readers of the *Gospel Advocate* may know what we are doing at Franklin under the leadership of our brother, Hall L. Calhoun, who is an earnest, devoted gospel preacher and an untiring worker. From September 19, 1897 to September 19, 1898, he preached in Franklin 114 sermons; elsewhere, 103. Total, 217. Funerals attended, 18; marriage services, 4; additions elsewhere, 64; withdrawn from by letter and death, 12; net gain in membership during the year, 34. September 19, 1898, found

us entirely out of debt—did not owe any man anything but good will. During the year we raised something over twenty-three hundred dollars which includes all expenses . . . improving the house and keeping it in order, home and foreign missions, preacher's salary, etc.; and we raised it all without fairs, suppers, or concerts. It was contributed and paid into the church treasury and paid out by the church treasurer. The church does foreign and home mission work, taking up collections for this work every fifth Sunday. We have, by voluntary contribution, collected on the last two fifth Sundays, over fifty dollars; but best of all, the general spiritual condition of the church is good and growing better. Peace, harmony, and good will prevail us. Now, I submit this to the churches everywhere, for all of them can, in proportion, do as well if they desire and determine. It can be done along the same old gospel lines. Why not do it brethren? At our morning services yesterday, a young lady made the good confession and is to be immersed tonight.[14]

The work of Calhoun prospered at every turn. The controversy over the organ in the church had been going on for some thirty-five years. Calhoun continued preaching for "organ churches" in protracted meetings. McQuiddy, who had become an uncompromising foe of the organ and missionary society, continued to take special notice of this practice of Calhoun in his account of a mutual arrangement between Sheffer and Calhoun:

Brother Sheffer, of Woodland Street and brother Hall Calhoun, of Franklin, Tennessee have made an exchange of service for meetings at Franklin and Woodland Street . . . Woodland Street congregation is one of the most digressive in the state, having the organ, Endeavor Societies, and being in full sympathy with the modern movements of organized effort.[15]

The nineteenth century came to a close with Hall Laurie Calhoun preaching for the church in Franklin. In the meantime, plans were made by A. G. Freed for Calhoun to come to the Georgia Robertson Christian College to be principal of the school and serve as chairman of the Bible faculty under Freed's presidency.

A statement in the *Advocate* dated May 10, 1900, sets the time for Calhoun's leaving Franklin:

Brother George Gowen of Lancaster, Kentucky, has gone to Franklin, Tennessee to accept the place made vacant by the resignation of the former pastor . . . brother Calhoun. Brother Calhoun has gone to Henderson, Tennessee to teach in the Georgia Robertson Christian College.[16]

The remainder of Hall Laurie Calhoun's life may be clearly traced. His role in the third generation of the Restoration movement takes on major dimensions of significance, a fact that is becoming more apparent within the historical time perspective of Restoration history.

The foregoing information chronicles the major events in Calhoun's life between 1893 and 1900. Other than a growing reputation as an outstanding evangelist, little else marked the impact of Calhoun's influence on the church. However, Calhoun was even then being caught up in cross currents of troubling religious controversies which had long plagued the Christian Church—the American Christian Missionary Society and the use of instrumental music in the worship of the church.

The supporters of the missionary society organized the Tennessee State Missionary Convention on October 6, 1890, with one purpose in mind, as stated by J. H. Garrison. He said at that time: "We will take Tennessee for organized mission work . . . within five years." A. I. Myhr was dispatched to Tennessee to head the new state society despite the protestations of David Lipscomb that Tennessee was not a destitute mission territory.[17] Myhr and his supporters moved resolutely ahead to accomplish their mission.

Their efforts met with some success and the intent was made clear. Myhr was aggressive and abrasive in his operations. His actions were of such a nature, in promoting the missionary society, that he came under the direct attack of E. G. Sewell and David Lipscomb. And as later event proved, Myhr was no match for Lipscomb and the *Gospel Advocate*.[18] As early as 1882, Sewell and Harding were urging that a separation be brought about to identify that part of the Christian Church fellowship which supported the organ and the society. Lipscomb, at the time, rebuffed his brethren who called for such division. He sought no compromise, but hoped that the church would not suffer division.

By 1897, Lipscomb was reconciled to the fact that division had already occurred and the supporters of the innovations would be satisfied with nothing less than a complete take-over of the churches. He strove to avoid the inevitable separation, but was rebuffed at every turn. And so in 1897, Lipscomb joined his brethren recognizing that division had already become an established fact. Lipscomb no longer accepted fellowship with that part of the Christian Church which deliberately chose to divide or take over churches which were not in sympathy with the missionary society and the organ.[19]

Two incontrovertible facts later emerge about Calhoun between 1893 and 1900 which were not apparent at the time. First, he preached for the "organ churches" with apparent approval of what they were doing and seemed to be much at home with them. Second, Calhoun openly supported the missionary society from the first time he addressed the issue at the turn of the twentieth century. He did so in speeches published in the official publication of the society, *The Tennessee Christian,* and in other published articles. He later served in official capacities with the Kentucky Missionary Society.

Calhoun's role in the Christian Church in Tennessee during this period was a minor one, but that would dramatically change in the years just ahead when he went to the College of the Bible as a faculty member. Forces were gathering even then that would propel Calhoun into key positions of leadership in the Christian Church which time proved to be of momentous dimensions. The theological storm which Calhoun helped to create in the Christian Church beginning in 1917 is still running at full tide among the Christian Church congregations. This complex story unfolds in the chapters ahead.

4

Georgia Robertson Christian College

The year 1900 was one of the most crucial years of decision for Hall Laurie Calhoun. He was then thirty-seven years old, a time when the lives of most men of many talents are peaking. This would not be true in the case of Calhoun whose career was in an upward spiral. He was standing on the threshold of a period which would be filled with important events of great significance. Calhoun was destined to play prominent roles in the Restoration movement which he could not have anticipated and some which he would not have chosen. No student who had graduated from the College of the Bible surpassed him in ability and achievement in the estimation of John W. McGarvey. Within six years after graduation from college, Calhoun had developed into an outstanding evangelist in the region of his birthplace. His talents were superb and matched with a complementing personality and character. David Lipscomb and James A. Harding knew him well and had endeavored to place him on the Nashville Bible School faculty. However, his paradoxical views on the use of the organ in the church house prevented his acceptance.

Calhoun studied diligently the instrumental music question following his conversations with Lipscomb and Harding in 1896. He then came to conclusions about 1899 that were totally unacceptable to Lipscomb and Harding. Calhoun was very much at home with the "organ churches" as his preaching appointments in the late 1890's indicated. Lipscomb patiently waited for Calhoun to take his stand in opposition to the use of instrumental music in worship. The fact that Lipscomb had brought J. C. Mc-

Quiddy and F. D. Srygley to the *Gospel Advocate* staff when their position on the missionary society was still unsettled shows that he sought to win promising young men to a biblical position that he was convinced was scriptural. Much to Lipscomb's chagrin, Calhoun had worked out his "unanswerable argument" to justify the use of the organ in connection with the song service.

By the fall of 1900, Calhoun had moved to Henderson, Tennessee, to teach in the Georgia Robertson Christian College. His wife, Mary Ettah, also taught in the college. The history of the college and the Christian Church in Henderson are inseparable and both of them were then under the control of the society and the organ brethren. Calhoun's first college teaching was done in the Henderson school. While he played no major role in the Henderson Christian Church and Georgia Robertson Christian College, a knowledge of their history is vital to understanding the personal complexities of Calhoun. Calhoun seemed to have found a compatible environment in Henderson.

A Christian Church was first established seven miles east of Henderson, in 1871, at Jacks Creek. The Jacks Creek church of Christ was founded by R. B. Trimble of Mayfield, Kentucky. This was the only Christian Church at that time in Chester County. Later a congregation was organized in Henderson. This West Tennessee town boasted of a fine college, the Masonic Male and Female Institute. The name "Masonic" as a part of the name had no special significance. On August 4, 1885, the Institute was incorporated as the West Tennessee Christian College by an act of the General Assembly of Tennessee. It was in the Christian Church in Henderson that A. G. Freed preached his first sermon. And on April 21, 1901, N. B. Hardeman and Joanna Tabler were joined in marriage by A. G. Freed in the same church building. It was December of 1877, that Knowles Shaw brought a portable organ with him to the Henderson Church to be used in a protracted meeting and it left with him. Shaw was known as the "singing evangelist." But Shaw was killed in a train wreck at McKinney, Texas; and the organ was brought back to the Henderson Church later, for reasons that are not clear, but was thought to be the result of an emotional reaction to Shaw's death.[1] Some opposed the use of the organ, but the opposition to discarding the organ was far greater. One woman is reported to have said that if the organ were taken out of the church that she would "go out a straddle of it."

In 1889, A. G. Freed went to Essary Springs, Tennessee, to

become head of the Southern Tennessee Normal College. Freed later moved to Henderson to become President of the West Tennessee Christian College. A new structure for the college was built in 1897, which was first called the "New College". Five thousand dollars of the funds for building the structure were supplied by J. F. Robertson of Crockett Mills, Tennessee. The college was named for his daughter who had died as a young girl. And so the "New College" received its memorial name for Georgia Robertson. Religious and moral training were primary in such colleges, and training young men for the ministry was of paramount importance. The building still stands on the campus of Freed-Hardeman College. It was restored in 1984 at a cost of $650,000, and converted to the use of the Department of Business of the college.

N. B. Hardeman joined the faculty of the Georgia Robertson Christian College during the first year of its existence, and served without pay. Hall Laurie Calhoun delivered the dedication sermon at the "New College" on December 7, 1897.[2] It may be correctly surmised that N. B. Hardeman and Hall Laurie Calhoun met for the first time and formed a personal friendship. We have no knowledge of the first acquaintance of Freed and Calhoun. However, Calhoun came to the Georgia Robertson Christian College as a faculty member in 1900 with highest praise from A. G. Freed. The college was then under the complete control of a Board of Trustees who supported the organ and missionary society.

Freed and Hardeman left the college in 1905 because of this fact. Georgia Robertson Christian College closed after two more years. Freed and Hardeman then opened their own school in Henderson in 1908 bearing the impressive title of the National Teachers' Normal and Business College. The primary purpose of Freed and Hardeman was not to train preachers, but the intent to do so was inherent in the objectives and curriculum of the college.

When Calhoun first came to Henderson, the organ could be heard every Sunday in the Christian Church which was located across the street from the Georgia Robertson Christian College. The organ controversy was far from being resolved at the time. The views of John W. McGarvey, A. G. Freed, James A. Harding, Benjamin Franklin, Moses E. Lard, and David Lipscomb all differed widely on the use of instrumental music and the support of the missionary society. To condemn Calhoun for his stand at this stage of the growing controversy would be premature. However, he seemed to stand apart in some of his views.

When Hall Laurie Calhoun began teaching in the Georgia Robertson Christian College, he closed to himself the opportunity to teach in the Nashville Bible School by refusing to accede to David Lipscomb's request that he repudiate the use of the organ in worship in 1896. Freed had not been without his critics; but his views on the organ had been made known to some of his close associates. John R. Williams defended Freed in the *Advocate* with the certain knowledge of Freed's beliefs about the organ. Freed finally took his uncompromising stand as later events proved. Freed's commendation of Calhoun was written into the college catalog for the school year 1900-01:

> It is with profound pleasure that we write a word in behalf of brother H. L. Calhoun. As a scholar, logican, and orator, he has but few superiors. His earnest Christian life and loyalty to the truth has made him great. And a good man and a safe teacher. We most assuredly believe that the G. R. C. College offers a Bible course second to none.[3]

Calhoun was listed as the Principal (chairman) of the Bible Department. Freed was listed as President of the College, and Hardeman was listed as an Associate. Calhoun's teaching responsibilities included: Sacred Literature, Hermeneutics, and Hebrew. His wife, Mary Ettah, was scheduled to teach Biblical Geography and Church History.

The college catalog sets forth the views of Calhoun on the purpose and objective of the Bible Department which reflected his training under McGarvey in the College of the Bible. Calhoun stated that an education without the knowledge of God's word was incomplete. The Bible curriculum was based on that of the College of the Bible and the textbooks included: *McGarvey's Class Notes on the Sacred History, McGarvey's Text and Cannon, Milligan's Scheme of Redemption, and Hurlburt's Biblical Geography*. Calhoun wrote in the college catalog what McGarvey had stated thirty-five years before:

> The demands for an educated ministry is so great that no young preacher who has it in his power to avail himself of such a course of study can afford to enter upon his life's work without having taken it in this or some other similar institution.[4]

Little is known of Calhoun's home life during his stay in Henderson. His mother had died in Martin, Tennessee, the year before he went to Henderson. His father died in July of 1901, releasing Calhoun to make plans for his future as he deemed best. His two oldest children, Mary Ettah and John, were enrolled that year in the Primary Department of the Georgia Robertson Christian College. Calhoun left Tennessee after the school year (1900–01) for reasons disclosed later, but he returned to Henderson twenty-four years later as Associate President of Freed-Hardeman College. The National Teachers' Normal and Business College was renamed Freed-Hardeman College in 1919.

That school year at Georgia Robertson Christian College (1900–01) was hardly underway when Calhoun became embroiled in a personal controversy with some of his brethren over the organ question. The controversy was not precipitated by Calhoun, but he was not without blame for the unpleasant turn of events. The principals in the controversy were M. C. Kurfees and David Lipscomb who took Calhoun to task in the pages of the *Gospel Advocate*. Calhoun had engaged in private conversations with Lipscomb, Kurfees, F. W. Smith, and others about the use of the organ in connection with the song service. Calhoun had worked out an argument he was convinced would justify the use of the organ in conjunction with the song service. Calhoun called his logical paradigm justifying the use of the organ in the worship his "unanswerable argument." Calhoun said he could not answer his own argument, and F. W. Smith also said that he could not answer the argument. Kurfees also stated, according to Calhoun, that it was the best argument that he had heard in defense of the instrument of music in the worship. However, Calhoun protested that he was not defending the organ. The "tragic flaw" in Calhoun's personality make-up is discovered in the absolute confidence that he had in the soundness of his logic.

The issue was painfully brought to a head in November of 1900. Kurfees, who was preaching for the Campbell Street Church in Louisville, Kentucky, placed in the hands of the *Gospel Advocate* correspondence which had been going on between him and Calhoun. Calhoun's argument for the use of the organ during the song service was set forth in a paper which he had read to several acquaintances including Lipscomb. It was reported erroneously that Calhoun had also read this paper at a meeting of the Tennessee Missionary Convention in Clarksville,

Tennessee. Kurfees assumed on this basis that Calhoun had gone public with his "unanswerable argument".[5]

Calhoun's support of the organ is exegeted from John 4:24. The argument runs thusly: (1) God must be the object to which the act of worship is directed. (2) "In spirit" means from the heart or sincerely or with the intention of doing homage which must be the spirit of the act. (3) "In truth" means according to the truth, or as God directs in the New Testament which must be the manner of the act. Calhoun meant to exclude the organ as an integral part of the worship because the scriptures did not teach its use and the organ is not a spirit that can worship God from the heart.[6]

Calhoun used the identical argument of John W. McGarvey that the silence of the New Testament scriptures forbade the use of the organ in worship. Lipscomb likewise accepted this reasoning. Calhoun concluded that the use of the instrument in connection with the singing is that of convenience, and should not be made an integral part of worship. He classed the voices of singers mingling with the organ as the sound of coughing or the barking of a dog outside the building that could be heard by the singers and organist. He said it would be wrong to consider instrumental music as worship.[7] Lipscomb adamantly opposed the use of the organ and never defended its use. Calhoun classed the organ in the same category with the song book and the tuning fork. This position is still maintained by the Independent Christian Churches.

It is clear that the concentrated study of Calhoun added nothing new whatsoever to the organ controversy. His argument made the full turn back to the old stand-by argument of the Christian Church that the organ was a mere aid to the singing as were the song books and tuning forks. The organ is auditory and the hymnal is visual; the tuning fork is to the ear what the song book and notes are to the eyes. Both are called expedients and are to be used only as helps in worship. J. C. McQuiddy defended the *Advocate's* publication of Calhoun's paper on the grounds that it was public property since Calhoun had made it so.

Calhoun vigorously objected to the *Gospel Advocate* publication, saying the articles were actually an exchange of personal letters between Kurfees and himself and published without his knowledge or consent. Calhoun charged Kurfees with a breach of faith and trust. However, Calhoun had been quite open in discussing his thinking on these matters with interested parties in a more or less public fashion.

David Lipscomb had his turn in the *Advocate* that Calhoun had read the information to him while they were going to a gospel meeting riding in Lipscomb's buggy in April of 1899. Calhoun then asked Lipscomb to review the material. Lipscomb promised to do so after four or five weeks due to a crowded schedule. Calhoun chose to keep the article and promised to send it to Lipscomb later. Eight or ten weeks passed and the article had not been sent by Calhoun. Lipscomb wrote in the *Advocate* of a hearsay statement from an unnamed source that a Christian preacher said: "Brother Calhoun had written an unanswerable defense for the use of the instrument in worship, and had read it to a number of opponents, and all of them except brother Lipscomb cannot answer it, and he cannot find the time." Lipscomb took exception to the rumor that was being circulated. He wrote Calhoun for the article to reply to it. Calhoun said that he did not want Lipscomb to publish it. Lipscomb consistently maintained that if the instrument had no place in the worship, then it should not be used at all. He was concerned with the presence of the instrument in the meeting house and concluded it would cause some to look with favor on the instrument. Lipscomb then moved to make the details of the exchanges public in the *Advocate*.[8]

The controversy with Calhoun ended in the early months of 1901. Kurfees objected to Calhoun's implied attack on his character. Kurfees was apologetic, but declared that he had nothing to retract. The matter was dropped from the pages of the *Gospel Advocate*. However, the issue appeared again in 1904 in the Newbern, Tennessee, trial depositions by Calhoun who gave testimony to support the introduction of the organ and missionary society in the Newbern Church. The full story of this follows in another chapter. Calhoun then recalled under cross examination particular details about those earlier exchanges with Kurfees, Lipscomb, and Harding.

Before 1903, Freed and Hardeman held membership in the "organ church" in Henderson. Freed seemed to be leaving the impression that he was opposed to the organ in worship, and some thought Freed was "running with the fox and holding with the hounds". McGarvey, who was held in greatest esteem, never made the organ a test of fellowship, nor had Hardeman and Freed made the organ a test of fellowship before 1903. That Calhoun

Arvey Glenn Freed

Ernest Clifton McDougle

Georgia Robertson Christian College

joined Freed and Hardeman as a member of the teaching staff of Georgia Robertson Christian College at this time tells its own story.

It is difficult to assess the role of Calhoun in the music controversy at the turn of the century. How were Freed and Hardeman being understood in 1900, and did Calhoun belong in their camp? The battle lines were clear in some quarters, but in others they were not. Lipscomb, Harding, and Sewell, who had made their positions clear and unequivocal in 1897 in the *Advocate,* continued adamant in their opposition to the organ and missionary society. The "organ churches" were gaining ground in Kentucky, Ohio, and Missouri; and for the most part, their leaders were militant in the defense of the innovations. Despite the key note of the Restoration movement, "In matters of faith unity," and "in matters of opinion liberty," there was little charity shown toward the opponent of instrumental music and the missionary society, and *vice versa.*

The Tennessee churches seemed to be ripe for the "Digressives" to take over. The success of the "Digressives" in other regions encouraged them to mount an aggressive campaign in Tennessee. The name "Digressive" was attached to the organ and missionary fellowship by those who were opposed to the innovations. Following close on the heels of the Kurfees-Calhoun debate in the *Gospel Advocate* over the organ issue, a much larger controversy seemed to be brewing. Since the story must be told to explain Calhoun's change on the organ about twenty-five years later, this time slot is necessary to explain the split in the Christian Church in Henderson over the organ in January of 1903. It was during this period that the final split between the church of Christ and the Christian Church occurred. Calhoun was gone from Henderson and attending the Harvard Divinity School in Cambridge at the time. However, Calhoun had by then fully made up his mind on the organ and missionary society issue and had cast his lot with the Christian Church.

When the Christian Church split over the organ in 1903, both Freed and Hardeman, and for that matter, all of the Christians in Henderson worshipped with the organ as had Calhoun in 1900–01. There was no other "Disciples" church in Henderson. However, there had been opposition all along to the organ. Freed came in for considerable criticism among the brethren in West Tennessee and Kentucky for his identification with the Henderson Church. When Freed first came to Chester County, the nineteen year old N. B. Hardeman was in full fellowship with the "organ church" as he had not known anything else. And it was Freed that educated Hardeman and L. L. Brigance out of the organ church.

The Henderson Church division developed out of an invitation extended by A. A. St. John for E. A. Elam to hold a meeting for the Christian Church in Henderson starting the second Sunday in January of 1903. The confidants of Freed and Hardeman were convinced of their adamant stand against instrumental music and the missionary society, but this was little known.

The correspondence with Elam was carried on by St. John who thought the time had come for a "full and dispassionate" investigation into the use of instrumental music in worship. Elam came with the understanding that the elders of the Henderson Church were in full agreement with the meeting. Elam arrived in Henderson and was met at the train by five men led by R. P. Meeks. Elam was asked if he had received a letter from the elders of the church advising him that they had decided that a meeting was not needed at that time due to bad weather, muddy roads, and for fear that Elam would stir up a strife over the organ. Elam had not received such a letter, and he declined the invitation to speak Sunday morning and evening since he considered that a muzzle had been imposed on him. The meeting, nevertheless, went on. The Baptist church turned over their meeting house to Elam and his supporters. The meeting lasted during the week and ended the following Sunday.[9]

The supporters of Elam who disapproved of the organ and the missionary society formed a Sunday school of eighty-six members. The group proceeded to build a meeting house and the membership of the Christian Church was left undisturbed.[10] *The Nashville American,* a daily newspaper in Nashville noted that the Henderson, Tennessee, Christian Church was "split by an organ." The *Gospel Advocate* paid attention to the news item with the editorial comment:

> There is something radically wrong with the spiritual condition of people when they love the tones of an organ more than they do Christian fellowship.[11]

The truth is that those who were opposed to the innovations simply withdrew without anger or bitter denunciation to form their own fellowship as a church of Christ.

Statements made prior to the meeting, during its progress, and shortly afterwards in the *Advocate* raised some danger signals. In the January 1, 1903, issue of the *Advocate*, an article signed by a "brother" who did not identify himself, challenged McDougle and Freed to state their positions on the missionary society and the organ. Freed was asked if he thought it was right for a preacher to go over the country preaching for churches opposed to the organ and missionary society and then return home to worship with a church that regularly used both.[12] That was a good question!

While the meeting was in progress, the *Advocate* noted that Elam was "doing some most excellent preaching". In this same issue for January 29, Freed responded to the "brother" defending himself and adding: "No more loyal set of boys (preaching students) can be found in the land than those taught and assisted by brother Freed." And he called special attention to Hardeman and Brigance.

However, Freed's statements did not remove the suspicion that he was soft on the presence of the organ. The article that related the details of Elam's arrival in Henderson and the presence of Freed, McDougle, Hardeman, and the preaching students during the meeting, also pointed a questioning finger in particular at McDougle: "Brother Ernest McDougle, co-president of the school with Freed, stood firm for instrumental music and the missionary society, using the usual subterfuge that they are only expedients and helps."[13] The critic was partially correct. McDougle was indeed with the organ church then and cast his lots with them afterwards. He was preaching for the Newbern Christian Church in 1905 during the famous trial and reported the court judgment favoring the organ supporters.

J. R. Williams, a West Tennessee evangelist who wrote a regular column for the *Advocate* titled "Notes from West Tennessee," came to Freed's defense in answer to the "brother's" questions: "Brother Freed has laid his plans and convinced me of the course he would follow; and right here I will state that in a very short time it may be seen what that course was to be."[14] The Baptist called Williams the "Campbellite Watchdog of West Tennessee."

The clinching words in defense of Freed came from G. Dallas Smith and he acknowledged that a great deal of complaint had been directed against Freed by well meaning brethren who did not understand him or the circumstances under which he labored. Many knew about the organ in the Henderson Church without knowing Freed's disapproval. Freed was consequently marked as being unsound in the faith. Smith did not propose to say that the course that Freed had pursued in Henderson was the proper one. Time would reveal that and indeed, time did reveal it. Freed's method was to educate the "organ" and "missionary society" out of the church. Freed had not for a "moment, lost his soundness in the faith." Wisdom is justified of her children and Freed was one of her most apt pupils.

David Lipscomb and E. A. Elam along with their associates, were standing firm in Nashville against the organ. A. G. Freed and N. B. Hardeman both eventually took a stand publicly opposing the instrument of music. The organ churches were entertaining high hopes that their position would sweep through the churches of Christ. And it appeared for awhile as if it might. In this, they were in great error, and they were not long in finding this out. They found it out for certain in 1923 when Ira M. Boswell met N. B. Hardeman in the Nashville "music debate" in the Ryman auditorium. Calhoun left the Christian Church two years later.

Calhoun obviously had chosen not to write to the *Advocate* about his personal plans for the future after his dispute with Kurfees. The Henderson Church division was two years ahead. One fact is clear, Calhoun had no intention to turn his back on John W. McGarvey and the College of the Bible. The unpleasant exchange with Kurfees and Lipscomb was perhaps a contributing factor that led to the negotations between Calhoun and John W. McGarvey with the prospect of Calhoun going to teach in the College of the Bible. Calhoun had little to do in the events related in this chapter which nevertheless, are essential to understanding Calhoun's place in the Christian Church.

The information is lacking of the opening of the communications between Calhoun and McGarvey that led to Calhoun's going to the College of the Bible. In a letter to McGarvey dated August 10, 1901, written from Newbern, Tennessee, Calhoun says: "I frankly confess nothing would make me happier than to fill such a position (teacher in the College of the Bible) in a proper way. And although I know my ability is not great should my services be asked for, I shall gladly do what I can to meet the demand."[15] The implications are clear that Calhoun was then negotiating with McGarvey in regard to his joining the faculty of the College of the Bible and he fully intended to leave the Henderson school.

Calhoun had good words to say about his teaching in the Georgia Robertson Christian College. He wrote: "I am engaged in teaching the very things that are taught in the College of the Bible. But my engagement is of such a nature that I am free at anytime I desire to be so." Calhoun was still living in Henderson at this time.

Calhoun's desire to go to the College of the Bible came to fruition. Mark Collis, chairman of the Board of Trustees, extended the formal invitation to Calhoun to come to Lexington for a formalization of a contract. Calhoun wrote Collis that he was engaged in teaching young men for the ministry in much the fashion as Collis must have suggested in his letter about their plans for Calhoun. Calhoun expressed his willingness to the Executive Committee that he would engage in such training deemed best by them. Calhoun made the request that if his services were not needed for a year or so, that he could increase his ability to do first class work by pursuing a course of study in some noted institution. Both the institution and the course of study would be decided by the Executive Committee of the College of the Bible.[16]

Although Calhoun's place in the events of this period was minimal, it must be kept in mind that the split between the Christian Church and the church of Christ was imminent. The *Advocate* had run articles beginning in August 1897 asserting that the organ and society churches were not worthy of fellowship. The separation was made public and final in the United States Religious Census of 1906. Calhoun was a party to the growing controversy in 1896 in the Nashville meetings with David Lipscomb and James A. Harding. And it is apparent that Calhoun had made up his mind about his church affiliation by 1901.

5

The Halls of Ivy

Hall Laurie Calhoun's choice of the Yale Divinity School for advanced biblical studies is easily explained. There were no graduate schools during the early twentieth century of high quality associated with Christian colleges and universities. He wanted to obtain the very best possible academic preparation before joining the faculty of the College of the Bible. President John W. McGarvey concurred in his choice. Calhoun was thirty-seven years old when he entered Yale in the fall of 1901. His credentials were impeccable. He had graduated with first honors from all of the schools which he had attended. He read and used Latin, Greek, and Hebrew with a high degree of competence.

Advances in ministerial education among the Disciples first began with Alexander Campbell establishing Bethany College in 1840. David Lipscomb described Bethany College as the "mother of ministers and college professors." Bacon College was the first institution of higher learning established by the Disciples in Georgetown, Kentucky, in 1836, but its primary thrust was not that of training ministers. The first institution exclusively devoted to training of ministers for the church was the College of the Bible established in 1865 in Lexington, Kentucky, as a part of Kentucky University. The Nashville Bible School was not organized until 1891 with David Lipscomb and James A. Harding as the co-founders. The National Teachers' Normal and Business College in Henderson, Tennessee, predecessor of Freed-Hardeman College, was organized by A. G. Freed and N. B. Hardeman, and opened its doors in September of 1908 to five hundred students. The name of the institution was changed in 1919 to Freed-Hardeman College.

The only formally educated preachers who were among the Disciples received their training in small liberal arts colleges. The denominations established similar schools for the preparation of their ministers. However, students began to seek admission to divinity schools of prestige such as Harvard and Yale, for advanced graduate study. Levi Marshall was the first Disciple to seek and be granted admission to the Yale Divinity School in about 1875. The Yale faculty members were hesitant to admit Marshall. The Disciples had the reputation of being "troublemakers." Marshall was requested to submit a statement of his religious beliefs and objectives before being admitted. He must have made a favorable impression on the faculty, for in 1890 Yale began advertising for students in the *Christian-Evangelist*.[1] Only five Disciples were enrolled at Yale in 1892. The number increased to eleven in 1901, the year that Calhoun entered the Yale Divinity School.

Under a financial agreement between the Board of Trustees of the College of the Bible and Calhoun, he was to pursue advanced graduate study and return to the College as a member of the faculty. He moved his family to New Haven, Connecticut, on September 26, 1901 and "took rooms at 219 York Street." Calhoun's walk from his residence to the campus, as he said, was about a three minute walk. His children, Mary, John, James, and his mother-in-law, Huldah Stacey made his family number six members. Mary and John attended a public school where all books, pencils, and tablets were furnished free of charge.[2]

Calhoun was accepted as a member of the senior class of the Yale Divinity School. To qualify for admission to Yale, a candidate must have completed three years in a reputable theological seminary with an earned bachelor of arts degree from a reputable college or university. A good knowledge of Latin, Greek, a modern language, English Literature, history, and philosophy was required.

Calhoun's Yale studies consisted of: Hebrew Old Testament, and Greek New Testament, Theological German (Wellhausen), Biblical Theology of the New Testament, Old Testament Introduction, the Epistles of the Captivity (Ephesians, Colossians, Philippians, and Philemon), the Church of the Eighteenth and Nineteenth Centuries, and Neo-Hegelian Philosophy of Religion.

Calhoun left little information about this year of graduate study in the Yale Divinity School and very little personal information about his family other than reports on their health. Calhoun proved his mettle to his Yale professors in that he received the Bachelor of Divinity degree in just one year, in a discipline that normally required three years. His wife, Mary Ettah, was also enrolled as a special student in the school taking courses in Church History and Sociology.

Calhoun had some time to look around in the first three months while he was in Yale and found his prospects for preaching appointments were not promising. The Christian Church, as Calhoun knew it, was almost unknown in New England. He made an interesting comment that the denominations were not so strict in New England, and he contemplated the possibility that he might arrange to preach for some congregation among them if he so desired. Calhoun wrote to McGarvey that he would do so if the congregations would leave him free to preach what he believed. There is no record, however, that he preached for any sectarian church.

Calhoun planned to talk with a certain brother of the Disciples about beginning their own worship in New Haven. Ten young men of the Disciples' persuasion were then attending Yale and some had preaching experience. Calhoun thought that the possibility of regular preaching in New Haven depended on their finding a meeting place. He wrote McGarvey that he was studying hard and trying to be prudent. He spent the holidays at the close of the year 1901 preaching for the Danbury, Connecticut, Christian Church. The Danbury Church was established during the early years of the Restoration Movement.

McGarvey suggested that Calhoun study Elocution while he was a student at Yale. Calhoun had already begun to do so, and was studying two hours each week under Samuel Silas Curry, the foremost celebrated speech teacher of the time. Curry was a Harvard Ph.D. having earned his degree in 1880. He was born forty miles northeast of Chattanooga, Tennessee. He was profoundly religious and began his career as a Methodist preacher.

Curry founded the School of Expression in Harvard University and served as Dean. Dr. Curry did not like the name "Elocution." He later established his own School of Expression in Boston and served as its president. Curry's philosophy of expression was highly popular at the time. And his influence was such that similar "schools of expression" sprang up all over the country. His School of Expression still exists under the name Curry College in Milton, Massachusetts.[3] Special attention is paid to Calhoun's study under Curry due to criticisms which were made of Calhoun's teaching a course in Speech during the 1917 controversy that rocked the College of the Bible. Stevenson wrote that the course which Hall Laurie Calhoun taught in the College of the Bible was privately referred to as "hot air" among the students.[4] His critics refused to acknowledge that Calhoun was a superb pulpiteer qualified with both the experience and training to teach the finest arts of public speaking.

Calhoun wrote a letter to McGarvey in January of 1902 telling him that he was preaching a good deal, and was pleased with the reception New England people gave to New Testament evangelism. The year Calhoun spent in Yale does not seem to have been marked with any noteworthy happenings. The letters that Calhoun wrote to McGarvey are the only reliable source of personal information that is available of his stay in New Haven. Calhoun mentioned that all of the members of his family were in excellent health and enjoying themselves. Calhoun, near the end of his life, told of an honor that came at the time of his graduation from Yale. He was one of the four honor students chosen to represent his class and he was selected to deliver an adress on the occasion. Calhoun completed his study at Yale in June of 1902 and was awarded the Bachelor of Divinity degree.

Calhoun transferred to Harvard University at the beginning of the 1902 fall term. He gave no reason for the transfer. We know Calhoun had contemplated doing so; but on this fact, hangs a tale. In the published volume of Harvard Divinity School *Addresses* delivered on the observance of the one hundreth anniversary of the Harvard Divinity School, Calhoun's message was given a prominent place. Deal Francis Greenwood Peabody introduced Calhoun to the Harvard alumni celebrants at the dinner in Harvard Union. Dean Peabody reflected that Calhoun, then an unknown relatively young man, wrote to him that he would like to come to Harvard and added "that everything was being done for him to make him happy at Yale." Professor Peabody replied that since the young man was content where he was and getting what he needed, he should not be encouraged to come to Harvard.

When the Harvard Divinity School opened in the fall, Peabody looked up from behind his desk to see Calhoun at his side, and without preamble, Calhoun said: "Well you see I am coming anyhow." Peabody commented that Calhoun had come from the distant state of Kentucky and this was his first sight of him. Professor Peabody said this verified an opinion he had long held, that if Harvard wanted worthy students, it should be made hard for them to get there. He went on to say: "Well, that young man not only came at his own risk, but was promoted from various positions until he received our highest award and became a Williams Fellow." Peabody added it took a very plucky fellow to do what Calhoun did.

Calhoun proceeded to apply for his doctorate in the Old Testament, under the paternal direction of the celebrated Old Testament scholar, Dr. George Foot Moore, and furthermore, he obtained it.[5] A Harvard student was indeed fortunate who met the approval of Moore and win his respect. The full significance of this is not apparent without explanation. Dr. George Foot Moore, graduate of Yale (1872) and Union Theological Seminary (1883), went to Harvard in 1902 and was made professor of the History of Religion in 1904. Moore's eminence as a critical scholar in the fields of Hebrew and Old Testament was international. A universal knowledge was attributed to Dr. Moore by those who knew him best. He became indeed a legendary personality, and much that was believed about his superior academic qualifications was warranted. His personal attractiveness and distinction as a scholar made his position one of great respect and dignity. Moore introduced the latest conclusions in his classes of German Higher Criticism, its methods, and standards, supported by his enormous learning.[6] Hall Laurie Calhoun went to both Harvard and Yale to study Higher Criticism and did so under the most eminent of the age.

Calhoun and his family took up residence at 71 Sacramento Street in Cambridge, Massachusetts, which he said was about a "four minute walk from his classrooms." In a letter dated November 27, 1902, Calhoun wrote McGarvey of his current plans. He at that time had been accepted as a candidate for the Masters of Arts degree in the Harvard Divinity School.

Calhoun was enrolled in Old Testament Criticism and the History of the Hebrew Religion taught by Moore; New Testament Introduction taught by Dr. James Hardy Ropes as well as a course in the Johannine Writings; a course in the Syriac language taught by Professor Haynes; a course in Sociology taught by Dean Francis G. Peabody; and two courses in Elocution taught by Professors Minter and Hill. Calhoun had thirteen one-hour recitations each week. He commented that Dr. Moore was the strongest man he had come in contact with after going East. Calhoun described Moore as a radical higher critic from whom he was getting it straight in that year. He said that Moore is "by no means so radical in his views as Professor Bacon of Yale." However, he added that Moore "is heartily in sympathy with much that seems to us very far from correct." Calhoun described Harvard as an old great university, but added that a person should have his faith well-grounded before going there. Though he enjoyed his work at Harvard, he commented that he did not believe all that the professors said.

Calhoun wrote that he had never been more kindly treated. Of his children, he wrote that they had the whooping cough. Mary and John had the disease in Tennessee, and after their move to Cambridge, caught it again, and James now had contracted the disease. Mary whom he called "little girl" had been quite sick but was much improved. Calhoun said except for whooping cough, the health of the family had been almost perfect.

While Calhoun was at Harvard, he preached on a temporary basis every Sunday at Worchester, Massachusetts, a town forty miles west of Boston. And he asked McGarvey to send his book *The Authorship of Deuteronomy* to be placed in the Harvard Divinity Library. Calhoun stated that before the school was to open in September, 1902, he was voted a $200 scholarship. But instead of the academic scholarship of $200 he received the Hopkins Fellowship for that year carrying a stipend of $300. (The Hopkins Fellowship was a portion of the charity of Edward Hopkins (d. 1657) awarded to theological students at Harvard). Calhoun said living expenses were much higher at Harvard than at Yale. And he received the Williams Fellowship in 1903 which contributed more adequately to the support and comfort of his family. The highest award honor that Harvard could bestow upon a student was the Williams Fellowship which carried substantial monetary benefits. The Williams Fund, to honor John Davis Williams, was established in 1848 from his bequest to the Society for Promoting Theological Education.

Calhoun received another singular honor as a student at Harvard. His fellow students elected him President of the Semitic Club. The club was composed of both students and faculty which met on specified dates. Faculty and students read and discussed scholarly papers prepared for the club sessions.

His first year of living in Cambridge was during the anthracite coal strike which resulted in very hard times. One cold wintry morning, Calhoun found the Dean of Harvard Divinity School standing on his front portico. The Dean solicitously inquired if Calhoun had fuel (coal) enough to provide for the comfort of his family. As it turned out, Calhoun had thoughtfully filled his cellar with coal during the summer before the strike began.

One of the most interesting and challenging encounters which Calhoun had while at Harvard was with Dr. George Foot Moore. McGarvey had sent to Calhoun the book which he had written titled, *The Authorship of the Book of Deuteronomy*. McGarvey had requested Calhoun to give the book to Professor Moore hoping that Moore would perhaps write a critical review of it. In the correspondence McGarvey had asked Calhoun what sort of man Moore was. Calhoun described Moore as over six feet tall, well-proportioned, neither thin nor heavy, with light hair, and blue eyes. Moore was described as very sociable. Calhoun said Moore could read Hebrew, Aramaic, Syriac, and Arabian languages as easily as he could read English.

McGarvey also asked Calhoun to write articles for his department in the *Christian Standard*. Calhoun accepted the invitation; however, Calhoun did not submit any articles on the subject of "destructive criticism" because of his reluctance to speak out against the liberal ideas of his professors for fear he would alienate himself from them. And he expressed the concern his professors might be less free to express their opinions in his presence. Calhoun also expressed the concern that his youth could be a hindrance due to the fact there were older men who were more capable. It should be remembered that Calhoun was in his fortieth year at this time. Calhoun went on to say that the more he learned of the "Modern Critical" views the more beautiful the great old gospel was to him. We are given cause to wonder why Calhoun, with the exception of a few scattered articles, never addressed "destructive criticism" as McGarvey had done.

At the time Calhoun left Tennessee and entered Yale, he could not have imagined the opportunities that would come to him. In February of 1902, Calhoun answered a letter in which McGarvey suggested that Calhoun return to Lexington and begin work in the College of the Bible the next fall. But Calhoun thought it best to spend another year in Harvard in pursuit of his doctorate. Calhoun said that he would never again have such an opportunity as was being offered to him at Harvard. He added that his information about the knowledge of "destructive criticism" was greatly increasing. Calhoun was also confident that he would again be awarded the Williams Fellowship. Furthermore, he had arranged to preach for a small Christian Church in Haverhill, Massachusetts, that would pay him $30 per month and traveling expenses during the remainder of his stay in Harvard.

Calhoun then added the clincher by stating that he had already arranged to be a candidate for the Ph.D. degree. Of the degree, he said this one would give him far more prestige that all of his other degrees combined. His professors advised Calhoun to study through the summer months of 1903 to insure the awarding of the degree the following June. Calhoun told McGarvey that two years of residence were required to qualify for the Ph.D. He reminded McGarvey that only he knew with what meticulous details that Calhoun prepared his lessons, and added that the Harvard professors assigned large amounts of work. Calhoun requested that McGarvey extend his leave of absence for another year. He promised that he would make up for lost time upon his return.

In another letter, Calhoun begged to be excused from appearing before the State Convention of the Kentucky Missionary Society during the summer. McGarvey wanted members of the churches in Kentucky to see and hear Calhoun who would soon be returning to the College of the Bible. Calhoun's tasks were indeed formidable. He told McGarvey he could not afford to fail to receive his degree. He did not want to offend or displease his beloved mentor, but he knew better than anyone else that he was moving into the crisis period of his graduate studies and he could not falter and he must not fail. The real heroes of academia are they who stay the course without compromise and who keep their self-respect and meanwhile win the respect of their professors.

As to be expected, McGarvey granted Calhoun his request to stay on in Harvard another year. He told McGarvey that his grades for four subjects that he knew about were "A's." And it was in this letter to McGarvey that he told him that he had succeeded in getting a brief review from Dr. Moore of *The Authorship of the Book of Deuteronomy,* which he enclosed in the letter. Moore seemed to have been in no great hurry to put his remarks regarding McGarvey's book in the hands of Calhoun. McGarvey asked Calhoun to call upon Moore and request his permission to publish his review of McGarvey's work, which Moore granted. However, Moore wanted it understood that he had not originally written the review for publication. Calhoun requested that if an article appeared in the *Christian Standard* that a copy be sent to Moore.

John W. McGarvey was obviously pleased that George Foot Moore gave attention to *The Authorship of the Book of Deuteronomy* with permission for McGarvey to print his remarks. McGarvey was also pleased that Calhoun had managed to get his work before Moore. McGarvey prefaced Moore's comments and his response to them in the *Christian Standard* with a commendation of Calhoun whom he described as "an honor graduate of the College of Bible and Kentucky University then studying on his Ph.D. at Harvard." McGarvey said in the article that the review was contained in a letter written to his "respected student" (Calhoun) by Moore. McGarvey then responded to Moore's comments. George Foot Moore accepted the Wellhausen Documentary Hypothesis that Moses was not the sole author of the Mosiac law. A number of unknown writers, it was claimed, identified as J, E, P, and D wrote related, though separate, accounts accruing over several centuries, eventually forming the narratives of the first five books of the Old Testament. McGarvey had carried on a relentless attack on what he called "destructive criticism" for many years. McGarvey gave attention to Moore's comments in two issues of the *Christian Standard*. He showed Moore proper respect, but he did not retreat from his opposition to "destructive criticism" in an effort to guard younger brethren against the cunning devices of men.[7]

Hall Laurie Calhoun was thirty-eight years of age when he arrived on the Harvard campus in 1902. Mary, his oldest child, was eleven; John was eight; and James, a toddler, was born while the family lived in Henderson. The life of Hall Laurie Calhoun in New England reads like a story book tale. The communities, of the city of Cambridge and Harvard University, were still basking in the golden haze of what one historian called the "flowering of New England." Still fresh in memory were the likes of Ralph Waldo Emerson, Oliver Wendell Holmes, James Russell Lowell, Henry Wadsworth Longfellow, Nathaniel Hawthorne, and many other scholars. And it was said in those days that the aristocracy of Massachusetts was such that the "Lodges spoke only to the Cabots, and the Cabots spoke only to God." A few of them were still in positions of great influences in 1902, and others who had come along were equally ostentatious. A person could meet on a given day the likes of the Lowells, the Peabodys, and the Adamses on Massachusetts Avenue in Cambridge.[8]

After the Calhouns were settled in their living quarters on Sacramento Street, Calhoun asked Dean Peabody where the children should go to school. Peabody told him that the best school in Cambridge was only four blocks from his residence and that it was perhaps the best grammar school in New England. This was the Agassiz Grammar School. Leading families in Boston moved to Cambridge so their children could attend the school. Peabody said the children were indeed fortunate to have the opportunity to attend such a great school. And he added to Calhoun's surprise that Maria Louise Baldwin, the headmaster, was a black woman. Then came another surprise that Maria was the first black woman headmaster of a school in New England. She was one of only two black women employed in the Cambridge School System.

Maria Baldwin was born in Cambridge. She was a brilliant and lovely child. Her rare talents, her love of poetry, and her poetic compositions, brought her to the attention of Henry Wadsworth Longfellow. As a child she came to him by invitation and he was charmed by her poetry reading, her understanding mind, and intelligent questions. From that time on, Longfellow helped in planning the education of Maria Baldwin. Alice Mary Longfellow, the poet's daughter, and Maria Baldwin complimented each other with a mutual friendship.[9]

Hall Calhoun broke the news to "Momsie," his wife, and children that the children would be attending a grammar school with a black woman as headmaster. "Momsie" was upset by the thought that the Calhoun children would be going to a school headed by a black woman. She remarked to Calhoun that here they were in the shadow of a great university and this was the best he could do for his children. Calhoun never faltered a moment as he recounted to his family at the dinner table the qualifications of Maria Baldwin, a friend to Harvard's great notables past and present. Calhoun said he had given the matter careful thought, and the children would go to the Agassiz Grammar School, and he would hear no more about the matter.

Mary Ettah remembered that day her father escorted her and John to the school. The gas lights were fading on the lamp posts in the early morning. An Irishman drove his shaggy old horse pulling a wagon piled with rags and old bottles which he had collected, crying out, "Any old rags and bottles today?" A fishmonger was busy in the streets chanting "fresh fish today!" and a scissors grinder was knocking on back doors looking for work and hoping to receive the remains of a breakfast. Little boys on their way to school were wearing knee pants and blouses with draw strings around the middle. Little girls wore chantilly dresses with white pinafores, long brown stockings, and high button-up shoes.

Calhoun and the two children appeared on the school premises and were met by Maria Baldwin. He said to her that he was in Cambridge for advanced graduate study. Calhoun explained to the headmaster that the family had lived and were reared in the South. Calhoun went on to explain that Dean Peabody had advised him to put the children in Baldwin's school. And that was the day of the beginning of a love affair between the two small Calhoun children and Maria Baldwin. No more cherished memories of Cambridge were held over a lifetime by Mary and John who often told the story.[10]

Hall Laurie Calhoun was confident in early March of 1904 that by June he would successfully complete his work in Harvard. On April 9, he had completed his doctoral thesis which was a formidable handwritten instrument numbering some seven hundred pages in two bound ledgers. The thesis was titled *The Remains of the Old Latin Translation of Leviticus*. Calhoun made a collection of the Old Latin texts of the book of Leviticus. The Old Latin Translation was made from the Greek version (the third century B. C. Septuagint) of the Old Testament. The importance of the study lay in the fact that a cricitism of the Greek text of the Septuagint would bring out the truer meaning of many passages and detect any corruptions which may have crept into Jerome's Latin translation. It is obvious that Calhoun possessed a high command of the Hebrew, Greek, and Latin languages to be able to write the dissertation to the satisfaction of George Foot Moore.

The invitation was extended to Calhoun and he accepted the invitation to deliver the baccalaureate sermon for the 1904 graduating class of the College of the Bible during commencement week in June. In the meantime, Calhoun was preparing for his final examinations in early June. There were five examinations which he must take—four of them were written and one was oral. And each examination ran to three hours in length. The first examination was in Hebrew and Syriac, the second in Biblical Geography and Civil History, the third in the History of the Religion of Israel, and the fourth in Biblical Literature and Criticism. The oral examination covered the four written examinations giving each professor the opportunity to satisfy himself as to the fitness or unfitness of the candidate for the degree.

Calhoun spoke of these matters in a letter to McGarvey and he requested that only such degrees as he had already earned should be listed after his name in the college catalog for the fall term. Calhoun said no student could be assured of earning a Ph.D. from Harvard until all examinations were completed and passed. He was the first preacher among churches of Christ to have earned the Ph.D. degree prior to 1925.

Calhoun and his family left Cambridge for Lexington in time for the commencement exercises on June 12 at the College of the Bible. By special permission, Calhoun was not required to be present in Cambridge for the graduation of his class at Harvard. After only three years of study, Calhoun returned to the College of the Bible as a member of the faculty with an array of graduate degrees not before attained by his peers in higher education among the Disciples. The memories of Conyersville, Nashville, and Henderson were fresh in his mind, and a part of his memories were pleasant while others were unpleasant. The future seemingly held boundless opportunities for him. Calhoun had the blessing of John W. McGarvey, and he was highly regarded by his brethren. The splendid education of Calhoun which seemed to promise so much, however, failed to sustain him in the greatest testing period of his life. McGarvey had led the fight against "destructive criticism" through his featured column in the *Christian Standard* from 1893 until his death in 1911. McGarvey meant for Calhoun to take up the gauntlet against the "destructive critics" after he had laid it down. A stranger turn of events could hardly have been imagined by McGarvey than the take-over of the College of the Bible in 1917 by the liberal theologians trained in the ways of Higher Criticism. Hall Laurie Calhoun was driven from the deanship and faculty of the College. McGarvey's beloved College of the Bible at that time lost its identity as the bastion of conservative orthodoxy in the fellowship of the Christian Church.

6

From Professor to President

Hall Laurie Calhoun arrived back in Lexington, Kentucky, on June 12, 1904, to deliver the baccalaureate sermon on the first day of commencement at the College of the Bible. A college publication announced that: "The College of the Bible is happy in the assurance that Hall L. Calhoun, of Tennessee, will be added to its faculty next September." The official statement further indicated that he had been on leave three years for advanced studies in Yale and Harvard (1901–1904). Calhoun's specific teaching responsibilities in the college were enumerated:

> He will come to his work with the degree of Ph.D. from Harvard. He will teach Hebrew and Ancient Civil History, and will have charge of the department of Public Speaking and Reading, hitherto, styled Elocution. Every student of the college will hereafter have the benefit of the most skillful training in this last department. Professor Calhoun has a natural gift of oratory and has had thorough training under the best teachers of the art in New England.[1]

John W. McGarvey had previously written and expressed to Calhoun a personal interest in setting up a new department in Public Speaking in the College of the Bible. He requested Calhoun to organize the department upon his return. The reputation of Calhoun as a pulpiteer and a scholar was greatly enhanced by his academic achievements in the Yale and Harvard Divinity Schools. That Calhoun had studied under the nationally celebrated Dr. W. S. Curry in Public Speaking was a plus for the students in the College of the Bible. The College of the Bible applauded his return with the comment that Calhoun had already established for himself a high reputation in his native state as a scholar and preacher.

McGarvey held Calhoun in the highest esteem from the first time Calhoun came to Lexington as a student in 1888 until McGarvey's death in 1911. Until Calhoun and his teaching came under attack in 1917 by President Richard Henry Crossfield and four of his faculty appointees, there had not been a hint that McGarvey's plan for his mantle to fall upon Calhoun had been altered. McGarvey planned for his son, John W. McGarvey, Jr., to write his biography and left personal notes surveying the episodes of his life for his son to edit and publish. McGarvey wrote near the end of his life in his *Notes For Memoirs* of his high esteem for Calhoun.

> Another acquisition in this period was the addition to the Faculty of Prof. Hall Laurie Calhoun. From the time that he graduated in our classical course in 1892 with the first honors in both the College of the Bible and the College of the Arts, it was a fixed desire in the minds of the Professors that he would some day become a member of the Faculty. Finally, when the time seemed to be drawing near that some vacancies would occur, and both Faculty and Trustees were impressed with the importance of having some choice spirits in training for the work which would ere long be laid down, the Faculty gave formal expression to the trustees of their judgement that of all their past graduates, Calhoun was their choice for such a position. In the interval he had been preaching and teaching in Tennessee, his native state, and steadily growing in reputation and influence. He was invited to Lexington to confer with the trustees, and as a result, he immediately went first to Yale University and then to Harvard to pursue a course of post-graduate studies leading to the degree of Ph.D. This he completed in three years, and although no vacancy had occurred in the Faculty, he was added to it and entered upon his work in the fall of 1904. From the beginning of his career as a Professor, the wisdom of his selection was vindicated, and his work was added greatly to the reputation of the College.[2]

It should be added that John, Jr., died before he could write his father's biography. The honor of writing McGarvey's biography fell to W. C. Morro who wrote *Brother McGarvey,* which was published in 1940. The design of this chapter is to highlight the major events of Calhoun's years between 1904 and 1917.

Calhoun and his family took up residence at 622 Headley Avenue in a commodious brick residence with a garden plot and a large yard for the children to play in. Calhoun's household included "Momsie," (his mother-in-law), his wife (Mary Ettah), and their children: Mary, John, James, and Margaret Lee. Dorothea, the youngest child, was born in Lexington in 1910. Also included was a servant who helped with the domestic chores.

The entire Calhoun family was well-ordered and family worship had been a life-long practice. Nothing was allowed to interfere with worship in the family circle. Guests were expected to participate in the devotion. The children recited a daily memory verse. Calhoun taught the class at home with the same care that he exercised in the college. Everyone read in turn from the Bible with special emphasis on the pronunciation of proper names. A special prayer was offered each day for a member of the family who was ill, starting on a journey, or getting married. Mrs. Alma Downing Browning was born July 20, 1890, and still lives in Lexington. She tells of visits which she made to the Calhoun home to spend the night with the daughters. She says that the family and guests arose thirty minutes before breakfast and spent the time in devotional activities. Mrs. Browning indicates that Calhoun was a strong disciplinarian which carried over into his dealings with guests.

The following account provides essential personal information about Calhoun for a better understanding of him. The chronological setting for the story is adequate justification to include it. Calhoun had hardly settled in Lexington in 1904 when the Newbern, Tennessee, "Church Trial" got underway. And Calhoun played a significant role in the litigations. Newbern is a town located in Dyer County of West Tennessee about fifty miles west of Conyersville. A suit was brought before the County Chancery Court to dispossess the original builders of the Newbern church house, and was entered in court proceedings as A. H. Meeks et al *vs*. J. J. McCorkle et al. The plaintiffs alleged that there had been a perversion in the use of church property in that the congregation had introduced innovations into the church fellowship—the organ, and the missionary society—contrary to the teachings of the New Testament. The Newbern church was erected in 1880, and the congregation operated without the presence of an organ in the meeting house until shortly before the date of the trial.

All the testimony in the church trial was presented in the form of depositions. When the case came to be heard by the judge on March 22, 1905, nearly three thousand pages of testimony were submitted. David Lipscomb, reluctantly, took the witness stand for the plaintiffs opposing the introduction of the organ into the Newbern church and affiliation with the missionary society. The Christian Church brought their most widely known and respected leaders to give expert testimony. Charles Loos, John W. McGarvey, and J. B. Briney testified in behalf of the defense.[3]

Dr. Hall Laurie Calhoun was also a star witness for the defense. His depositions were taken in the Northern Bank Building on December 19, 1904, in the office of Attorney Jeremiah Morton, in Lexington. Calhoun had recently arrived in Lexington from Yale and Harvard with an array of the most prestigious academic degrees offered in America.

David Lipscomb wrote at great length in the *Advocate* in some twelve articles from December 1904 to October 1905 about the Newbern lawsuit. The Newbern trial is curiously a little publicized chapter in Restoration History. Lipscomb was distressed that the matter was brought to court in the first place and deeply troubled by its outcome. The church of Christ was the loser; and for the Christian Church, it was just another take-over of church property. The Christian Church had enjoyed a great success from 1880 in winning numerous congregations of the Restoration fellowship to favor both the organ and the missionary society.

Judge John S. Cooper of Trenton, Tennessee, presided at the trial in Dyersburg, Tennessee, beginning March 22, 1905. The trial lasted until April, 1905. Judge Cooper sat for eight days listening to the depositions and arguments of the counsel. Precedents were set by the court decision: (1) The right of the local church to manage its own affairs through majority rule was established, and (2) The tests of fellowship in the Christian Church were undeterminable, (Judge Cooper refused to rule on these issues). There were no binding or excluding clauses in the deed to the property which would have prohibited the use of instruments of music. (If a donor wishes to encumber his gifts with conditions, he must say so). Judge Cooper's decision was clear and sweeping and decidedly in favor of the defendants.[4] This court case led many churches of Christ to write restrictive clauses in their property deeds. However, the family of James A. Harding had already written a clause in the deed to the property of the Fairfax church of Christ in Winchester, Kentucky, that forbade the use of an organ in 1887.

The failure of church historians to recognize David Lipscomb's great disappointment over the outcome of the trial is indeed puzzling. The split in the Henderson, Tennessee, church in 1903 over the organ and the results of the Newbern Trial must have convinced Lipscomb, J. W. Shepherd, and their associates that the clock had struck the midnight hour for the separation of the church of Christ from the Christian Church. The year following the Newbern Trial, the church of Christ received a separate listing from the Christian Church in the United States Religious Census for 1906.

The landmark court decision was announced through the *Christian Standard* and the *Christian Evangelist*. Their leaders exulted in receiving such a favorable court judgement. David Lipscomb regarded the trial's outcome as a betrayal of the Restoration movement. We may only conjecture the reasons for Calhoun's participation as a witness. He was favorably known in that general region of Tennessee and had preached in 1900 for the Christian Church in Newbern. Calhoun's newly earned eminence in the Christian Church may have also been a factor. Had there been any question about where Calhoun stood on the organ issue and the missionary society, the questions were resolved by his deposition.

The College of the Bible was an integral part of Calhoun's life, and his life story cannot be told apart from it. Calhoun entered upon his teaching duties in the College of the Bible in September of 1904 with great expectations and had every right to do so. He was destined to play major roles in the future course of the College of the Bible. The years between 1904 and 1917 were eventful years in the life of Hall Laurie Calhoun. The main thrust of his work was centered in and around the College of the Bible. He devoted considerable time to preaching and church related matters.

As previously mentioned, the College of the Bible was the brain child of John W. McGarvey. The original purpose of the College, as stated by McGarvey, remained constant until his death. The first line in the 1865 catalog of the College set forth the purpose of the institution: "The design of this college is to prepare young men for the Christian ministry." That objective did not change and few if any thought it would change even after McGarvey's passing.

The College of the Bible, as has been said in other places, was organized in 1865 within the larger corporate body of Kentucky

University. Robert Milligan assumed the presidency of the College and Professors John W. McGarvey and I. B. Grubbs, made up the first faculty. McGarvey taught the Pentateuch, Old Testament History, the Gospels, Acts, and the rest of the New Testament over a four year period. As early as 1866, the College of the Bible adopted a method to recognize student attainment. No degrees were to be offered. Ministerial students who chose not to study the Biblical languages received a certificate listed in the college catalog as the English Diploma. Students who received the A.B. degree in a liberal arts college or university and who took the required courses in the College of the Bible, including Hebrew and Greek, received the Classical Diploma. This diploma was equivalent to a Bachelor of Divinity degree on the graduate level in a standard theological seminary.

The story is told in another section of this biography of the controversy between John B. Bowman and John W. McGarvey which led to the temporary separation of the College of the Bible from Kentucky University resulting in the re-organization of the New College of the Bible in 1877. The new organization brought together Robert Graham, John W. McGarvey, and I. B. Grubbs who constituted the faculty. The three men (referred to by Stevenson as the "sacred trio") worked in the closest bonds of harmony and fellowship for more than twenty years. Graham was appointed president of the New College. However, McGarvey was and had been the guiding spirit behind the College of the Bible from the time of its inception. Graham seemed to be willing to yield the policy decisions and the preeminence to McGarvey.

At the end of the academic year 1894–95, Robert Graham resigned as president of the college but continued to teach during the next three years. McGarvey was elected to succeed Graham as president. Graham died January 20, 1914. In 1895, Benjamin C. Deweese joined the faculty to help carry a part of the teaching load. Samuel M. Jefferson came to the College to occupy the chair of Philosophy in 1900, a position he held until his death.

Hall Laurie Calhoun was honored to begin his work in the College of the Bible in company with the faculty who were members of the "Old Guard." Calhoun had been a member of McGarvey's classes as a student, and again sat in on his classes upon his return to the College in 1904. Stevenson said Calhoun attended McGarvey's classes in order to learn to immitate McGarvey in his classroom teaching. Suffice it to say, Calhoun had gone far beyond McGarvey in formal training and knowledge. As a matter of fact, Calhoun had no academic peer at that time in higher education among the Disciples.

William Charles Morro came to the College as a professor of Greek and Christian Doctrine in 1906. In order to present Calhoun in an unbiased perspective, we must say that he indeed did emulate his benefactor John W. McGarvey. Morro candidly presents the truth of this relationship and no person associated with the two men in the College of the Bible could have been more knowledgeable. Morro wrote in his book *Brother McGarvey* regarding Calhoun:

> In the spring of 1904 an announcement was made that at the opening of the fall session, Hall Calhoun would be added to the faculty. He had been a brilliant student graduating in 1892 . . . He was diligent, painstaking, a master of details. He was closely associated with McGarvey, and rendered him every assistance in his power in his teaching and his administrative work. In temperament, and type of mind, they were very congenial to one another.[5]

Calhoun was equally complimentary of Morro when he wrote in the *Christian Standard* of Morro's joining the faculty saying he "has proven himself a most excellent teacher, and he is deservedly popular in his work."

Stevenson wrote that "it must have been a severe disappointment to Calhoun when McGarvey passed him up in 1910 to make Morro the first dean of the College of the Bible." This statement is not documented and is highly questionable. The newly created office of dean was meant to be a permanent one and Morro was appointed to remain in the position indefinitely. There is no evidence that Calhoun gave the matter a second thought because he knew of McGarvey's plan to groom him for the presidency of the College. Morro wrote that the reason for the creation of the new office of dean and his appointment to it was to give assistance to President McGarvey in "his growing frailty."

Dean Morro left the College of the Bible early in the fall of 1911 to build a program of ministerial education at Butler University in Indianapolis. But Morro was disappointed with his new position due to a lack of support from the trustees and university officials. He eventually left Butler and went to Texas Christian University in 1914 where he died in 1941. Stevenson described Morro as having a "distinguished career as one of the leading liberal spirits of the brotherhood."

Calhoun was securely ensconced in the College of the Bible

until and immediately following McGarvey's death in 1911. Grubbs was forced to resign from the faculty in 1905 due to poor health. He died September 18, 1917 at the age of seventy-nine. While Grubbs was in the hospital he is quoted as having said: "The highest honor I have enjoyed on earth is that of having been a servant of Jesus Christ, and the next is that of having been intimately associated so many years with Robert Graham and J. W. McGarvey." However, there were developments that would radically change the complexion and course of the College of the Bible during the next few years. By an act of the General Assembly of Kentucky, the charter of Kentucky University was amended March 20, 1908, to confer upon the Curators of Kentucky University the authority to change the name back to Transylvania University.

In November, 1908, Richard Henry Crossfield was named as the president of Transylvania. Crossfield had graduated from Kentucky University in 1889, and received his English Diploma from the College of the Bible in 1892. This placed him in the same graduating class with Calhoun. Crossfield had earned the Ph.D. degree from Wooster University. Upon the death of McGarvey in 1911, Crossfield made a move to resign as president of Transylvania University to accept a "pastorate" of a Christian Church in Atlanta, Georgia. Crossfield tendered his resignation on November 3, shortly after McGarvey's death to move to Atlanta in June of 1912. Crossfield injected another reason for his move by saying that, "A vacancy in the presidency of Transylvania would open the way for the election of one executive of Transylvania and the College of the Bible, a thing to be greatly desired."[6] Calhoun was then serving as acting president of the College. There is little question but that Crossfield conceived the move so that he might be elected as joint-president of both institutions.

The vivid memory of the trouble between Bowman and McGarvey over the relationship between the College of the Bible and Kentucky University remained in the minds of many. Prior to Crossfield's suggestion to the university Board of Curators, Calhoun had been elected Dean in August of 1911, due to Morro's departure. Calhoun was made acting president of the College of the Bible soon after McGarvey's death on October 13, 1911. Calhoun's tenure as acting president lasted only through January of 1912; however, he retained the office of Dean and his professorship. When Calhoun became Dean and then acting president, this undoubtedly convinced Crossfield that the McGarvey pattern of doing things could very well continue. This and working with Calhoun, with whom he had experienced differences of policy in the past, greatly concerned Crossfield.

The trustees of the College of the Bible and the Curators of Transylvania University concurred with Crossfield's view and forthwith made the formal move on December 21, 1911, to authorize the selection of a man to serve as president of both institutions. It is not at all surprising that Richard Henry Crossfield was persuaded to withdraw his resignation and to accept the dual presidency at a meeting on January 17, 1912. He was not long in accepting the offer and in taking office on February 1, 1912. Calhoun and Crossfield had not been compatible from the time Crossfield first came to the presidency of Transylvania University. The relations between the two obviously were becoming more strained.

Calhoun had been charged with beginning a campaign of criticism in the fall of 1908 directed against President Crossfield and his administration of Transylvania University. Bushnell states that Calhoun's purpose was to intensify the feelings already existing between the College of the Bible and Transylvania which dated back to the McGarvey-Bowman conflict. Anyhow, Crossfield complained to the Executive Committee of the Board of Curators and threatened to resign if Calhoun did not cease his opposition. Calhoun was advised by the Curators to refrain from any further criticisms of the Crossfield administration.[7]

The immediate task confronting Crossfield, as the new president, was to rebuild the faculty in the College of the Bible, and he moved with dispatch to do so. The first faculty member to be selected, who more nearly represented Crossfield's own liberalism, was Alonzo Willard Fortune. He was elected on April 8, 1912, to teach the classes which Dean Morro had taught. Fortune immediately came under attack from his conservative adversaries. The attack led against Fortune was started by S. S. Lappin, editor of the *Chistian Standard*. Lappin accused Fortune with being an ultraliberal and one of the most ardent of all Campbell Institute men. A more sustained and vigorous opposition was mounted by John T. Brown, a Louisville evangelist. The continuing fray was carried on in the *Christian Standard* beginning on July 27, 1912 and continuing for five consecutive weeks. President Crossfield rode out the storm while giving his uncompromising support to Fortune.[8]

The second man to be elected to the faculty of the College of the Bible was William Clayton Bower. He was appointed July 1, 1912, to the chair of Bible School Pedagogy. Bower held the Master of Arts degree from Columbia University and had studied in the Union Theological Seminary. He did not complete the requirements for the Ph.D. degree while he held the pastorate of the Wilshire Boulevard Christian Church in Los Angeles because he stated "the Ph.D. degree was not an advantage to the minister." When he became Dean of the College of the Bible in 1921, Bower pointed out that: "My responsibilities in seeking to repair the damages of the attack among the constituency along with my administrative and teaching duties, made any further work toward the degree impossible." Bower, however, became the dominant leader of liberalism within the faculty of the College of the Bible as later events proved.

On February 20, 1914, on his way home from teaching a class, Professor Jefferson collapsed and died within a few minutes. Elmer Ellsworth Snoddy was elected immediately to take Jefferson's place. Snoddy taught philosophy in Transylvania University and theology in the College of the Bible. Snoddy was a highly popular teacher among the students and his peers. His appointment caused little or no opposition at the time, and neither did the appointment of Bower.

Dean Calhoun was the only one remaining from the older faculty. He taught the courses in sacred history formerly taught by McGarvey. Stevenson says of Calhoun: "So great was his reverence for his mentor that he taught from McGarvey's printed syllabi in a catechetical manner meant to be an exact immitation." Stevenson said his method of teaching was by indoctrination as opposed to the contemporary methods of the faculty.[9]

President Crossfield meant to dominate the policies and procedures of the College of the Bible, and he was able to do so with the support of his liberal faculty colleagues. Changes were made in the academic offerings. The Bachelor of Divinity degree was offered for the first time in the 1914–15 academic year, a degree which required three years of seminary training. The Classical Diploma was discontinued in 1918. The English Diploma continued to be offered until the session of 1922–23. Academic degrees then displaced the diploma. Dean Calhoun saw the handwriting of liberalism on the wall and was disturbed and apprehensive as to its meaning. He felt himself standing alone in 1917 as a representative of McGarvey conservatism as later events proved.

It is clear that Calhoun had crossed his "Rubicon" in 1901 at the time he became a member of the College of the Bible faculty. McGarvey was his revered and honored mentor and personal friend. What became apparent in 1901 is the fact that Calhoun chose to stay with the course of the Christian Church, the College of the Bible, and John W. McGarvey. Calhoun's return to Conyersville in 1893 had found him more at home with the liberal element in the Christian Church than with the likes of David Lipscomb and James A. Harding.

Upon Calhoun's return to Lexington, he preached for the Nicholasville Christian Church (1904–06). The Nicholasville Church was established in 1828 by George Elley and named the Baptist Church of Christ. William Shreve, the father-in-law of Tolbert Fanning, was one of the first elders. Calhoun began to keep a ledger of all his church work. He wrote in the ledger the titles of his Sunday sermons and the number of additions by letter and conversion. Calhoun preached twenty-seven sermons and lectures from the Nicholasville pulpit from January 7, 1904 until March 25, 1906. He preached one sermon in a Methodist pulpit and one in a colored (black) church. He named three preachers who spoke from his pulpit. And twenty-one members were added to the church through baptism, commitment, and letters. The list of sermons, places, and the number of members added were carefully recorded in each quarter of the year. Calhoun's summers were filled with revivals. The success of Calhoun in his summer protracted meetings was reminiscent of his efforts during the Conyersville years. Calhoun listed remunerations for meetings during the summer of 1906 as $40; $126; and $100, which were typical.

Calhoun began work in January of 1907 with the Providence Christian Church south of Lexington. The Providence Church was organized as a Baptist Church in 1817. Jacob Creath was instrumental in changing it to a Christian Church under the influence of the teachings of Alexander Campbell. Calhoun's "pastorate" with the Providence Church continued until he left Lexington in the summer of 1917. A new church building had been erected and dedicated during the summer with stained glass windows and two of the windows bear the name of Calhoun and his wife. Only two years of the Providence church work were entered into his hand-sized ledger. Calhoun's handwriting was neat and precise. All sermon titles were faithfully recorded and the names of new members, by baptism, re-commitment, or letter were likewise entered.[10]

Chestnut Street Christian Church

Providence Christian Church

Calhoun named preachers who preached in Providence while he was there and among them were Samuel M. Jefferson, John W. McGarvey, and Alfred Fairhurst. Among the sermons which Calhoun preached, the titles are of particular interest. In the early years of his preaching he paid little or no attention in his sermons to the missionary society or the organ. In his deposition in the Newbern Trial, Calhoun stated that he had not supported the missionary society with personal contributions nor by paid membership. Calhoun later supported and became a leader in the society cause.

The first written report of support that Calhoun gave to the missionary society appeared in the *Christian-Evangelist* in 1902. Calhoun wrote of a farewell reception, while he was a student at Harvard, that was given by the St. James Christian Church in Boston for E. C. Davis and his wife, Adelaide Gail Frost and Florence Mills. They were missionaries who were being sent to foreign fields under the auspices of the Christian Woman's Board of Missions. The missionaries were going to the Hamipur District of India. A voluntary offering of $36.78 was taken up for them. Calhoun reported that these were the first missionaries of the Christian Church to sail from Boston.[11]

A year after Calhoun began teaching in the College of the Bible, a report was printed in the *Christian Standard* that he was attending the Congress of the Disciples at St. Louis, Missouri, and was scheduled to deliver one of the principal addresses in support of the missionary society. In December of 1908, Calhoun preached in the Providence pulpit a sermon on the Christian Woman's Board of Missions, and other sermons were preached later in support of the missionary society. In fact, he preached a sermon on this subject each year. Calhoun followed closely in the footsteps of John W. McGarvey, who had been an active supporter of the Kentucky Christian Missionary Society and had become an officer at the age of thirty-three. McGarvey and Calhoun thought to disfellowship the Christian Churches which used the organ would be a greater wrong than to accept the organ's presence. Both accepted and supported the missionary society.

The only available information of Calhoun's interest in missionaries are in the Reports of the Kentucky Christian Missionary Society Convention. In 1909, Calhoun was commended by the convention for his preaching at the Arlington Church Mission on Sunday nights and for returning to the society the stipend paid him. In 1910, he gave a comprehensive report at the annual convention on the country church problems. And during the 1914 Convention, Calhoun lauded churches which had contributed greatly to the missionary society. A statement in the Convention report commended the efforts of Calhoun: "If we had two or three hundred Calhouns, we might make anew many country churches. Perhaps we will have to endow a chair for the education of men for the country church and seat Professor Calhoun in it. Country Church Pedagogy should be the name of it." In the 1915 Convention, it was reported that the Providence Church located in Jessamine County, had conducted mission meetings at Burnside and other points. Under Calhoun's leadership, the Providence Church held Kentucky's first "Rural Church and Bible Institute." The conference was attended by representatives from one-hundred Christian Churches.

The theme of the 1916 Kentucky Convention was the "Rural Church," and the keynote sermon was preached by Calhoun. He was then a member of the Executive Committee and the Recording Secretary of the Board. However, time was running out by 1917 in Kentucky for Calhoun. In the 1916 Convention, he was asked as the Recording Secretary to find two businessmen to be added to the executive committee. The minutes of the decision of the convention were dated on September 19, 1917, at the conclusion of the bitter College of the Bible verbal battle which had been published in the *Christian Standard* through the summer months. It was noted in the minutes that Calhoun had failed to appoint two men to the executive committee. Calhoun is not mentioned at all in the 1918 Convention proceedings, but his successor as minister of the Providence Church was mentioned by name.[12]

The Disciples attached superlative importance to religious education through various media. The teaching of the Scriptures was paramount and secular education was highly honored. In 1869, the Christian Church became a part of the International Sunday School Association program, an interdenominational agency. The Christian Church took action which led to the issuing of the first Uniform Lessons in 1872. The Disciples adopted the plan of the International Uniform Lessons and eventually had a representative appointed to the Lessons Committee. Isaac Errett served as a member of the committee from 1884 to 1888. He was succeeded by Benjamin B. Tyler who was elected president of the Sunday School Association in 1902. Calhoun's turn to serve the International Sunday School Association as a representative of the Christian Church came in 1907 when he was appointed to the Old Testament Committee of the Sunday School Lessons Committee to succeed Tyler.[13] Calhoun continued to serve in this capacity until 1917. Calhoun's crowning joy in his work with the Lessons Committee came in the summer of 1913 when he and his wife traveled to Zurich, Switzerland. Calhoun's expenses on the trip were paid as a member of the International Sunday School Committee. Mary Ettah's expenses were paid by the Providence Christian Church. They visited Egypt, Palestine, Greece, France, and England before returning home.

Calhoun enjoyed an unprecedented and singular honor in 1916 conferred upon him by the Harvard Divinity School. Harvard College was founded to train ministers and magistrates of a godly commonwealth. The date most commonly accepted for the beginning of the Harvard Divinity School is 1816 though Harvard College was founded in 1621. That Calhoun studied just two years at Harvard to earn the most prestigious degrees which the University had to offer says all that is necessary of his knowledge and ability as a student.

The celebration of the one-hundredth anniversary of the Harvard Divinity School took place on October 5, 1916, on the Harvard Campus. At the three o'clock afternoon session in the Divinity School Chapel, President Emeritus Charles W. Eliot delivered the main address. The main evening session was held at the dinner meeting in the Harvard Union with Professor Francis G. Peabody presiding. A select and representative group of Harvard Divinity School graduates from widely separated places as Montreal, Canada, and far away Kentucky had been invited to speak on the occasion. The faculty of the Harvard Divinity School chose to bestow one of the honors to speak upon Dr. Hall Laurie Calhoun. Among the celebrated dignitaries representing Harvard at the dinner was Abbot Lawrence Lowell, President of Harvard University.

Professor Peabody, who was presiding, introduced Calhoun when his turn came and recalled that while Calhoun was at Harvard he had been: "promoted from position to position until he received our highest award and became a Williams Fellow . . . he proceeded to apply for his doctorate in the Old Testament under the paternal direction of Professor G. F. Moore, and what is more, he got it."

Hall Laurie Calhoun on that auspicious occasion gave a courteous and generous acknowledgement for the great honors that Harvard had bestowed upon him.[14] That he should have done otherwise is unthinkable. (No statement that he made in his brief address could rightly be construed as a compromise of his religious convictions). Professor Peabody remarked that Calhoun maintained his orthodox views uncompromised by his studying in the Harvard Divinity School. And it was a wonder to the Harvard professors that he had been able to do so. In less than a year, Calhoun was charged during the 1917 Controversy in the College of the Bible with saying one thing in Cambridge and another in Lexington. One of the charges made was to show Calhoun's inconsistency when he said, "Let us do all the good we can, to all the people we can, and just as long as we can." Furthermore, his critics found fault with him for proposing that it mattters not whether we teach and believe that Christ was humanly divine or that he was divinely human just so we teach and believe that he was divine.

Nineteen-hundred and sixteen was a momentous time in Calhoun's career based upon his positions of prestige in the Christian Church. He was serving as Dean of the College of the Bible, a member of the International Sunday School Association, "pastor" of an old established Christian Church, a world traveller, an honored graduate of the Harvard Divinity School, and known to his contemporaries as the chosen protege of John W. McGarvey.

In less than one year, however, radical changes would take place in the College of the Bible. The College of the Bible was being shoved into the new theology of higher criticism. In the ensuing struggle during the months between March and September of 1917, Calhoun was the principal figure in a bitter controversy between the conservative and liberal parties in the Christian Church. When the last words were written, Calhoun would enter secondary positions in the Christian Church which he finally left in 1925. The leadership he sought in the College of the Bible and the opportunity to become a spokesman for the Christian Church as McGarvey had been was denied him.

7

A Firestorm in the Bluegrass

The first salvo of the Battle of the Book that shook the College of the Bible for two-hundred days was fired on the last days of March by a student, Benjamin F. Battenfield. A circular letter was mailed by Battenfield on March 12, 1917 to approximately three-hundred Christian ministers and other Disciples. The letter precipitated the fundamentalism-modernism controversy that wracked the College of the Bible during the spring and summer months of that year.[1]

The Battenfield letter was a well calculated appeal to the Disciples to protect the College of the Bible against the control of the "destructive critics." At the same time the letter was mailed, a group of students presented a petition to the Executive Committee of the Board of Trustees signed by Battenfield and nine others. The statements which accompanied the letter petitioned the Board to conduct an investigation of the charges made in the letter.

The letter charged that President Richard Henry Crossfield and four professors, A. W. Fortune, W. C. Bower, George W. Hemry, and E. E. Snoddy held advanced critical views and were opposed to Dean Hall Calhoun and Professor Benjamin Deweese who held to the original fundamental beliefs of the College of the Bible. The letter stated that perhaps three-fourths of the students accepted the new doctrines espoused by the liberal faculty. Snoddy was quoted as saying: "I am a hard evolutionist," and "The first chapter of Genesis is poetry." Bower was accused of having called Jehovah "the tribal God of the Jews". In another

Hall Laurie Calhoun

Richard Henry Crossfield

Morrison Hall

comment, Bower was reported as having said: "The Pithecanthropus Erectus is the missing link between man and the lower animals." Fortune was quoted as saying: "The men who wrote the New Testament were inspired and not their writings." Fortune was accused with believing theistic evolution and denying the doctrine of the physical resurrection of the body of Christ.[2]

The Battenfield letter also divulged that a secret meeting was held by students who were "laying" for Dean Calhoun "to catch something against him" to bring about his dismissal. However, some of the students present at the meeting registered their support of Dean Calhoun, and the opponents retreated from their first intractible position.

President Crossfield immediately staged a counter attack in a printed document of five pages to refute Battenfield's allegations. Crossfield's circular letter was mailed on March 17, five days after Battenfield's letter. Crossfield's document contained four exhibits: Exhibit A contained Battenfield's letter and the petition to the Trustees signed by the students. Exhibit B was a letter signed by the five accused professors: Crossfield, Bower, Snoddy, Fortune, and Hemry. The circular said that the Battenfield statements were, in the main, false and misleading. The letter said in part: "we take occasion to affirm our fidelity to the fundamental truths of Christianity as revealed in the Bible, and to the historic principles of the Disciples of Christ."

Exhibit C contained a letter of denials from students who were accused in the Battenfield letter of making heretical statements. The accused students further denied any attempt to eliminate Dean Calhoun from the faculty, and then went on to express "our absolute confidence in Dr. Crossfield and the professors." Furthermore, eighty-seven percent of the student body of Transylvania and the College of the Bible under undue influence signed a protest against the Battenfield letter that favored the accused. Student officers, the editor of the *Crimson Rambler*, captains and managers of the athletic teams, and other student leaders signed the protest against Battenfield.

Exhibit D was a letter signed by Professor Deweese and was meant to leave the impression that Deweese favored Crossfield and the accused faculty. However, the letter by Deweese extended his courtesy to Crossfield and the other faculty members and firmly added: "They know my views and respect my convictions. These views are in line with those emphasized by the

William Clayton Bower

Alonzo Willard Fortune

George Watson Hemry

Elmer Ellsworth Snoddy

founders of the college, and when called upon to state them, I am free to do so without any hindrance."[3]

The foregoing statements and exhibits contained the essentials of Crossfield's circular and were calculated to counter the allegations in the Battenfield letter. The transactons had not as yet been made public. Only persons privy to the content of the letters were cognizant of the trouble brewing in the College of the Bible. President Crossfield calculated to keep the controversy within the confines of the college if at all possible. Crossfield and the accused had denied categorically the accusations leveled against them.

The College of the Bible controversy was made public on March 31, 1917, in a published article in the *Christian Standard* under the title "The College of the Bible in the Limelight Again." The entire circular letter by Crossfield was published. Another letter from C. R. L. Vawter addressed to Crossfield was appended to the circular from Crossfield who wrote patrons of the College of the Bible to help ward off the effects of the Battenfield allegations. However, Vawter's response was damaging to Crossfield and his colleagues. Vawter called upon Crossfield for a simple "yes" or "no" answer to the charges. Vawter wrote: "In all that you have submitted to me, there is not a single word to indicate that your views are other than those of the 'destructive critics.'" Vawter said to Crossfield that if the charges were untrue, "you will come out unscathed."[4]

Editor George P. Rutledge of the *Christian Standard* brought the whole matter into the open for a show down fight. The same March 31 issue of the *Standard* carried an article captioned "Dean Calhoun Speaks." Calhoun's statements was dated March 24, 1917, and said: "In response to certain inquiries which have come to me, I feel that candor compels me to state that for more than a year, I have been fully convinced that destructive criticism was being taught in the College of the Bible." Rutledge, complimenting Dean Calhoun, called upon the Disciples to write to Mark Collis, Chairman of the Board of Trustees, asking for him to demand the fullest and most impartial investigation possible of charges brought against Crossfield and members of the faculty.

Editor Rutledge and General Manager Russell Errett of the *Christian Standard* sent out their own circular letter to Disciple leaders pressing their demand for a committee to be named, in no way officially connected with Transylvania or the College of

Russell Errett

George Perry Rutledge

Mark Collis

Ralph Lafayette Records

the Bible, to conduct the investigation. In the April 7 issue of the *Standard*, a barrage of letters which had poured into the *Standard* office favoring the proposed impartial investigation were printed as well as a few letters which were not in favor of the investigation. An editorial in the same April 7 issue charged that ministers then being trained in the college under the influence of destructive criticism would be the leading ministers for the next quarter of a century and that the new theology would wreck the cause of the Restoration plea.

Rumors were rife in the College of the Bible that Dean Calhoun and the *Christian Standard* were in collusion with Battenfield and the other students who had signed Battenfield's letter. Battenfield in a statement dated March 27, stated that Calhoun and the *Christian Standard* were not responsible for the letter which he had written and had no knowledge of it. The *Standard* added its own comment that nothing was known of the letter until it came to the desk of the editor.

J. B. Briney, a noted evangelist of the Christian Church, added his commentary in the opening skirmishes of the College of the Bible: "the expected has happened . . . for ever since the investigaton of the charges brought against Professor Fortune by John T. Brown, I have been satisfied the question would come up again, for nothing is ever settled until it is settled right."[5]

Eight full pages in the *Standard* were given to letters on the pros and cons of the proposed impartial investigation. Few letters favored R. H. Crossfield. The *Standard* denied attacking the College of the Bible and maintained the journal would act only as a clearing house for all the information. "The *Standard* contends for the faith which was once for all delivered to the saints," so the editor claimed.

The "fat was in the fire." It was not envisioned in the initial stages how bitter and prolonged the struggle would be. When the investigation by the Board of Trustees did get underway, however, it was a far cry from what the *Standard* had originally contemplated. Calhoun seemed not to realize that he had attacked the power structure of Transylvania University and the College of the Bible. The accused were literally fighting for their lives. The *Standard* was determined to expose the radical liberals in the College.

The April 14 issue of the *Standard* further aggravated the growing controversy. Peyton H. Canary, a student in the College of the Bible, submitted to the *Standard* an affadavit of accusations against the faculty and Chancellor Homer W. Carpenter. Canary accused Snoddy, Fortune, and Bower with personally intimidating him in a classroom confrontation in the presence of one other student, J. T. Pugh. Canary also said that Chancellor Carpenter had accosted him on the campus. Canary stated that Carpenter, Chancellor of Transylvania University, was militant toward him and was trying to crush him into silence.

The Lexington fuss was becoming daily more murky. The skirmishes between the factions grew acrimonious. The efforts of President Crossfield to squelch the burgeoning controversy were futile. Editor Rutledge and Dean Calhoun said they had nothing to conceal. Had Crossfield and the accused professors faced up to the charges that they were indeed theological liberals, the issues could have been openly addressed and resolved in one fashion or another.

On April 5, the accused members of the faculty permitted the *Crimson Rambler* to publish an article favorable to them, but nothing was printed from the parties who had charged them with disloyalty. Miss Maurine Dallas Watkins, who had enrolled in Hamilton College in 1914 and had entered Transylvania University the following year, was editor of the *Transylvanian,* the monthly newspaper of the university in 1917. Watkins had decided not to print the material relating to the controversy in the monthly publication, but changed her mind when the weekly *Crimson Rambler* carried the account favorable to President Crossfield and his faculty. Watkins wrote a length reply in the *Transylvanian* answering the statements which had appeared in the *Crimson Rambler*. Editor Watkins objected to the *Crimson Rambler's* impugning the character of the student petitioners and accusing Canary with making derogatory remarks about some ladies of the student body and the wives of the faculty for immodest dress. The faculty refused to name the persons who accused Canary for making derogatory remarks or to give the time and place when the alleged remarks were made. Watkins claimed this was unjust and unfair to Canary.

Watkins disdained the protest petition reputed to have been signed by eighty-seven percent of the student body who had little or no knowledge of the allegations impugning the character of Battenfield and his associates. The signatures included students even in the Preparatory School and Transylvania freshmen students. Watkins stated that the five original petitioners, who withdrew their names from the Battenfield letter, had been called upon by the Administration of the University and College to reflect on the possible consequences if they failed to do so.

Edwin Marx, president of the University Press Association and editor of the *Crimson Rambler,* was a leader of the students who met secretly, according to the Battenfield letter, to dismiss Dean Calhoun, and who enjoined the Executive Committee of the Association to deny Editor Watkins the privilege to print the article favorable to Battenfield, his petitioners, and Dean Calhoun. Watkins was then joined by her associate-editor, Peral Mae Cornelison, in signing an article of explanation which appeared in the April 14 issue of the *Standard.*

Letters continued to pour into the *Standard* in favor of the impartial investigation of the College of the Bible from all over the country. The readers of the *Christian Standard* must have found great interest in the weekly revelations appearing in the *Standard.* Numerous articles and letters over several weeks were published in the *Standard* of one kind or another, and very few were favorable to the accused faculty.

However, President Crossfield and his colleagues also had their supporters. An editorial in the *Christian Century,* an ultra-liberal journal, with uncertain ties with the Disciples, called for a showdown in the College of the Bible fuss under the headline: "Let's Have It Out." A clear cut definition of policy was demanded without compromise. The editorial stated that academic freedom was at stake and demanded that modern concepts such as evolution and historical criticism be taught. The *Christian Century* severely castigated Calhoun: "In all the sorry history of self-appointed heresy hunters, there has never been a more astonishing and pathetic spectacle than this of a graduate of Harvard Divinity School bringing charges of 'destructive criticism' against the teaching of his colleagues." The journal went so far as to impugn even the sincerity of Calhoun.[6]

The *Standard* published and took quick notice of the editorial by publishing it in full with a lengthy attack upon the *Christian Century* saying in one place: "The *Christian Century* is not representing the Restoration Movement. It has flagrantly misrepresented the movement for years, and we are prepared to prove whenever the challenge is picked up."

There was a lull in the number of articles and letters in the *Standard* relating to the controversy for the week of May 5 and May 12. The Board of Trustees found itself being forced to take action. The hopes of Hall Laurie Calhoun, George P. Rutledge, and their associates were that the Board of Trustees would clear up the College of the Bible controversy through an impartial investigation. The *Christian Standard* stated that a report had been received that the Board of Trustees would go into a special session to consider the allegations of the Battenfield circular letter and the charges made by Dean Calhoun. The report proved to be true because such a meeting was in the planning stage.

The Board of Trustees held its first meeting in an executive session on May 1, 1917, to investigate the Calhoun-Battenfield charges. The Board made the policy decision that the Board would retain the sole jurisdiction in the case. During the second session on May 1, Calhoun was requested to appear before the Board to state and explain his charges against the accused faculty. Calhoun appeared before the Board and offered to prefer charges and present evidence to support them if and when a plan of procedure was adopted to guarantee a thorough and fair investigation.

Calhoun, at the request of the Board, suggested such a plan for conducting the investigation. He recommended that at least ten men who were in no way officially connected with the college be invited to be present to hear the entire proceedings. Each side would have a leader and an assistant leader and that a stenographic report of all the proceedings would be made. Hardly had Calhoun finished presenting his proposal when certain members of the Board said that Calhoun was undertaking to dictate how the investigation would be conducted. He was merely making an effort to do what the Board had asked him to do.

The next day, May 2, Calhoun was presented a document from the trustees which declared in essence that it was the right and duty of the members of the Board to conduct the investigation according to their own format. President Crossfield and the accused faculty members were defended by statements from the trustees. The Board stated that the accused supported and desired the investigation as to their character, scholarship, and teaching skills. An investigation was agreed to and the hearing was ordered to proceed without further delay.

On this same day, Calhoun was summoned by the Board to appear and to begin his testimony as a part in the investigation. He was informed that he could not put direct questions to the accused; but would be permitted to present his questions in writing to members of the Board who in turn would ask the questions. The Board of Trustees refused to accept Calhoun's suggestion for outsiders to be present and participate in the investigation. Calhoun was reluctant to submit to the procedures proposed by the Board. However, he agreed to the format because he wanted to get the investigation underway. The Board began proceedings the same day, at 7:30 p.m. without making much progress.

Calhoun again presented himself before the Board to open his part of the investigation on Wednesday morning, May 2. W. S. Irvin, an attorney, was asked by Calhoun to sit with him during the proceedings with the understanding he could only take notes, find pages, and hand items to Calhoun. W. C. Bower, who was present as one of the accused described later what actually went on.

The first session was held in Morrison Hall. There was a long table in the center. On one side sat Mark Collis, President of the Board of Trustees. On the opposite side sat Hall Laurie Calhoun and an attorney with a large bag of law books. Seated at the end was a stenographer. Seated along the south wall were the accused, and around the other walls were the trustees. After prayer, Collis turned to Dean Calhoun that he should proceed with the charges and the supporting evidence.

Calhoun was the first to arise on the occasion of the meeting to address the group. In the early course of the proceedings, Bower stood up and addressed the chair charging that the proceedings amounted to an ecclesiastical set-up for a heresy trial. Bower stated that he refused to be a participant in such a heresy trial. He offered to submit his resignation to the Board if his services to the College of the Bible were not acceptable. Bower then declared: "I refuse to be tried for heresy." Some of the trustees agreed with Bower that they did not want a heresy trial while others thought Bowers was over-reacting to the situation. This maneuver of Bower was apparently designed to confuse the members of the Board and bring a halt to the proceedings, which it actually did.

On the following day, May 3, Calhoun again met with the Board and the accused professors. The "gag rule" fastened on Calhoun curtailed his freedom to present his charges in an open and impartial manner. He consulted with his friends, and they were of the unanimous opinion that Calhoun should not continue further in such a star chamber arrangement. The same day, on Thursday, May 3, Calhoun appeared for the second time before the Board at 2 p.m. He told the board that he could not continue the investigation upon terms which were virutally dictated by his opposition. Calhoun at that time orally tendered his resignation to the Board of Trustees. However, the Board did not accept his resignation at that time.

The following Monday, May 7, a committee of two members of the Board waited on Calhoun in his classroom about 12:30 p.m. Calhoun was informed that his resignation had not been accepted and that he was still a professor in the College of the Bible and Dean of the faculty. Calhoun was informed that he could continue the investigation without embarrassment. Calhoun was presented by the committee the following document setting forth the rules of the procedure:

1. Resolved, that the Board of trustees of the College of the Bible is competent to conduct the investigation of the conditions in the college.
2. They requested Dean H. L. Calhoun to appear before the Board and present his charges against the members of the Faculty of the College in their presence.
3. That all parties shall be given full opportunity to present all testimony in support and defense of the charges.
4. That all members of the Board may interrogate all parties to their satisfaction and that the members of the Board may call for any witnesses or students for examination as to the charges.
5. That the chairman of the Board shall rule on the relevancy of all questions, with the right to appeal to the Board.
6. That all questions put to the members of the faculty shall be put by members of the Board, but all parties may interrogate any other witnesses.
7. That the Board in executive session shall then come to its conclusion and formulate its report.

On Monday afternoon May 7, Calhoun agreed, against his better judgement, to go on with the hearing. He was convinced that the proceedings would follow the rules set by the Board of Trustees, or not at all, and he was anxious that his charges be heard by the Board. Calhoun called only one witness, Irvin Taylor Green. He questioned Green for about twenty-five minutes. Green was then questioned through the Board by Bower and others. The proceedings broke down in a stormy exchange of charges and counter charges leaving Green's testimony unfinished when the Board recessed. Green proved to be the only witness that Calhoun ever called before the Board.

The next session convened at 7 p.m. the same day. Nothing

had been settled in the afternoon session, and the breach between Calhoun and his opposition had widened beyond repair. Calhoun said that some of the Board members were eminently fair in their manner and treatment; but, unfortunately, their number was too limited for them to exercise any influence on the proceedings. He appeared before the Board on that evening of May 7, stating that he would not "continue to have any part in such unfair and unjust proceedings" as were in progress. Calhoun tendered his resignation to the Board of Trustees and withdrew from the meeting. The Board accepted his resignation, and he never returned to the room where the hearing was being conducted.

The Board of Trustees continued meetings through Wednesday, May 9. Battenfield and Canary were called before the Board on May 8. Both agreed to testify only on the condition that Calhoun be present. Alfred Fairhurst, a board member and retired faculty member, questioned Snoddy on his views of evolution. And six students favorable to the administration testified that their faith had been strengthened under the teachings of Snoddy, Bower, and Fortune. At the fifteenth session held on May 9, Bower and Fortune read statements of their defense and then were questioned at length by the Board.

The last two sessions of the Board of Trustees were devoted to formulating the final report. The report declared that the proceedings had not intended to be, in any sense, a "heresy trial." The Board completely exonerated the accused members of the faculty declaring that the teachings of the faculty were in harmony with the best tradition of the Christian Church. The Board heard no students who said their faith had been shakened by the teachings of the accused faculty.

In one of the clauses of the final report is this statement: "The Board believes that the disposition to preserve the good of the past, combined with the ability to improve the task of the present should be the underlying principle to its trusteeship of the institution." President Crossfield and the Board of Trustees had unwittingly set the stage, without meaning to do so, for a bitter controversy which contributed to the formal separation between the conservative and liberal ranks of the Christian Church.

Calhoun served notice to his brethren that the investigation would continue despite the efforts of the Board of Trustees in its report to put the matter to rest. Witnesses would be heard and a full expose of "destructive criticism" being taught in the College of the Bible would be set forth. Calhoun said he had done his best to keep the College of the Bible from falling into the hands of the destructive critics. He quoted John W. McGarvey and Isaiah B. Grubbs as saying that "they would rather see the College of the Bible sunk in the bottom of the ocean than that it should become a place where destructive criticism is taught." But such was the case and Calhoun said, "it is with a heavy heart that I sever my connection with a school which I have loved better than life itself." Calhoun had lost his cause to the liberals and he never sought to disguise the fact.

Whatever may have been the apprehensions of President Crossfield as to the future course of action to be pursued, he was not long in waiting. The direction of the action began to unfold in the next issue of the *Standard*. On May 10, 1917, Professor Ralph L. Records, head of the Chemistry Department in Transylvania University resigned his position in protest declaring: "The College of the Bible to my personal knowledge, has been committed to the teaching of destructive criticism by the recent action of the Board of Trustees." Records submitted his resignation to the Board of Curators of Transylvania University saying the continued existence of Transylvania depended, in a large measure, upon the future of the College of the Bible.

Calhoun began an investigation in the *Standard* of the charges, which the Board had by-passed. Each article was captioned in bold capital letters: "DEAN CALHOUN APEALS TO THE BROTHERHOOD." Professor Records was his first witness and furnished the opening article to be published. Records made twelve lengthy statements of the reasons for his opposition to the conditions which existed within the College of the Bible and the reasons for his resignation: He claimed that students were saying to him that they were losing their faith in the Scriptures. Other ministerial students of a liberal bent told Records that they could no longer preach what they believed due to the ignorance of church members. Records supported the fact that Calhoun was truthful in his allegations. Some of the students of the new thought endeavored to win Record's favor by speaking of the "mossbackism" and "foggyism" of certain professors trying to show that the charges against President Crossfield and his colleagues were untrue.

In personal conversations with some of the accused faculty, Records was convinced that they favored the liberalism set forth in the tenets of "Higher Criticism." Intimidations by the administration and faculty, according to Records, were directed toward students reluctant to sign the protest petition against Battenfield's letter with such statements as: "Well, your name will be given to the President," or "Your scholarship will likely be removed," or "You will find it difficult to receive a scholarship." The petition in protest to the Battenfield letter was submitted to a meeting of the faculty of Transylvania University for their signatures of approval, whereupon, Records refused to affix his name. One of the accused faculty spoke up and asked that "the opposition to be noted."

Records stated that he was "staked out" on an evening when he met with a religious editor, presumably George P. Rutledge, in a Lexington hotel, for conversations with him lasting until nearly midnight. On his way to his preaching appointment on the following Sunday morning, he learned from others what his actions had been on the previous evening. Records concluded that his loss of faith in his *alma mater* was to be found in the conduct and action of the Board of Trustees, which committed the College of the Bible to the support of destructive critics.

Calhoun wrote in the *Standard* that the "so-called" thorough investigation of the College of the Bible had come to an end on May 9, 1917. He told how the Board had spent six days in the sittings (May 1–3 Tuesday through Thursday, and May 7–9 Monday through Wednesday) in seventeen sessions. Calhoun commented that the Lexington newspapers published glowing accounts of the thoroughness of the probe during the decisive days of the proceedings and reported the Board had fully exonerated the accused faculty.[8]

In the June 2 issue of the *Standard*, Calhoun introduced Ben F. Battenfield as his second witness. Battenfield was an older student in the College of the Bible in 1917. He had preached since 1900. E. E. Snoddy had been one of Battenfield's teachers (1899–1901) in Hiram College. Battenfield came to the College of the Bible in 1910 to study the Bible under the likes of McGarvey. Battenfield also enrolled in the classes of Bower, Snoddy, and Fortune. It would be impossible at this point to detail the testimonies of all the participants. Some fifteen students of the College of the Bible gave their testimony in the pages of the *Christian Standard*. All of the students were reputable and mature persons. Three women were among the witnesses. These students who played key roles in the proceedings were singled out and punished in one fashion or another.

The story of Peyton H. Canary, Jr., points up the sorry spectacle that marked that College of the Bible "fuss." Canary had grown up on a farm in Western Kentucky. He was at the time twenty-five years of age and had preached before coming to the College of the Bible. And in 1917, Canary was in his senior year. He was singled out by Professors Bower and Snoddy and Chancellor Carpenter, who, according to Canary, sought to intimidate and crush him. Canary was charged and indicted by the faculty and dismissed from the College of the Bible for "gross insubordination and for making scurrilous attacks against members of the Faculty." This information was published on April 14, 1917, in the *Standard*.

Crossfield and his faculty left the impression that the students who protested were inexperienced and immature. However, this was not the case. Irvin Taylor Green had graduated in 1907 from Transylvania University. He had taught in the public schools of Western Kentucky and served as a school principal and superintendent. He had preached in Murray, Kentucky, before coming to the College of the Bible in 1916. Green had classes under the accused professors and gave supporting information to what others had said. The proceedings which broke down were described by Green in the *Standard* as a farce from beginning to end.

The experiences of Maurine Dallas Watkins serve to point up the bitterness in the initial stages of the controversy following in the wake of the Battenfield letter. Watkins, who had graduated from the Junior College Department of Hamilton College, had entered Transylvania. She, too, had classes under both Snoddy and Calhoun in the College of the Bible. Watkins refused to sign the student protest against the Battenfield letter because she had heard Snoddy say, with other similar remarks, that he was an evolutionist.

Peral Mae Cornelison, associate editor of the *Transylvanian*, also registered her disapproval of the transactions designed to discredit Calhoun. She had been enrolled as a student at Transylvania since September 1914. Cornelison, who had originally signed the protest petition against the Battenfield letter, later demanded the removal of her name upon learning the true nature of the petition. Cornelison remembered that Bower had said in one of his classes that Snoddy was a thoroughgoing evolutionist. She registered for one of Snoddy's classes after hearing Bower's statement due to her curiosity and interest to learn more about evolution. She gave the most detailed account of Snoddy's statements. Not even Snoddy himself ever denied the allegations. Cornelison had learned from Watkins her reasons for refusing to sign the letter and adopted the same position. Cornelison was compelled to put her request in writing for the withdrawal of her name from the petition against Battenfield and was informed that there could possibly be consequences for her action. Watkins and Cornelison were later removed from their editorial positions.

Hall Laurie Calhoun took the witness stand in his own behalf in the August 4, 1917, issue of the *Christian Standard*. Calhoun gave the reasons why he had come to the College of the Bible as a student in 1888 and what had caused him to return to the faculty in 1904. He named the Campbell Institute group and Herbert L. Willett and Charles Clayton Morrison of the *Christian Century* as leaders among the liberals who were bent on destroying the fundamental principles of faith in the Christian Church brotherhood.

Calhoun cited the recent capture of the College of the Bible as the boldest and most unblushing manifestation of the false teaching. Calhoun stated that at the time of Crossfield's election to the presidency of Transylvania University, his supporters claimed that Crossfield stood against destructive criticism and was true to our plea and to the Book. Calhoun stated that it was to his certain knowledge that John W. McGarvey had been opposed to Crossfield's ever becoming president of Transylvania University. Calhoun said that Crossfield had told him that "McGarvey's method of teaching was a farce." Calhoun cited other statements of Crossfield indicating that he "did not accept the Genesis account of creation as being true." Crossfield denied the allegation.

Professor Fortune, according to Calhoun, succeeded best among the faculty in keeping his liberal views concealed. Fortune believed the "inner consciousness" to be the final seat of religious authority. Bower personally told Calhoun that he did not accept the Genesis account of creation and the origin of man. Calhoun said that Snoddy was "less learned, but more dogmatic in his teaching than Professors Fortune, and Bower and made wilder assertions than they."

J. B. Briney expressed his feelings in a *Standard* article saying, "perhaps a greater outrage was never perpetrated upon an unsuspecting people" than had been perpetrated upon the men who were the founders of the College of the Bible. Briney said of Calhoun and Records that "they were neither fools not knaves."

And since they were neither, then something was "rotten in Denmark."9

In the issues of August 11 and 18, 1917, of the *Standard,* Calhoun and Records kept up their relentless attack on Crossfield, Bower, and Snoddy. Little is said about Professor Hemry who was identified with the accused faculty. In the main, he was ignored and considered to be of less importance. The College of the Bible controversy was winding down during the closing weeks of the summer. The September 8, 1917, issue of the *Standard* ran the last accounts of the student accusations directed against the accused faculty.

The opposition to Hall L. Calhoun and his supporters struck rock bottom on Sunday morning, September 2, 1917. Peyton H. Canary, Jr., and his wife had called for letters from the Broadway Christian Church where they held membership because they were leaving for Bethany College. A communication came to Mark Collis, minister of the Broadway Church, saying that some of the elders objected to giving the letters to Canary appending their names. Collis spoke words of commendation on that occasion for Canary and his wife, and Collis said the matter should be acted upon by the congregation. The congregation gave visible assent of their desire to vote on the matter. By a standing majority vote of the members, the motion was carried to award the letters to the young couple. Collis wrote and delivered to Canary and his wife letters of commendation.

Calhoun devoted some little attention to G. W. Hemry toward the end of the controversy because he believed that Hemry was more restrained in his critical views of the Bible, and did not go as far in his teachings as his more erratic brother-in-law, W. C. Bower. And in his last published appeal to the brotherhood, Calhoun took his final shots at Bower. Calhoun was fully aware that it was due, in a large measure, to the generalship of Bower that the College of the Bible had been lost to the destructive critics.

Calhoun had seldom addressed himself to Crossfield, but he did so in his closing remarks in the September 15 issue of the *Standard.* He showed little regard for Crossfield's role in the college takeover, and even less for his scholarship. Calhoun said it was not necessary to say much if anything about Crossfield other than to point out his disloyalty to the College of the Bible and to show the unfair treatment that the students who were opposed to Crossfield had suffered at his hands. Calhoun by this time had moved from Lexington to Bethany, West Virginia. An editorial in the *Christian Standard* thanked Calhoun for all his efforts beginning in the March 31 publication of the journal and concluding September 15.

Even after Calhoun had concluded his "appeal to the brotherhood" to save the College of the Bible from the destructive critics, the *Christian Standard* had "only begun to fight." The exposes and attacks on the destructive critics continued on into 1918. The first world war in Europe was raging at the time. The *Standard* compared the Lexington professors to America's German enemies. They were lampooned as teachers of "German Rationalism" and "German Kultur." The editors heaped insult on insult by saying that the teaching in the College of the Bible should be labeled "made in Germany."[9]

Calhoun addressed for the last time in December of 1917, the College of the Bible controversy. W. C. Bower had delivered an address on September 9, 1917, to his congregation at Newtown Christian Church near Lexington, Kentucky, attacking the veracity of Calhoun. Calhoun had been given ample time to review the Bower's *apologia* and to prepare his response. Bower's address explained nothing and clearly substantiated the statements which Calhoun, Records, and the students had made. Had Bower simply stated that he was a liberal, stamped in the mold of what McGarvey described as "destructive criticism," the smoke would have been cleared away and the fire would have become visible.

Calhoun countered the Bower address with an article published in the *Christian Standard*, December 29, 1917. The article was titled: "What Lies Behind the Camouflage." Calhoun said the obvious: "back of all the camouflage—*a virtual admission* . . . The simple truth is that professor Bower denies the truth of large parts of the Bible. Even to his own interpretation of it."

There is really no place to end this never-ending chapter on the 1917 "Battle of the Book" that shook the very foundations of the College of the Bible in Lexington, Kentucky, for well over two-hundred days. The shock waves of the aftermath of the earthquake have not yet subsided.

8

On Campbell's Mountain

The dissension within the faculty of the College of the Bible in 1917 was catapulted into the public limelight with stunning suddenness by the circular letter written and mailed by Ben F. Battenfield to prominent ministers and leaders in the Christian Church. President Richard Henry Crossfield sought to lessen the damaging influence of the Battenfield letter with a circulation of his own including the Battenfield letter with rebuttals to the allegations made by Battenfield. The Crossfield circular, too, was restricted to the same ministers and prominent leaders in the Christian Church.

As the swift moving events proved, the issue would not be summarily dismissed as a "tempest in a teapot" created by a few trouble-making students. President Crossfield had indeed passed beyond the point of "no return" in his calculated maneuvering to take the College of the Bible into the mainstream of liberalism. Crossfield was the executive officer of both Transylvania University and the College of the Bible. The liberal faculty members selected by him were in place and in his corner and would not be moved to the president's certain knowledge.

Calhoun was faced with a growing awareness of the gradual waning of the conservative traditions which had been established by John W. McGarvey and his associates in the College of the Bible. His suspicion of this change pre-dated the 1917 turmoil in the College. Calhoun was in error, however, in believing that the traditions of the conservative forces which created and had sustained the College of the Bible for fifty years would be adequate to defeat the calculated designs and purposes of President Crossfield and his faculty colleagues to introduce the methods and theology of "destructive criticism" in their efforts to gain control of the College of the Bible.

Calhoun's awareness that he stood alone as a conservative in the College of the Bible came in a series of startling and shocking revelations. Calhoun must have been dismayed in the realization that the control of the institution was fixed in the hands of the Board of Trustees which supported President Crossfield. The Chairman of the Board, Mark Collis, initially stood with Calhoun's opposition though he renounced that stand later.

Since the Board of Trustees chose to exonerate President Crossfield and the accused faculty, Calhoun was left with no meaningful options. His abrupt and final resignation as Dean pointed up the gravity of the growing firestorm which had been smoldering in the College of the Bible. Had Calhoun been left alone in the conflict, he would have faded from the Lexington scene with scant notice; however, this was not to be. The *Christian Standard,* the successor to Alexander Campbell's *Millennial Harbinger,* would not stand idly by and see the College of the Bible diverted from the "Old Paths" without a fight. George P. Rutledge, editor of the *Standard* and Russell Errett, business manager of the journal, immediately manned the ramparts and mounted the attack against President Crossfield, his liberal faculty, and the Board of Trustees in an attempt to divest control of the College of the Bible from their hands. Their efforts were marked by utter failure as later events proved.

With Calhoun's resignation, the rumor mills worked overtime. Speculation was rife. The future of Hall Laurie Calhoun and the College of the Bible became the concern of the whole brotherhood. Some reckoned, supposedly on good information, that a rival school to the College of the Bible would be established with Calhoun designated to be its head. The site of the anticipated college was said by some to be Lexington while others thought it would be located in the Providence Christian Church.[1] The speculations in a short while proved to be rumors only.

The rumors were put to rest by an announcement from T. E. Cramblett, President of Bethany College. He sent a telegram to the *Christian Standard* announcing that a new Graduate School of Religion was in the organizational stages in Bethany College and a faculty already had been selected. The telegram was dated June 9, 1917, from Bethany, West Virginia, and stated:

Hall L. Calhoun, R. L. Records, Walter S. Athearn, J. Walter Carpenter, and Wilbur Cramblett, will be among the faculty of the new graduate "School of Religion," at Bethany next season. Provisions have been made to finance the new enterprise.[2]

The decision of T. E. Cramblett and the Board of Trustees of Bethany College to create a full-fledged graduate school of religion was not necessarily precipitated by the controversy in the College of the Bible. The leaders of the *Christian Standard* and Bethany College did not exult over the 1917 debate that crippled the College of the Bible, but they were gravely concerned over the outcome. There may be little doubt that the unhappy circumstances in Lexington gave good reason for the Board of Trustees of Bethany College to include Calhoun in their plans to establish a graduate school of religion. Cramblett and his associates meant to take up the torch of conservative tradition which the liberal leaders of the College of the Bible had cast aside.

As a matter of fact, the Board of Bethany College had been discussing the establishment of graduate programs since early 1915. This was evidenced by the fact that Bethany College had created a School of Arts and Sciences, a School of Religion, a School of Agriculture and Home Economics, a School of Education, and a School of Fine Arts. The Board appointed a dean for each of the schools. Cramblett envisioned Bethany College as eventually moving toward university status. This move was being made however, at a time when Bethany College was not accredited by a regional accrediting association even on the undergraduate level.[3]

President Cramblett was convinced that he had good reason to believe that "Old Bethany," the mother of a U.S. President, a Speaker of the House of Representatives, preachers, lawyers, doctors, and other distinguished public servants, with its illustrious history and traditions, was entitled to attain such a promising academic future. A more detailed announcement of the proposed Graduate School of Religion later appeared in the *Standard* which stated in part under the caption: "Bethany Answers the Call." The announcement of intentions set forth the thinking and objectives of President Cramblett and the Board of Trustees. The articles lamented that for years young ministers had been left to do post-graduate work in Chicago, Yale, Harvard, and other liberal institutions of higher education. Some indeed had returned to preach the simple gospel and others

Thomas Ellsworth Cramblett

Bethany College

returned to ridicule the gospel story. Others had become indifferent to the old plea for unity, and even to discredit the integrity of the Bible. The article pointed up the fact that no finger of suspicion had ever been pointed at Bethany College or those who were trained there.[4]

During the summer months of 1917, the attacks against the liberal elements in the College of the Bible were carried on unrelentingly through the pages of the *Standard*. The embattled College of the Bible was still taking a terrific beating at the hands of its conservative critics. The brotherhood was kept apprised by President Cramblett and the Bethany Board of Trustees as they laid the ground work for the proposed graduate school of religion scheduled to begin operations that fall.

The *Standard* was winding down its attack on the College of the Bible during the late summer of 1917 which had been spearheaded by Calhoun. An article appeared in the *Standard* stating in greater detail that the Board of Directors of Bethany College, who had unanimously voted to establish a high grade standardized Graduate School of Religion, had now moved resolutely ahead to complete the plans. The Board stated its intention to assemble the best trained and the most efficient men for the work available known in the brotherhood for their outstanding loyalty to the Bible as the infallible revealed will of God.[5] The newly created School of Religion had been organized and ready to go.

The Graduate School of Religion in Bethany College began operating in September of 1917 without additional fanfare other than the usual announcements of the opening of other schools and colleges published in the *Standard*. A college publication announced and described the beginnings of the Graduate School. A faculty of eleven men, in addition to the president, had been employed ready to begin the new program. The minutes of the Board of Trustees record the plans for establishing the graduate School of Religion which would offer the Bachelor of Divinity degree, names of the proposed faculty members and the salary schedule for the graduate faculty.[6] The rising and falling fortunes of the Bethany Graduate School of Religion will be covered at another place in this chapter.

Little is known, because Calhoun wrote nothing, about his move to Bethany College. He joined the faculty of the College in the seventy-seventh year of its existence and when he was fifty-four years of age. The College had operated from the beginning within the liberal arts philosophy of higher education. For many years, Bethany had offered four year courses of study leading to baccalaureate degrees. Hundreds of men who were preaching for the church had received their preparation in Bethany College. Those who were qualified to do so were encouraged to seek and obtain the best possible post-graduate seminary training for their life's work. From the time Calhoun had gone to Yale in 1901, graduate students from among the Disciples at Yale numbered annually from four to twenty-three. T. E. Cramblett said that not all of those who attended returned to the pulpits grounded in the faith and committed to continue the Restoration plea, that of speaking where the Bible speaks. Cramblett said for every student lost to liberalism the brotherhood had lost an investment in effort and money.

When Calhoun resigned his position as Dean of the College of the Bible in 1917, and left Lexington, Kentucky, for Bethany College, he realized that many of his fondest dreams had been shattered. He had been promised, and he expected, that he would succeed McGarvey as president of the College of the Bible and then he would be in a position to protect the College from an invasion of liberalism as McGarvey had been able to do for forty-five years. His opportunity to serve as acting president of the College lasted only a few months following McGarvey's death.

Calhoun left Lexington with a heavy heart and dejected spirit not knowing what would follow him from Lexington or what awaited him at Bethany. He sold his home on Headley Avenue and appointed a lawyer, R. D. Norwood, "my true and lawful attorney," to look after his legal affairs. Calhoun evidently felt that he was apt to become involved in some legal matter arising from the academic conflicts with his peers and the personal testimony given by him in the Board hearing and the articles published in the *Standard*. Calhoun was also leaving the Providence Christian Church, one of the outstanding congregations in the brotherhood.

It is in order at this juncture of Calhoun's career to present a brief but comprehensive sketch of the history of Bethany College. The story of Bethany College is well known in some circles and little known in other circles as a chapter in Restoration history. When Calhoun went to Bethany, the college which Campbell had established was flourishing. The forerunner of Bethany College was the Buffalo Seminary, inaugurated at Bethany in 1818, and housed in the home of Alexander Campbell known then as the "Mansion."

The establishment of an institution for the promotion of higher learning had long been a cherished dream of Campbell. When he was fifty years old, he announced and published his plan to organize Bethany College. The charter for Bethany was procured in 1840 by John C. Campbell of Wheeling, West Virginia. The first session of the college began in the fall of 1841. Campbell maintained that as the Bible is the basis of the highest and truest culture it should form an integral part of a college education. For a long time, Bethany College was the only institution of higher learning in America using the Bible as a textbook. The early days were marked with success; the college became the training ground for leaders of the Disciples of Christ. James A. Harding, co-founder of David Lipscomb College, received his training at Bethany.

Bethany College is located in Brooke County, West Virginia, fifteen miles north of Wheeling, and forty miles south of Pittsburg, Pennsylvania. Traveling to Bethany in the days of Alexander Campbell and until after the turn of the twentieth century was by horseback or horse-drawn vehicles. The fortunes of Bethany College had risen in the early years of its existence; but in the closing years of the nineteenth century, it moved into a period of slow decline.

T. E. Cramblett came to Bethany College in September of 1901 to take over the presidency. The College then had been in existence for about sixty years. Despite its honorable past and living traditions, the buildings had become shabby and were sadly in need of repair. Weeds had been permitted to grow in areas over the campus. The village of Bethany had a scant population of no more than three-hundred citizens and had made no improvements of any kind. The nearest railroad lay seven miles away. The continued existence of "Old Bethany" seemed threatened. The Board of Trustees had mustered courage for a final four year pull before they were willing to give up. However, the "flowering of Bethany" under the tutelage of Alexander Campbell was still glowing in memory.

President Cramblett immediately began a campaign in 1901 to save Bethany College. His efforts were crowned with success at every stage. The friends of the college were already in place. T. W. Phillips in high position and great wealth became the first "princely giver" in the effort to save Bethany. Cramblett was credited with being the financial saviour of Bethany College. He soon established himself as the leading citizen and patron of the Bethany community. First of all, water and lights were brought to the village on the "banks of the Buffalo" in 1904. Eventually, a trolley car line was built from Wellsburg to Bethany, and began operations on a Baccalaureate Sunday in June of 1908, when the first electric car rolled into Bethany. The entire village turned out to see the sight. The faculty and graduating students did not even take the time to doff their academic caps and gowns.[7]

In seventeen years through the labor of one man, Bethany College had survived. New buildings were erected, splendid facilities were provided, enrollments grew and endowments increased. Hopes for the future matched the splendid achievements of the past. And against this background, it becomes clear why President Cramblett and his associates held such high hopes for the success of the new graduate School of Religion. With the failure of the conservative leadership in the College of the Bible, to withstand the encroachment of liberalism in the College, T. E. Cramblett was recognized as the logical successor to John W. McGarvey among the membership of the conservative element in the Christian Church. Cramblett's opposition to "destructive criticism" had been known from the time he took over the helm of Bethany College in 1901, when he wrote in the *Standard:*

> Bethany has never been tinctured with so-called 'Higher Criticism.' And so long as we have any voice in its management of her, she never shall be. To permit such would betray innovation and to betray the trust committed to Bethany by her founders.[8]

T. E. Cramblett never faltered for a moment in keeping this promise until the time of his passing. A notice in the *Standard* in November gave a scant report on the Graduate School of Religion which stated: "The Bible Department is starting off in fine shape . . . Bethany was founded as a school for the training of ministers, and never since its founding has it been better equipped for the job."[9] However, Bethany College would be faced with serious and pressing problems just as the graduate program was being set in motion. World War I, the world's great shame, was in its death throes which made every other consideration seem secondary. As young men died in military camps and on the battlefields of France, little else mattered. In spite of the war raging in Europe, Bethany College resolutely pursued the development of the School of Religion. In 1918, Bethany College was troubled by problems growing out of the war that nearly closed its doors. The details follow later in this chapter.

A progress report of the School of Religion in the early period of operation is recorded in the minutes of the Board of Trustees which met January 4, 1918. President Cramblett reported to the Board that the "School of Religion which was re-organized a year ago, has given of its power to meet a real need." He expressed confidence that with the return to normal conditions (Post World War I), the college would attract an increasing number of young men who would prepare themselves for Christian ministries. W. S. Athearn for an unexplained reason did not accept the deanship of the School of Religion to which he was elected. The honor instead went to J. Walter Carpenter. There is no indication as to why Hall L. Calhoun was not elected to the post, and there is no evidence that he sought the office. However, Calhoun was more highly qualified than Carpenter by training and experience. Calhoun was honored by being appointed as the Thomas W. Phillips Professor of Old Testament Literature and Hebrew. He was further complimented by President Cramblett's statement as a professor "who with his other gifts is an efficient teacher of oratory." Calhoun was asked to conduct one class at the undergraduate level on the subject of speech. There is no question but that Calhoun was deeply involved in the development of the plans and the curriculum for the Graduate School of Religion.

When Calhoun went to Bethany College, he was accompanied by Ralph L. Records. He resigned in 1919 from Bethany College to return to Indiana to care for his aging parents. Later he became the president of the Cincinnati Bible Institute. Peyton H. Canary and Irvin T. Green also left the College of the Bible to enroll in Bethany College. Canary and Green graduated in the 1918 commencement with the Bachelor of Arts and Masters of Arts degrees respectively. Green eventually became a valued member of the Bethany faculty. Another note of interest is the fact that S. S. Lappin, former editor of the *Christian Standard,* was head of the Extension Department. Lappin was involved in the attack against Willard Fortune at the time of his appointment to the faculty of the College of the Bible. He seriously opposed Fortune because of his liberal leanings. Calhoun must have rejoiced in having Lappin as an associate.[10]

A cursory examination of the Bethany College catalogs which were published between the time that Calhoun went to Bethany in the fall of 1917 and the time he left Bethany in the spring of 1925 shows that Calhoun's scholarship and talents were brought into full play. For the school year 1918–19, Calhoun taught advanced courses in the English Old Testament and courses in the Hebrew Old Testament. His professional teaching assignments during the second calendar year, were increased to include courses in Old Testament Criticism, as well as courses in New Testament Criticism. No other person among the Disciples of Christ was better qualified. He must have taught his courses with highest approval in the graduate school since no one said otherwise.

The school year (1918–19) at Bethany College was marred by two significant events. One was sudden and indeed sad. The untimely death of T. E. Cramblett was a serious shock. The other event was a tragic student strike against the administration and Board of Trustees of the College. President Cramblett and the faculty had indicated strong confidence in the expanded program at Bethany. Success had seemed to mark the efforts of President Cramblett from the first day he arrived on the Bethany campus. However, Bethany College suffered an unforeseen blow in the early months of 1919. A student strike, in no way connected with the School of Religion, resulted in great disruption of the college and the suspension of classes.However, few students or classes were affected in the School of Religion by the student walk-out.

World War I was having profound effects on the colleges and universities of the nation. And especially disturbing were the reports of the deaths of a large number of young men who died or were killed in service. In the spring of 1918, the Secretary of War mailed a circular letter announcing the Department of War proposal to furnish military instruction in colleges. The proposal required a minimum enrollment of one-hundred men in a program of military science that was called the Student Army Training Corps. The discussion by the Board to adopt the S.A.T.C. caused slight disruption at Bethany College during the fall months of 1918. By the start of the second session in 1919, the situation had become critical. At a meeting of the Executive Committee of the Board of Trustees, on January 22, 1919, it was decided to reject the S.A.T.C. and to ask the federal government to organize and provide a Reserve Officers Training Corps in Bethany College. Since the unit required a minimum of one hundred men to qualify for approval, this meant all male students who were enrolled in Bethany College were required to join the R.O.T.C. for the remainder of the school year. This resulted in a student strike lasting through most of the school term. The matter was eventually resolved when the Board voted to withdraw from the R.O.T.C. The whole matter was a mistake from the beginning to the end on all sides. By May 4, 1919, two-hundred and thirty students out of an enrollment of two-hundred and fifty droppd out of Bethany. Moreover, dissatisfaction over R.O.T.C. reached the ranks of the professors causing most of them to resign. Following the action of the Board to abolish military training, many students returned to the campus and the unfortunate circumstances were gradually dissipated.[11]

A pall was cast over the campus when President Cramblett was taken suddenly ill with blood poisoning which had set up in a wound in his hand. His death was announced on June 15, 1919. The consequences of the passing of President Cramblett was not immediately apparent to Calhoun, or the faculty, nor the Board of Trustees. Calhoun and Cramblett were kindred spirits and that relationship was recognized and appreciated by their contemporaries.

The Board of Trustees was faced with the task to appoint a worthy successor to T. E. Cramblett who would carry on the traditions of "Old Bethany." The Trustees were not prepared for such a momentous decision. The Board of Trustees met and quietly settled the matter in Pittsburg, July 17, 1919. The Trustees, by a unanimous vote, requested Cloyd Goodnight to leave the prominent pulpit of the First Christian Church in Uniontown, Pennsylvania, where he had served for seven years to accept the presidency of Bethany College.[12] At the time Cloyd Goodnight was nominated as the successor of T. E. Cramblett as President of Bethany College, his identity with the Campbell Institute in the University of Chicago was seriously questioned. Goodnight who was questioned by the Board of Trustees disclaimed any sympathy with the ultra-liberal Campbell Institute or with "Destructive or Higher Criticism." He admitted that he had been associated with the Campbell Institute but claimed he left it when he learned of the liberal leanings.[13] Cloyd Goodnight moved immediately to heal the wounds and restore stability on the campus which the strike had inflicted. It was a slow process to restore the level of enrollment, but recovery was assured.

There is no clear evidence that Calhoun had been involved in the proceedings in any significant fashion. His professorial duties with the college were carried on as set forth in the college catalogs. Recovery from the 1919 student strike was followed by another development that would bring an end to the School of

Religion in Bethany College. The college administration and Board of Trustees were taking decisive steps that would bring academic accreditation by the Southern Association of Colleges and Secondary Schools. The academic schools which had been organized in Bethany were discontinued and replaced with academic departments with chairmen instead of deans to meet the requirements of the Association for an undergraduate college.

The completion of plans to apply for accreditation for the college was rapidly being realized. On December 2, 1921, Bethany College was admitted to membership into the Southern Association of Colleges and Secondary Schools. The accreditation standards indicated that Bethany College lacked qualified personnel, adequate physical facilities, and a sufficiently large student body to warrant college course offerings on both the undergraduate and graduate levels.

At a Board meeting of the Trustees on January 30, 1922, President Goodnight announced that: "We are confining ourselves for the present, strictly to work leading to the B.A. and the B.S. degrees. The M.A. degree will not be conferred after this year, since we are not in a position to offer an adequate amount of that type of graduate work."[14]

Calhoun never commented on the direction that Bethany College was taking while he was on the faculty. The implications were apparent. Calhoun would no longer teach courses on a strictly graduate level. His vast scholarship could not be brought into play by teaching only on an undergraduate level. In all probability, Calhoun could see that the administration of Bethany College was losing interest in "Ministerial Education" by becoming a liberal arts college as the programs envisioned by him and Cramblett were relegated to the background.

Year by year, the college catalogs and the minutes of the meetings of the Board of Trustees reflected Calhoun's steady decline in a position of prominence in Bethany College. The college catalog for 1920–21 dropped the appellation, School of Religion. Calhoun taught his usual undergraduate courses within the newly created Department of Old Testament. A new course was listed in Old Testament Geography which was assigned to him. Additional teaching responsibilities for Calhoun including a full set of speech courses were listed in the Public Speaking Department. The number of Bible and speech courses which Calhoun taught during the school year 1923–24 were reduced, no doubt, due to the student demand for such courses.

The last year which Calhoun taught in Bethany (1924–25) followed the same pattern as the year before. In this last year at Bethany, Calhoun was joined on the faculty by his wife, Mary Ettah. She was an accomplished speech teacher with great knowledge who had graduated from the Curry School of Expression in Boston. The courses which Calhoun had taught were listed in the minutes of the Board meetings, but his name did not appear for the 1925–26 school year when the faculty was elected. His replacement had not been secured. Calhoun had left the ranks of the Christian Church after a quarter of a century of identification with that religious constituency.

Calhoun was a highly respected teacher while he was in Bethany. No criticism of Calhoun's method of teaching was voiced, such as was voiced in the 1917 controversy at the College of the Bible. A careful perusal of the minutes of the Board of Trustees from 1917 to his departure, wherever his name appears, reflects the high esteem in which he was held as a professor and to the quality of his instructions. There is one curious note. The minutes of the Board show that he and Records were not listed on the faculty roster at the first meeting following the student strike. However, Calhoun's name was listed on a later roster; and Records was listed as having been granted a leave of absence.

Calhoun had declared his intention to leave Bethany in the early part of 1925. It is a fact that Calhoun's annual salary was dropping behind other faculty members with less training and shorter length of tenure. In the spring of 1924, Calhoun reached the point that he was disenchanted with Bethany and the growing liberalism in the Christian Church even then threatening in the foreseeable future to capture Bethany College. He had turned his attention to seek ways and means to leave Bethany College and separate himself from the Christian Church. He was determined that his leaving would be mutually agreeable and that he would not arouse the animosity of his peers in Bethany College, nor his brethren within the Christian Church fellowship. He made satisfactory arrangements with President Goodnight which called for him to resign his teaching position in Bethany College and to terminate his employment at the end of the school year in the spring of 1924. Calhoun also withdrew from his preaching assignments with the Christian Church without any publicity.

The eight years Calhoun lived in Bethany were pleasant ones. He preached away from the campus on week-ends for churches in traveling distance from the village of Bethany. His summers were fully engaged in protracted meeting work. Calhoun left no record of his preaching activities during this period. Calhoun and his family lived in a thirteen room home in Bethany which had been built by President Cramblett. The rooms upstairs were rented to teachers. His grandson, Orvell Crowder, now a chaplain in Phillips University, recalls visiting his grandfather during the Bethany years. He remembers the visits as happy ones. Occasionally, the older members of the family would bring up unhappy memories of the period that the Calhoun children were growing up in Lexington. A major chapter in Calhoun's life spanned the year 1924–25, the year that he gave to making plans to go back to Tennessee to serve as Associate President with N. B. Hardeman of Freed-Hardeman College (1925–26). The details of this story are forthcoming in the following chapter.

9

Back Home in Tennessee

Whatever hopes Hall Laurie Calhoun may have had in going to Bethany College to combat the growing forms of liberalism as set forth in the tenets of Higher Criticism were dimmed after the death of President T. E. Cramblett with each passing year. Why did Calhoun leave Bethany College and return to the state of his nativity? This is the question, but the answer does not come easily. There were no known public pressures or personal criticisms directed against Calhoun while he was at Bethany. The minutes of the meetings of the Board of Trustees show no particular displeasure with either his teaching methods or personal beliefs. At the time Calhoun left Bethany in the spring of 1925, no public denunciation from Calhoun was directed against Bethany College in any form, nor was Calhoun criticized by his peers while in Bethany or after he left. Calhoun taught with distinction in the West Virginia mountain college. Memories of his competence in the classroom linger to the present among those who knew him. He seems to have been completely ignored by the college and church power structure once he was gone.[1]

One source of explanation for Calhoun's leaving Bethany is found in the personal notes of Mary Ettah Calhoun written after her husband's death. The value of her comments can be measured by what Calhoun had done and written earlier. He and his wife gradually became aware of the growing trend toward liberalism in Bethany College and the Christian Church soon after the death of the senior Cramblett. It will be recalled that some members of the Board of Trustees had questioned the appointment of Cloyd Goodnight as the successor of Cramblett to the presidency of the College since he had been a member of the Campbell Institute at the University of Chicago at one time.

Other matters pertaining to the College also troubled Calhoun. Wilbur H. Cramblett, son of the lamented T. E. Cramblett, came on the faculty at the time Calhoun did. And later, much to Calhoun's dismay, the fact dawned on him that Wilbur H. Cramblett was cast in the liberal mold. He was educated in Yale University where he received the Ph.D. degree. It was clearly apparent that the rising star in the future fortunes of Bethany College would be Wilbur H. Cramblett. He proved himself to be a highly capable administrator, and became increasingly the most popular faculty member in Bethany College. Following the sudden and unexpected death of Cloyd Goodnight on October 3, 1932, the Board of Trustees, as was expected, appointed Wilbur H. Cramblett President of Bethany College. He became one of Bethany's most successful and honored presidents.

Calhoun learned first hand the theological views of Wilbur H. Cramblett. Wilbur did not hold the conservative views of his father and was frank in saying so. Calhoun confronted Cramblett as to his biblical positions. He freely admitted that his education at Yale had liberalized his old concepts and ideas of Christian doctrine. Cramblett assured Calhoun that no one would interfere with his teaching what he believed, but indicated that other professors would be allowed equal freedom to teach the "new theology". He urged Calhoun to remain in Bethany and represent his views to students who chose to sit in his classes. Calhoun realized the full implications of such an arrangement and found it totally unacceptable. He remembered the wreckage which had been wrought in the College of the Bible, and he refused to be used in a new round of dialectics to represent to the students the other side of "higher criticism."[2]

The second factor that caused Calhoun to consider leaving Bethany College centered in the person of a prominent young minister, John Barclay, who served his first "pastorate" (1923-24) in the Bethany Memorial Christian Church in Bethany. Barclay had graduated with highest honors from a high school in Lexington, Kentucky. He was the first high school graduating student in Lexington to receive the Yale Cup, an award based on scholarship, leadership, and character. Barclay had studied as early as 1916 in the College of the Bible, which he said later, provided him with a taste for the new trends in theology. In 1919, Barclay became a student in the University of London where his earliest liberal concepts of theology were confirmed by the British theologians, Peter Forsyth and Alfred E. Gaire.

Barclay graduated from Transylvania University in 1920 *cum laude*. For the next two years, he studied in the College of the Bible. He went immediately from the College of the Bible to Union Theological Seminary in New York where he studied under Harry Emerson Fosdick, an arch liberal of that era. Barclay said: "The College of the Bible had advanced so far in its acceptance of the modern scholarship of the Bible that the teaching there had conditioned his mind for the liberal view that found expression at Union in New York.[3] Barclay exposed his liberal views from the pulpit without disguise and introduced Sunday school literature in the Bethany Church cast in the liberal mold.

It is clear that with this knowledge of the trend of events Calhoun's decision to leave Bethany was not suddenly precipitated. He began to lay careful plans to leave the school and the Christian Church. Calhoun said nothing to the students; however, he explained his position to some of his fellow teachers. He decided there would be no "Bethany version" of a repeat of what had happened in 1917 in the College of the Bible. Calhoun regarded the liberalizing of both institutions as a betrayal of the Restoration movement. He had little hope there would be a reversal in Bethany College of the liberal theological trend that had troubled the College of the Bible. He was unwilling to make an issue of the forces of "destructive criticism" already invading Bethany College. And had he raised his voice in opposition, it would have made little or no difference.

Calhoun saw the handwriting on the wall, and the message was clear. Bethany College would go the way of the College of the Bible without a voice being raised in opposition. Calhoun suffered painful memories of his defeat at the hands of President Richard Henry Crossfield at Transylvania University. Calhoun resolved that he would not fight that losing battle again. He informed the Administration of Bethany College of his intentions to resign. Both parties agreed that Calhoun's leaving would not be an excuse for any disquieting circumstances that would disturb Bethany College, or result in personal hurt to Calhoun.

Another part of the story details the reasons for Calhoun's leaving Bethany College in 1925 to become Associate President of Freed-Hardeman College. Calhoun's position as he believed would be that of a coequal of N. B. Hardeman in the administration of the Tennessee college. This is fully documented through

Nicholas Brodie Hardeman

Freed-Hardeman College

the correspondence carried on between Hardeman and Calhoun and through the *Gospel Advocate* articles which kept the church of Christ brotherhood informed on the moves being made.[4]

It was the spring of 1924 when Calhoun had reached the point that he was definitely disillusioned with Bethany College and disenchanted with the liberalism in the Christian Church. He turned all of his attention to seeking ways and means to separate himself from the Christian Church. He desired that his leaving would be mutually agreeable, and that he would not arouse the animosity of his peers in the College, nor the opposition of his brethren in the Christian Churches. He made what he considered were satisfactory arrangements which called for him to resign his teaching position and to withdraw from his preaching assignments in early 1925. The Minutes of the Board of Trustees and Calhoun's reports reflect that the agreement was kept amicably by both sides.

Calhoun's first public move to affiliate with the churches of Christ came in September of 1924 when he visited with F. W. Smith who was preaching for the church of Christ in Franklin, Tennessee. N. B. Hardeman was at that time conducting a gospel meeting for the church where Calhoun had preached from 1897 to 1900. However, correspondence between Calhoun and Hardeman indicates that Hardeman had written Calhoun in early February of 1924 proposing that Calhoun consider joining him on the faculty of Freed-Hardeman College. Calhoun's answer to Hardeman in a letter dated February 18, 1924, was a response to what he called Hardeman's "very kind letter" and indicated Calhoun's appreciation for Hardeman's sincerity, growing influence, and clear head. Thus Calhoun's visit to Franklin in September may have been prompted by his February correspondence with Hardeman.

Calhoun recalled to Hardeman the days at Georgia Robertson Christian College (1900) when they were so "pleasantly and intimately associated." What Calhoun said in the letter is strangely odd, to say the least, when once his views on his growing criticisms of Bethany College is known. He admitted to Hardeman that "my heart has often yearned for the old associations and does so now." However, at this point, he did not indicate to Hardeman any intent to leave Bethany. Calhoun wrote:

> I am trying to do my duty as I see it and am teaching and preaching the Bible as the only infallible rule of faith and practice in religion.

> My work at Bethany has been pleasant and is growing more so. I have every reason that human assurance can give that Bethany is going to stand true to the Book and I have been strongly urged to remain here and help hold the school true to the Bible in the face of the tide of unbelief that is sweeping over the land. It is sometimes difficult to decide what is best.

This letter to Hardeman written by Calhoun about sixteen months before he left Bethany is typical of his indecision, complexity, and frustrations. He was caught in a dilemma with Bethany College and the Christian church just as he had been in many of the situations in which he found imself after he first contemplated becoming a preacher. There are clear inconsistencies between what he said his status was in early 1924, and what he said his position with Bethany College was in 1925. It is difficult to harmonize what Calhoun said about the freedom which he had at Bethany in his teaching assignments that "they had been pleasant and were growing more so." Later, he publicly renounced the practices of the "digressives". He did not say who gave him the "human assurance" that Bethany was going to stand "true to the Bible." Certainly it did not come from Wilbur Cramblett.

It is strange that with Calhoun's growing disappointment with the Christian Church that he would say: "I have been strongly urged to remain here and help hold the school true to the Bible." We are also led to wonder who so encouraged him. Calhoun makes another paradoxical statement in the context of the same letter: "It is sometimes difficult to decide what is best, but I have asked for divine guidance and I am trusting it will be given." The wonderment of this statement is couched in the fact that he had not questioned before the divine guidance in his preaching for the "digressives" for longer than a quarter century. In the context of Calhoun's letter in February of 1924, it is certain that he was undecided and had mixed feelings about leaving the Christian Church and Bethany College.

The course of action which Calhoun finally decided to take is set forth in the Freed-Hardeman College Bulletin dated April, 1925. Hardeman wrote in retrospect in the publication of the meeting he had with Calhoun in the fall of 1924:

> While at Franklin last fall, I met Brother H. L. Calhoun under whom I had been a pupil in Georgia Robertson Christian College some years ago. He then told me of his purposes and intents. A

correspondence followed from which it was learned that he would consider becoming a member of Freed-Hardeman faculty.[5]

This personal meeting between Hardeman and Calhoun took place at Franklin, Tennessee, in the early fall of 1924.

Following this meeting in Franklin, Hardeman wrote Calhoun a letter dated October, 1924, expressing his kind feelings toward Calhoun and giving his approval of the course of action Calhoun was taking. In a letter to Hardeman dated in Bethany November 7, 1924, Calhoun detailed his revealed intention to serve all connections with Bethany College and the Christian Church:

> I want to leave here with everyone connected with the College saying that I left like a Christian man. I have talked fully to the President and told him that I intend to leave not later than June and he asked me to keep my intention private until after Christmas and said he thought it best to do so.

Calhoun then in the same letter said he would base his further course of action on "what the Lord seems to want me to do, to do it, I shall be willing to consider going anywhere that may seem to be His will." We are again made to wonder how Calhoun planned to ascertain precisely the will of God in the matter.

The letters that Hardeman wrote to Calhoun are not extant. However, much of the content of Hardeman's letters is implied in Calhoun's replies to Hardeman. Calhoun wrote to Hardeman on November 28, 1924, acknowledging a letter from Hardeman dated November 17, 1924. Calhoun's stated intention to leave Bethany no later than June of 1924 would not be publicly announced until later in the school year in response to President Goodnight's request. Calhoun expressed his love for West Tennessee and the confidence that he and Hardeman could work closely together.

In a letter dated December 6, 1924, Hardeman wrote (letter not in hand) what must have given Calhoun cause for serious concern. Hardeman evidently was pressing Calhoun to go public with his decision. Calhoun answered:

> I do not know exactly what to say in answer to your last letter. In fact, I do not see anything I could say as yet. It seems to me that you and I ought to see each other somewhere and talk matters over fully to be sure everything is plainly understood by us both.

The reply indicates a high level of apprehension on the part of Calhoun who was on the brink of breaking with the Christian Church. He says in the same letter: "I appreciate your keeping matters quiet for the present. I hope before long to speak as I please." And Calhoun asked Hardeman to suggest "a place by which we might have a conference at some time in the not so distant future." The time and the place were soon to be arranged. Calhoun and Hardeman met in the apartment of M. C. Kurfees in the Watterson Hotel in Louisville, Kentucky, on December 22, 1924. Kurfees was present and joined in the discussions as they went over the whole situation.

Kurfees also had graduated from the College of the Bible. However, he was seven years the senior of Calhoun. Kurfees was serving as minister of the Campbell Street Church in Louisville at the time of the conference with Calhoun and Hardeman. He died in 1931 after preaching forty-five years for the Campbell Street Church and its successor, the Haldeman Avenue Church. Hardeman spoke at Kurfee's funeral. It will be remembered that Kurfees and Calhoun had exchanged pointed letters in 1900 over Calhoun's "unanswerable arguments" favoring the presence of the organ in worship. Hardeman wrote in the *College Bulletin* that at this personal conference with Calhoun "almost every item of school work and Bible teaching was discussed".

The conference seemed to have produced unity in the thinking, belief, and purpose between Calhoun and Hardeman, with Kurfees concurring, with their plans regarding their future in Freed-Hardeman College.

Calhoun returned to his home in Bethany following the Louisville meeting with Hardeman and Kurfees, and on December 26, 1924, wrote Hardeman a letter in which he said: "I reached home promptly after our very pleasant conference in Louisville last Monday. In thinking over matters since then, it has occurred to me that a definite statement, in writing, of my views along certain lines might not be amiss." Calhoun proceeded to set forth his "views" in this letter and the letter was later published in an article which appeared in the *Advocate* in the January 22, 1925 issue titled "Hall L. Calhoun's Statement of His Position."[7] Calhoun was exceptionally clear and concise in stating his position. Significant among his "statements" are the following:

1. I believe the Bible to be the inspired word of God, true in its statements of facts, authoritative in its commands and that it is our only and all sufficient rule of faith and practice.
2. I believe that in the church of Christ the worship is prescribed inclusively and exclusively; that we are told what to do in our worship and these are the things we must do and that we may not change them either by addition, subtraction, or substitution.
3. I do not believe that instrumental music is any part of the ordained worship of God or that it is permissible to use it as worship.
4. I believe that humanly organized missionary societies lead to ecclesiasticism and human authority in religion.
5. I believe that destructive criticism and evolution are trying to over-throw Christianity and that instrumental music and humanly organized missionary societies are seeking to corrupt it.
6. It is my earnest wish to spend the remainder of my days working for pure New Testament Christianity among those who are of similar faith and practice.

It is interesting and significant to note that Hardeman had in hand a letter from F. W. Smith, dated Nashville, Tennessee, December 26, 1924, when he received Calhoun's statement. Smith was replying to a letter which he previously had received from Hardeman. Smith expressed his conviction that he believed Calhoun was sincere and earnest regarding his changed attitude toward the societies and instrumental music in Christian worship. Smith related the details of correspondence which had taken place between Calhoun and H. Leo Boles, President of David Lipscomb College at the time, who put the question to Calhoun: "Will you teach that instrumental music in the worship and Human Societies for the spread of the Gospel is unscriptural?" And Calhoun answered with an unequivocal "yes." Smith described Calhoun as one of the most scholarly men in the church, and as a preacher and teacher of God's word with few equals.

Letters in the Hardeman-Calhoun file reveal that Hardeman had written both Kurfees and Smith asking them to answer certain questions and give their candid opinions of Calhoun. Hardeman may have entertained some reservations about Calhoun and needed supporting documentation in writing from these two other noted brethren who knew Calhoun well before presenting Calhoun to the friends and supporters of Freed-Hardeman College. The letter of Kurfees followed that of Smith dated from Louisville, Kentucky, December 29, 1924. Kurfees said in brief that "I regard him as a man of unimpeachable honor and integrity. I am sure that he would never intentionally misrepresent his position or convictions on any subject for any consideration."

Kurfees, however, made a qualifying statement of Calhoun's stand on controversial issues:

> I am thoroughly convinced that, while he may not go to the identical extreme of some of us in our conscientious attitude toward these things, it is, nevertheless, his devout and sincere purpose to stand aloof from them and I believe he will do so with genuine fidelity and integrity. I would perfectly be willing to risk him in any situation where the truth needs defense and error needs opposition.

Kurfee's statement reveals both the paradoxes and even self-contradictions that were typical of Calhoun extending over a lifetime. Kurfees knew of Calhoun's disposition to procrastinate when it came to taking a firm stand on a public religious issue.

Armed with the responses from Smith and Kurfees, and the letter from Calhoun himself stating his "views," Hardeman proceeded to set in motion efforts that would precipitate the famous mass meeting held on the campus of Freed-Hardeman College on January 1, 1925. Hardeman wrote a statement which appeared in a *Bulletin* of the College:

> When these things (correspondence and Louisville Conference) became known, a meeting of the brethren and friends was called, the prospect of securing Brother Calhoun was announced and the large number present by unanimous vote urged the Board of Trustees to engage our services for the session 1925–26.[8]

A. G. Freed and N. B. Hardeman had organized the National Teachers' Normal and Business College in 1907. The Board of Trustees re-named the school, Freed-Hardeman College in 1919. In 1923, both Hardeman and Freed left the Henderson School due to personal differences. Freed went to David Lipscomb College and Hardeman gave his full efforts to evangelism. Hardeman also made a trip in company with Ira Douthitt to the Holy Land during this time. During the two year period (1923–25), W. Claude Hall served as President and C. P. Roland served as Dean of the College. Hardeman wrote that: "During the past two years, many friends of Freed-Hardeman College have insisted upon my return to it. Different members of the Board of Trustees have also added their influence along this line."

Hardeman had decided to return to the College as early as September of 1924 which had prompted him to approach Calhoun about joining him for the 1925 fall semester. Though both Hardeman and Calhoun had agreed on a relationship as Associate Presidents of the College, they saw the need to create a large body of support, enthusiasm, and commitment on the part of friends of the College from the region which it served. Thus the mass meeting of preachers, elders, leaders, and friends was called for January 1, 1925. It remained for L. L. Brigance to report the meeting in the January 21, 1925, issue of the *Gospel Advocate*. Brigance began his service as librarian in Georgia Robertson Christian College in 1902. In 1905, he married a cousin of Hardeman and remained with Freed-Hardeman College until his death on February 4, 1950.

Brigance wrote his description of the meeting "at the request of the board president, E. P. Smith, and other members of the Board of Trustees at Freed-Hardeman College". A large number of interested brethren from five adjoining states attended the new year's meeting and all of the trustees were present with the exception of one. The meeting was called for the purpose of planning greater things for the school. The speakers of the occasion included E. P. Smith, chairman of the Board of Trustees, who spoke of the difficulties and problems faced by the College in past days. Smith was serving as the superintendent of public schools in Martin, Tennessee, at the time. Smith told of the request that members of the Board and others had made on Hardeman to return to the school which bore his name. Hardeman then spoke in terms of his past and continuing commitment to the College. He spoke to the heart of the meeting as he related the details of his correspondence with Calhoun and his meeting with Calhoun in the Watterson Hotel in Louisville with Kurfees present. Hardeman's speech was deeply moving and was received with expressed emotions of tears and expressions of joy. Roland and Hall gave their voices of approval. The Board unanimously voted to engage N. B. Hardeman and Hall Laurie Calhoun to serve the school in the role of associate Presidents. The Board in a called executive session "passed a resolution to turn over the school to Hardeman and Calhoun to run with the understanding that W. Claude Hall and C. P. Roland would be retained." Calhoun was not present for the Henderson meeting.

Hardeman immediately sent a telegram to Calhoun notifying him of the meeting and the decisions made by the Board and requested a statement from Calhoun that could be read to the brethren and made public. Calhoun's response to Hardeman's telegram is hedged with conditional reservations. He said that he thought before the matter was made public that all business details should be definitely settled. He was apprehensive that President Goodnight would not want the decision made public at that early date. Calhoun also suggested that his wife, Mary Ettah, could teach some classes in expression which was a matter that had not been under consideration.

Calhoun was never coy nor reserved, however, about financial support which he desired. He informed Hardeman that he was refusing all invitations to hold meetings from "digressive" churches. Calhoun suggested that he would like for Hardeman to help arrange meetings for him during the summer months of 1925 with "loyal" churches in the South. Calhoun expressed the wish that he and Hardeman could meet at a later time to work out their plan for the College in minute detail. In spite of his hedgings, the course Calhoun would follow is apparent in his letter to Hardeman dated January 6, 1925, from Bethany.

Hardeman exercised great patience in dealing with Calhoun during the last critical period of negotiations. As a matter of fact, Hardeman and the College had a very high stake in Calhoun's joining the faculty of the College. Calhoun added a quality of excellence in academic training that no other preacher or teacher in the churches of Christ possessed. His prestigious degrees and his reputation as a preacher and teacher were superlative and precisely what Freed-Hardeman College needed at this crucial juncture. Hardeman needed Calhoun's help to give the College academic credibility and to gain the confidence of the brethren following the break-up with Freed. Calhoun likewise needed the image which affiliations with the College and Hardeman would give him among the churches of Christ after breaking with the Christian Church.

Hardeman's patience and importuning finally paid off. He wrote Calhoun a letter dated January 26, 1925, describing the campus, actions of the Board of Trustees, the contract offered them, with a copy of Brigance's article to be published in the *Gospel Advocate*. A letter dated January 12, 1925, was written by Calhoun to Hardeman from Bethany. Whole heartedly and without mental reservation, he wrote Hardeman, that he was saying yes to all the proposals. He agreed for the Brigance article to be published in the *Advocate* and elsewhere. Calhoun declared that he would no longer keep secret his intentions and invited Hardeman to give publicity to their plans as Hardeman deemed best.

Calhoun expressed appreciation to Hardeman for having certain churches invite him for meetings during the summer months of 1925. He informed Hardeman that he would leave Bethany to come to Henderson during the "Bethany Easter" vacation beginning on Friday, April 10, to last until the following Wednesday. That would provide ample time for Hardeman and Calhoun to have their discussions. He suggested that he could preach for the Henderson Church on Sunday, April 12, if the church wished. Calhoun expressed hope that he could receive a stipend from the Henderson Church that would help with his travel expenses. Mary Ettah would accompany her husband and they wanted to arrange for a definite place to live upon their arrival in Henderson. It turned out that they would live in the girl's dormitory, Oakland Hall.

Hardeman wrote Calhoun another letter dated January 22, 1925, which Calhoun answered on February 2. His reply represented his complete willingness to rely on Hardeman's wisdom, judgement, and suggestion for a course of action which they should follow: "I shall depend upon you until I get in line. I know you will help all you can." Calhoun went on to tell Hardeman that he had been contacted for summer meetings in Tennessee and Mississippi. He agreed to have his picture made to appear with an article he would write for the fall college catalog.

Calhoun had learned that T. Q. Martin of St. Mary, West Virginia, was scheduled to conduct a meeting for the Henderson church during the week he would be in Henderson. Martin had known Calhoun since their student days in the College of the Bible dating back to 1889. Martin wrote that "the lamented J. W. McGarvey once said to me, 'I have selected Brother Calhoun as the man upon whom my mantle shall fall.'" L. L. Brigance wrote a report of the Martin gospel meeting and the happy reunion between Martin and Calhoun. While Calhoun did not preach for the Henderson Church on Sunday due to the meeting in progress, Brigance said that Calhoun made a wonderful speech at one of the opening exercises of the College while there. In the same article, Brigance complimented Calhoun's wife:

Sister Calhoun, although a highly cultural woman, is, nevertheless, plain, simple and motherly. She impresses you as a good, Christian wife and mother who is interested in the church, her husband and children, and, the proper education and training of the young.[9]

Hardeman, Brigance, and all others associated with Freed-Hardeman College seem to have done everything possible to assure Calhoun of their full support. They all sensed his apprehension and trepidation in leaving a structure of religious education to which he had been committed for twenty-five years and a pattern of worship in the Christian Church which he had defended against great odds for nearly thirty years.

The last two letters of record which Calhoun wrote Hardeman are dated March 4 and April 30, 1925, as a matter of wrapping up the details of his leaving Bethany and going to Henderson. He said "interesting things continue to happen here since my statement has become generally known." He did not say what the interesting happenings were. Calhoun named the places where he would hold meetings in the summer of 1925. He wrote of his plans for his "Easter vacation" visit in Henderson. He planned to spend the night with his sister, Mrs. Agnes Morris, in Troy, Tennessee, and preach there on Saturday night. Dr. A. B. Roberts was an elder of the Troy Church and a member of the Board of Trustees of Freed-Hardeman College. He planned to preach in Corinth, Mississippi, on Sunday, and to return to Henderson by train to spend the night in the Hardeman home by what he called the "kindness" of the Hardemans. The final bit of information given by Calhoun was related to his plans to leave Bethany for good on Saturday, June 6, 1925. Calhoun said "leaving at this date takes us away before commencement which comes the following week." It is easy to understand why the Calhouns did not want to remain on the Bethany campus during commencement week to face the pressure of questions and the coldness which must have developed toward him among the faculty, brethren, and students.

No sooner than the plans had been laid and the announcements made that Calhoun was leaving Bethany College, and the Christian Church, that vocal opposition began to mount. In the February 21, 1925, issue of the *Christian Standard,* an all out attack was made against that statement of severance from the "Disciples" made by Calhoun which was published in the *Gospel Advocate.* The *Standard* began its comments on the statement prefaced with praise and worthy compliments of Calhoun as a man and his successes as a teacher and preacher while identified with the "Disciples." However, the *Standard* did not stop with complimenting Calhoun's "sincerity" and "high motives," but went on to say that Calhoun left "one distinct body to join another distinct and separate people."

The *Standard* admitted that questionable practices had indeed grown up in the Christian Church because of the use of the organ and because of the missionary society, but denied this was reason enough for Calhoun to separate himself from those who used the instrument in worship.[10] Calhoun made no reply to the *Standard* attack. This was left to his close personal friend and confidant, F. W. Smith, who at that time was on the editorial staff of the *Gospel Advocate*. In the March 5, 1925, issue of the Advocate, Smith castigated the *Standard* for its inconsistency in attacking Calhoun's position: "The *Standard* should clear its own skirts by taking the same course Calhoun had pursued." Smith concluded by saying: "H. L. Calhoun has come among the people that not only know him, but who love him and appreciate him; and best of all, he is not only at home, but feels at home. The *Gospel Advocate* will stand by Brother Calhoun."

The *Tennessee Christian* lost no time at all in an open and public attack on Calhoun's position by "editorializing" on his "statement" and also publishing a copy of a speech which he had made in 1897 before the Tennessee State Convention on the subject: "Is Organized Missionary Work Scriptural?" At the time Calhoun made the speech, he considered his arguments in favor of the missionary society as "unanswerable." He claimed that there was no more authority for the Gospel Advocate Publishing Company than there was for the Tennessee Christian Missionary Society. He proposed that both were "right insofar as the organization is concerned, because both are expedients." The editor of the *Tennessee Christian,* who had been a classmate of Calhoun in the College of the Bible, wrote that: "We would like to see Brother Calhoun attempt to reply to himself and will be pleased to give him space in the *Tennessee Christian* to do so, if he wishes."[11]

Calhoun did not accept the invitation to reply to the editor in the *Tennessee Christian*. However, he did take advantage of the courtesy of the *Advocate* in the November 5, 1925, issue to comment on the address which he had delivered before the Tennessee convention. Calhoun's article in the *Advocate* was titled: "Why I Did It." He wrote:

> There was a time in my life when I regarded humanly organized missionary societies and instruments of music in the worship as expedients. I once delivered an address before the Tennessee State Missionary Society in which I took the position in regard to humanly organized societies.

Calhoun went on to say: "It is quite natural (that some) should like to see how the man that produced such an argument can answer it." Concerning the "principles set forth in the address regarding matters of faith, expediency, and indifference," Calhoun said they were true and would stand for all time. As for the application of the principles to organized missionary societies, Calhoun stated: "I have changed my opinion. I no longer regard humanly organized missionary societies as expedients." Calhoun concluded with the statement: "Neither humanly organized missionary societies nor instruments of music in the worship of God is a matter of faith, therefore, their use in the worship and service of God is sinful." That Calhoun would say that the use of the organ in Christian worship is "sinful" was first said by John W. McGarvey who condemned the organ in worship. McGarvey had written in the *Apostolic Times* before 1870:

> It is impossible to find a plainer case of innovation, in the evil sense of the term, than is presented in the use of instrumental music in Christian worship.[12]

However, McGarvey would preach in churches whose custom was to use the organ and did so to the end of his life.

The *Bulletin* published by Freed-Hardeman College in April, 1925, carried the pictures of Hall Laurie Calhoun and Nicholas Brodie Hardeman on the front page. Calhoun wrote enthusiastically of his genuine pleasure in coming to Freed-Hardeman College. He set forth his concepts of a meaningful "ministerial education" by listing the following areas of study:

1. A course embracing a thorough study of the entire English Bible, and
2. Rigid drills in the writing and speaking of correct English, and
3. Strong course in the science and art of public speaking, and
4. A comprehensive course in polemics, and
5. An extensive course in general and church history, and

6. A good course in vocal music, and
7. Careful training in the preparation and delivery of sermons, and
8. A course in public and private decorum, and
9. Courses in Hebrew and Greek.

In those statements, it is clear that Calhoun is reverting in memory to his college days under John W. McGarvey. Calhoun seemed to have had an inordinate desire to make the Department of Bible in Freed-Hardeman College what he aspired to accomplish as Dean of the College of the Bible and later as a teacher at Bethany.

The College catalog for the academic year (1925–26) was published in July of 1925. Courses were listed which were to be taught by both of the Calhouns. The *Bulletin* listed Calhoun and Hardeman as "Associate Presidents" of the College. Hall Laurie Calhoun was designated as head of the Department of Classical Languages and Bible. Comments in the *Bulletin* set forth the high hopes for a flourishing new era in Freed-Hardeman College under the direction of Calhoun, Hardeman, and their faculty colleagues.

Before the Calhouns settled in their living quarters in Oakland Hall and assumed their teaching assignments, Calhoun traveled to Albany, Alabama, where he conducted his first gospel meeting after separating from the "Digressives". Calhoun had once and for all abandoned a comfortable relationship with the Christian Church which had lasted for some twenty-five years. He was endeavoring to re-establish himself in a favorable light among the New Testament churches of the South. He spent the whole summer of 1925 conducting revivals for the churches of Christ in the South. He had closed his meetings and had come to Freed-Hardeman College by September of 1925. He took up his post in the college with the "enthusiasm" of a "little boy." He not only wanted to endear himself to the churches of Christ which he had turned away from in 1900, but he also wanted to contribute in the fullest to a strong program of ministerial education at an emerging and promising Christian College.

Calhoun taught in Freed-Hardeman College in the manner as he had taught in the College of the Bible following the precise methods of his mentor, John W. McGarvey. He seemed to have equated his "orthodoxy" not only with what he taught, but also with the manner in which he taught. He seemed to want to teach what McGarvey taught just exactly like McGarvey taught it. R. L. Colley, a student in Calhoun's class in Old Testament History at Freed-Hardeman, said Calhoun followed the class notes of McGarvey and wrote them on the blackboard for the students to copy and memorize.

On the first Sunday of October, 1925, Calhoun began a revival meeting in the Henderson church of Christ which continued through the third Sunday night. L. L. Brigance gave the highest commendations to Calhoun's presence and performance in the pulpit. Calhoun had begun preaching for the Henderson Church on the second Sunday in September and continued to preach twice each Sunday through the school year (1925–26). He was paid the handsome sum of forty dollars weekly which was considered a very liberal salary for the time.

Soon after the school year opened in 1925, it became evident that additional funds would be needed to pay the salaries of the teachers and to meet operational expenses of the College. A number of brethren in Henderson were requested to meet with Hardeman, Calhoun, Brigance, and Roland to discuss the matter of securing a loan in the amount of $25,000 from A. M. Burton, president of the Life and Casualty Insurance Company in Nashville. The loan was made and secured by a personal note signed by the agreeing parties and by "a mortgage on the college property." Calhoun and Hardeman were two of those who signed the note. By March of 1926, the financial picture of the college became increasingly unsteady. In addition to the Burton loan, $20,000 more would be needed to employ faculty and to meet ordinary and recurring expenses for the next school year (1926–27). Hardeman, Calhoun, and Brigance agreed among themselves that they would assume financial responsibility for the coming year regardless of the amount of their salaries but with one exception that: "A minimum salary was guaranteed for Roland."[13]

The 1925–1926 academic year was drawing to a close. M. C. Kurfees delivered the baccalaureate sermon on May 23, 1926. Kurfees wrote a complimentary account of Hardeman and Calhoun which was published in the *Gospel Advocate*. He compared Calhoun and Hardeman to John McGarvey and I. B. Grubbs under whom Kurfees and Calhoun had studied during their student days at the College of the Bible. Though Kurfees made no statement to that effect, it seems Calhoun was having serious health problems and was becoming a deeply troubled man as the school year drew to a close. Later events proved the poor health condition of Calhoun was not imagined. He had consulted a local physician (Dr. W. O. Baird) regarding his health problems. Dr. Baird advised Calhoun that he must have a rest from the worries that were making him unhappy.

The causes that led to Calhoun's physical breakdown in the early spring of 1926 are not difficult to identify and assess. Calhoun's leaving an environment which had sheltered and secured him for over twenty-five years and his going to another that seemed to be uncertain and unstable, created personal problems for him with which he could not cope.

Calhoun was not schooled nor skilled in administrative responsibilities demanded of one to serve as co-president of Freed-Hardeman College. He had come into a situation in which he felt very insecure while at the same time Hardeman was very secure and felt at home. Calhoun baptized every girl in the dormitory during the year who was not a Christian when she came to the college. However, tension later developed between him and the residents of the dormitory, no doubt due to the manner in which he disciplined the students. There was an "almost constant stream of criticism from the girls" according to a statement of Hardeman. This statement was written by Hardeman after the departure of Calhoun in the spring of 1926 from the College. Calhoun was a strict disciplinarian in his own home, and he probably applied the same system of discipline to the management of the resident students in Oakland Hall.

In order to be relieved of the pressures growing out of student displeasure with Calhoun, Hardeman agreed for Calhoun to move out of the dormitory into a private dwelling for the 1926–27 term. Calhoun also seemed deeply concerned about the salary he would draw from the college, the indebtedness he had assumed, and the fact that the Henderson Church had decided to use different faculty members to preach and to drop Calhoun as a full-time preacher. Dr. Calhoun and his wife had drawn a combined salary of $5,000 for the nine months period between September and May. However, the Henderson Church later changed its plans, probably at the insistence of Hardeman, and agreed to let Calhoun continue preaching for the church because of his concern that he would be unable to secure other preaching appointments with substantive financial support. There were few, if any, churches which would pay Calhoun what the Henderson Church was paying him.

On Thursday evening, May 27, at the closing commencement exercise of the school year, "in the presence of Calhoun and with his consent," Hardeman made a public announcement of the arrangements which he and Calhoun had made for the following year. Later Calhoun informed Hardeman that the arrangements which had been made and which Hardeman had announced were not satisfactory to him. Instead of moving into a single family residence which he was expected to do, Calhoun packed his family belongings and engaged the Mobile and Ohio Railroad to ship them to Nashville. Calhoun left Henderson on June 2, for Nashville and submitted to Hardeman an "unconditional resignation from all connections with Freed-Hardeman College."

Hardeman went to Nashville after receiving the resignation letter and met with Calhoun, Dr. J. S. Ward, F. W. Smith, A. M. Burton, and Mrs. Calhoun. During the conference, Calhoun seemed to be willing to withdraw his resignation. Hardeman was unwilling to accept Calhoun's proposal to withdraw his "unconditional resignation." It became increasingly clear that Calhoun had left Henderson and had no desire to return despite some indication that he would reconsider his decision. Calhoun evidently had been in touch with George R. Bethurum, 1913 Primrose Avenue, Nashville, Tennessee, who was an elder of the Belmont church of Christ before he left Henderson in as much as his personal belongings were shipped to the Primrose address.

In spite of the fact that Calhoun had indicated his desire to be relieved of the financial obligation to pay his promised $1,000 on the Life and Casualty Insurance note of $25,000 and to pay $1,500 on the $20,000 which had been committed to pay faculty salaries and operational costs for the 1926–27 year, he did pay both the amounts. Calhoun deposited with the Secretary-Treasurer of the Board of Trustees a check in the amount of $1,500 and paid the $1,000 on the Burton note for which he received written credit. Hardeman insisted that Calhoun honor this part of his financial agreement with the College and was unwilling to release Calhoun from the obligation.

Hardeman wrote shortly thereafter that: "I have never knowingly done Brother Calhoun any wrong. I have gone my full length for him. I am far from an enemy now. I am truly sorry for him. I hate to give him up, but I am forced to believe it is best."[14] Nevertheless, Calhoun moved his family from Henderson to Nashville in June of 1926. He had scheduled meetings for the summer months of 1926. He began his first revival on June 6 at the Russell Street Church of Christ, where S. H. Hall was the minister.

Calhoun had once and for all time burned his bridges behind him at the College of the Bible, Bethany College, and Freed-Hardeman College. He would recover from a serious, undetermined illness during the summer of 1926. He would spend the last decade of his fruitful life in the "Athens of the South" with the Belmont and Central churches of Christ with growing fame and appreciation from a vast radio audience in the pioneer days of radio preaching.

10

The Crowning Years

Hall Laurie Calhoun went to Nashville in the early spring of 1926 at a critical period in his life when he was sixty-two years of age. His disappointment in the loss of the College of the Bible to the "destructive critics" and his cherished dream to succeed John W. McGarvey as President of the College that had vanished were staggering blows to him. The support of the conservative leaders in the Christian Church and the editor of the *Christian Standard* failed to turn the tide in his favor. The Board of Trustees gave their unqualified support to President Richard H. Crossfield and his cohorts in the 1917 controversy.

Calhoun's hopes were further dashed when a strong School of Religion failed to become a reality in Bethany College. Calhoun witnessed with growing concern the drift of Bethany College into the liberal camp of the Disciples of Christ. This gradual drift started soon after the death of President T. E. Cramblett. Calhoun found himself, late in life, with no place to go and no incentive to stay in the Christian Church.

Calhoun's well laid plans to be in a position of academic influence and power among the churches of Christ when he became Associate President of Freed-Hardeman also failed to materialize. Calhoun little knew that at this time the churches of Christ were in the long hard pull to identify themselves as distinguished from the Disciples of Christ denomination; nor was it clear to him at the time that the Christian Church was rapidly losing ground in the state of Tennessee. David Lipscomb and his associates through the *Gospel Advocate* and the Nashville Bible

School had stemmed the tide of digression better than even they knew. And the likes of A. G. Freed, N. B. Hardeman, H. Leo Boles, Joe S. Warlick, Grover C. Brewer, and others stopped the further encroachment of the "Digressives" into the ranks of the loyal churches. The first Tabernacle meeting which Hardeman conducted in the Nashville Ryman Auditorium in 1922 and the instrumental music debate with Ira M. Boswell a year later greatly convinced the churches of Christ that they were indeed standing on valid and scriptural ground. Boswell at that time was preaching for the Georgetown, Kentucky, Christian Church. He was typical of the Christian Church preachers at the time who led the New Testament church in Central Kentucky away from the truth. Boswell, however, supported Calhoun during the 1917 controversy. The Christian Church leaders had previously boasted that they would debate the music question in Tennessee from Carter County in the East to the banks of the Mississippi River in the West. After the Hardeman-Boswell Debate, the "Digressives" lost heart and never called for another music debate in Tennessee with the exception of a written discussion on the issue between H. Leo Boles and M. D. Clubb which was printed in the *Gospel Advocate* during the period between April and July in 1926. M. D. Clubb and Hall L. Calhoun had been classmates in the College of the Bible.

Calhoun soon learned that his departure from the Christian Church in 1925 was largely ignored by their leaders. For more than twenty-five years, he had occupied positions of preeminence among the Disciples. As a matter of fact, Calhoun would not again sit in a position of leadership with them after the 1917 controversy. Calhoun's departure from Freed-Hardeman College in June of 1926 was not a sudden impulse, and his leaving was due, in part, to the personal disappointment that the college had not made the progress which he had envisioned. He had been gone too long from the churches of Christ to understand their structure and the forces that were at work among them. That churches of Christ were even then on the threshold of phenomenal growth in the years just ahead was not readily apparent.

Hardeman was convinced that Calhoun's leaving Freed-Hardeman College would put the school in a severe financial bind. That Calhoun agreed to assume his part of the financial obligation of the money owed The Life and Casualty Insurance Company brought little consolation to Hardeman. He seemed to have been greatly offended that Calhoun decided to leave the college after one year as Associate President. However, Calhoun's leaving seemed to have made very little difference among Hardeman's supporters and friends. Hardeman had been convinced in early 1924 that the presence of Calhoun on the Henderson campus would help counter the influence and status of the Christian Church in Tennessee.[1] He also knew that the prestige of scholarship that Calhoun brought to the College could not be matched among the leaders of the Disciples or the churches of Christ.

Calhoun had been engaged to conduct a fifteen day meeting beginning on June 6 for the Russell Street church of Christ in Nashville. He suddenly became ill, and the meeting was closed after eight days. His illness was diagnosed as a "nervous heart" by the attending physician. He was unable to eat or sleep. The precise cause for his illness was difficult to determine. He was advised to take a complete rest for one month. He entered a local sanitarium in Madison, Tennessee, to initiate his recovery.

S. H. Hall, minister of the Russell Street church, reported the success of the meeting and the circumstances of Calhoun's illness in the *Advocate*. He paid high tribute to Calhoun and his preaching:

> We have never had a man come to us that has impressed us more favorably and who did more good for the time spent with us . . . Brother Calhoun, I presume, stands above any preacher we have from the standpoint of scholarship, yet his sermons were so simple that they interested children, as no other preacher whom it has been my privilege to hear. And while thus simple in the choice of words and in his illustrations, they were fascinating to the strongest minds in the audience. His equal, I have not seen in this respect.[2]

The health of Calhoun worsened. Dorothea came to Nashville later in the summer to be with her parents. She had been staying with Margaret Lee, her sister, who was expecting the birth of her first baby. Her mother had cautioned her what to expect when she saw her father and to express no visible signs of surprise. She was shocked at his haggard appearance because he had suffered a considerable loss of weight. Calhoun was so physically, mentally, and emotionally incapacitated that his family and close friends were concerned that he might never preach again. He remained in a wretched state of health through the summer months. His oldest son, John, came to Nashvlle to be with his father and help him regain his health. John encouraged his father to eat nourishing food. And for exercise, John persuaded his father to sit on an "orange crate" in the yard and pull weeds along the fence row. Calhoun gradually improved during the summer, and his health was restored in a good measure by the summer's end.

Before Calhoun left Henderson for the Russell Street meeting, he secured a shipping card from the Mobile and Ohio Railroad to move his family possessions and personal belongings to the George R. Bethurum dwelling at 1913 Primrose Avenue, Nashville. The Calhouns took up residence next door in the upstairs rooms of the home owned by Mrs. Francis Sinclair, the sister of Bethurum's wife.

The spring and summer months of 1926 were among the most critical of Calhoun's life. He literally passed from one crisis to another. Having occupied significant positions of eminence in the Christian Church for a quarter of a century, it appeared that Calhoun may now have come to the end of his career. There may be little doubt that his leaving Freed-Hardeman College, under less than favorable and agreeable circumstances, contributed to his prolonged state of depression and anxiety.

Calhoun's return to Nashville in the spring of 1926 for the Russell Street meeting may have also brought back frustrating memories. The church there played a significant role in the early history of the turmoil over the introduction of the organ in Christian worship. In the early 1870's, David Lipscomb and E. G. Sewell moved their families into the Edgefield section of East Nashville. Lipscomb and Sewell organized the Woodland Street church.[3] Only a few years had passed until the organ and the missionary society were brought into the Woodland church. The Woodland Street church became one of the "ring-leaders" among the "digressive churches" in Tennessee. Calhoun was closely associated with the Woodland Street church and with its minister, W. H. Sheffer, who was one of the more notable "digressive preachers" in the state. Calhoun and Sheffer had been classmates in the College of the Bible. Calhoun had conducted meetings for the "organ church" in Union City, Tennessee, in 1896 when Sheffer was then the regular minister. During that four weeks meeting in Union City, sixty-five members were added to the church. J. C. McQuiddy directed criticism in the *Gospel Advocate* against Calhoun at that time writing: "The church can show no more authority for the organ in worship than for infant baptism."

Lipscomb and Harding had decided against bringing Calhoun on the faculty of the Nashville Bible School in 1896. Calhoun began preaching for the Franklin, Tennessee, church in 1897 which had not introduced the organ, nor has it to this day. However, Calhoun and Sheffer exchanged pulpits at this time for Sunday preaching appointments after Sheffer became the regular minister of the Woodland Street church. The fact that Calhoun preached for the Woodland "organ church" did not escape the notice of J. C. McQuiddy who recorded his reaction in the *Advocate*. Those who left the Woodland Christian Church when the organ was introduced, including Lipscomb and Sewell, formed the Russell Street Church of Christ. Calhoun was keenly aware of this bit of history when he went to Russell Street for the meeting. However, Calhoun outwardly seemed to regard the Russell Street revival in June of 1927 as just another protracted meeting.

Although the information to the contrary is not available, Calhoun must have discussed his future plans with Bethurum before leaving Henderson and going to Nashville. It is highly unlikely that Calhoun's definite plans extended any further than his meeting work which had been booked for the summer of 1926. He did not know the congregations of the church of Christ, nor did he know their local, state, and national leaders. He was at a loss to know where and to whom to turn. The illness of Calhoun in this most indecisive period placed him in a state of limbo so far as future plans were concerned.

The expressed fear that Calhoun would never be able to preach again was dispelled by the early fall of 1926. He was invited by Bethurum to preach at the Belmont church of Christ. Calhoun, at first, decided against accepting the invitation. Instead, he accepted an invitation to preach a sermon at the Woodson Chapel church in rural Davidson County. He was elated that his physical and mental powers as a gospel preacher were undiminished.[4] Shortly thereafter, Calhoun was settled in with the Belmont church as the full-time minister to the great satisfaction of the entire membership. The church grew rapidly and the audiences were increasing until there was never enough room to accommodate all who came to hear the master preacher.

Forceful leaders of the brotherhood were at work whose influence would have far reaching implications for the growth and development of the church in the city of Nashville. Even at the time that Calhoun began his work with Freed-Hardeman College, some distinguished church leaders were planning to establish a congregation of the church of Christ in downtown Nashville. The idea was by no means new. In 1921, James A. Allen and his father had failed in an effort to establish a church in downtown Nashville. A. M. Burton, one of the founders of the Life and Casualty Insurance Company, formulated a list of reasons by which to justify the organization of a downtown church. This effort on the part of Burton set in motion a series of events that led to the fruition of Burton's dream. The brethren intended to establish and organize a downtown Nashville church which would function as nearly as possible just like the Jerusalem church did during the first century.

The first Hardeman Tabernacle meeting in Nashville had stimulated great excitement among the members of the churches of Christ and throughout the general population of the city and surrounding region in the 1920's. Burton was inspired by the teachings in Matthew (25:31–46) and Luke (14:12–14) to lead a group of his brethren to establish the Central church of Christ in the center of the business district in Nashville. His intent and plan were simple. The new church would fulfill the preaching and benevolent demands of the Scriptures with a pronounced and distinct emphasis on the benevolent work of the church. Burton prepared a series of papers setting forth the proposals for a downtown church. A meeting of interested brethren was called for the first Sunday in October, 1925. E. H. Cullum presided over the business session. The Central church of Christ was organized and E. H. Ijams was selected as the regular minister. J. E. Acuff, C. E. W. Dorris, E. H. Ijams, and Dr. J. S. Ward were named elders of the Central church. These brethren were all held in highest esteem. E. H. Cullum was appointed church treasurer.

On July 9, 1925, the property at 145 Fifth Avenue North was purchased in anticipation of erecting a meeting house for the newly established Central church of Christ. A new auditorium, seating one thousand people, was completed in December. On a Saturday, December 26, 1925, the congregation which had been organized on October 4, moved into the new auditorium with forty-seven people present. N. B. Hardeman preached the first sermon in the new building.[5]

The Central church prospered and multiplied. A noonday service was conducted daily from the time the church first opened its doors. At a time when radio was still in its swaddling clothes, arrangements were made in December, 1925, to broadcast the sermons from the church auditorium over a small radio station

(WDAD). The station was purchased from the original owners in August, 1927, jointly by the Central church of Christ and the Life and Casualty Insurance Company. The station's call letters were changed to WLAC in recognition of the first letters in the name of the insurance company. From that time until the middle 1950's, the Sunday and weekly church services at Central were carried daily over the radio station WLAC.

The Central church was indeed a church of a special kind. In addition to quarters for the worship services and preaching ministry, the church provided a reception and reading room, a library, a kitchen, and a dining room to feed the hungry. There was also a social service department. In the three years following the establishment of the Central church, the new auditorium was opened, a five-story Boys' Building was under construction; and the church was operating a free medical and dental clinic and providing free clothing and a free lunch room. There was a day home for children and a Girls' Home nearby for caring for nearly one hundred girls. These are to name some of the Christian services provided by the Central church.[6]

In a special celebration of the third anniversary of the thriving downtown church, Hardeman conducted an eight day meeting in the Central building which started on October 7, 1928. WLAC had been up-graded to a powerful five-thousand watt station which could be heard all over the nation and beyond its borders. Hardeman was hailed in a daily newspaper as a "loyal and giant preacher of the Restoration Movement." Burton estimated then that perhaps a million people could have heard Hardeman.[7]

Calhoun at the beginning was not related in any way to the newly organized Central church, but he was destined to become the most effective and memorable preacher in the history of the downtown congregation. His superb talents as a preacher and reputation as a sound Bible scholar placed Calhoun in a unique position among his peers. After Calhoun left Freed-Hardeman College, he found himself in a conference with A. M. Burton and others concerning a business transaction involving the payment of a note to the Life and Casualty Insurance Company signed by Calhoun earlier. At this time, Burton and Calhoun established a warm mutual friendship that lasted until Calhoun's death.

Calhoun and his wife moved from the residence on Primrose Street in the late summer of 1926. Because his health was slowly improving, the Calhouns purchased a dwelling on Belmont Boulevard across the street west of David Lipscomb College owned by Myzella Burton, the recently widowed daughter of A. M. Burton. Distraught over the sudden death of her husband, she left the home just as it was when her husband died and never returned to it. The Calhouns purchased the household furnishings including even the china dishes on the dining table.

Much could be said about Calhoun's emergence as one of the most successful evangelists ever to preach in Nashville from the days of Tolbert Fanning, James A. Harding, and David Lipscomb. He was greeted daily by a large radio audience over station WLAC. These were the "Depression Years" and people had considerable time on their hands. Many tell that a person could walk down main street on a week day in any Middle Tennessee city and he was met from door to door by the voice of Calhoun preaching the noonday radio sermon. Many people remained at home during the noon hour to hear him. Calhoun was a Bible preacher without showing a trace of sectarian haranguing which attracted large unbiased audiences to his simple and powerful Bible sermons. Many were baptized as a result of his radio preaching based upon reports that came to the Central church. The rise of Calhoun to a position with a strong public image grew out of his radio ministry. Calhoun preached daily for almost eight years to a large and appreciative radio audience. His knowledge of the Bible was profound and his simplicity and eloquence as a teacher was matchless. Calhoun was blessed with a voice and a professional skill which are marks of all great orators.

A signal honor came to Calhoun in the spring of 1927. He was invited to deliver the baccalaureate sermon for the graduating class of David Lipscomb College on May 29 at 5:00 p.m., in the auditorium of the Central church. He was introduced on that occasion by the president of the College, H. Leo Boles. An overflow crowd filled the auditorium and every office, classroom, and the library where loudspeakers were set up.[8]

Calhoun had already touched all bases in the Christian Church, and he was now on the threshold of enjoying comparable recognition among the churches of Christ. An announcement appeared in the *Gospel Advocate* in October of 1927, that H. L. Calhoun would write the *Teachers' Quarterly* for the religious journal.[9] A perusal of these publications reveals the magnificent talents of Calhoun as a master teacher, preacher, and writer coming out of a scholarship that was as profound as it was minute. The new publication was designed to help teachers at all levels, including the elementary as well as the advanced, in the preparation and conduct of their classes. Orvel Calhoun Crowder said that the content of the *Teachers' Quarterly* portrays his grandfather at his best as a teacher. An interesting fact about Calhoun is that he wrote little for the *Christian Standard* and other Christian Church publications.

However, a veritable flood of articles poured from the pen of McGarvey who encouraged Calhoun to write and submit articles to the *Standard*. In view of Calhoun's talents and his opposition to "destructive criticism," we wonder why Calhoun had so little to say in print outside of the 1917 Lexington Controversy. Calhoun wrote numerous articles for the *Advocate* over a wide range of biblical subjects in the last years of his life. His enormous knowledge of the writings of the finest scholars in the field of Higher Criticism raises the question of why he did not write endlessly, as had McGarvey, against the tenets of liberal theology.

Due to the fact that the Central church radio ministry was the first of its kind, Calhoun's star role in the success of the undertaking is significant. The very first noonday services at Central were forty minutes in length and later were reduced to thirty minutes. After the radio broadcasts were firmly established, the thirty minute services started daily at 12:25 p.m. and concluded at 12:55 p.m. The format consisted of songs, opening prayer, scripture reading, sermon, invitation hymn, and a closing prayer. And beginning in October of 1928, a Sunday evening devotional was also conducted weekly over WLAC.

The Central radio ministry was at first conducted by different preachers. J. Petty Ezell was engaged by the Central church on March 1, 1927, to preach daily for the noonday service over station WDAD. However, Ezell left the Central radio ministry toward the end of 1927. The radio services were then conducted for a brief period by various preachers who lived in the Nashville vicinity. Calhoun was first invited to speak over WDAD in June of 1926, during his revival with the Russell Street church. About one year later, the announcement was made in the June, 1927 issue of the *Advocate* that Calhoun would conduct the noon radio services for a period of two weeks. Not long afterwards, Calhoun assumed the responsibility full-time for all of the Central radio services until his passing save for occasional guest-speakers. Unfortunately, no recordings were made of the sermons that Calhoun preached at a time when it could easily have been done. Outside of the testimony of many who heard Calhoun in the pulpit and over the radio, there are printed copies of his sermons to supplement this lack.

As Calhoun spent the summer of 1926 slowly regaining his

health, old friends such as F. W. Smith and George Bethurum gave Calhoun steady encouragement during this trying period; and there was widening circles of new friends to assure him. After Calhoun took up full time-work with the Belmont church, he resumed the practice of recording his ministerial activities: sermon titles, new converts, persons placing membership by letter, dates and names of weddings and funerals, titles of radio sermons, and stipends.

And beginning in late 1927, Calhoun was holding a limited number of revivals as far away as Texas and Oklahoma. One of the meetings is especially memorable. Adron Doran directed the singing in a gospel meeting conducted by Calhoun in Puryear, Tennessee, two miles west of Conyersville. The meeting began July 3 and closed July 16, 1928, with weekday services at three p.m. and eight p.m. Five persons were baptized during the meeting including Joe Morgan, the son of local preacher, W. E. Morgan. Joe was later appointed Superintendent of Public Instruction (Commissioner of Education) by the Governor of Tennessee. He left this office to become President of Austin Peay University in Clarksville, Tennessee. Joe is now retired as President Emeritus.

Doran had completed his freshman year in Freed-Hardeman College at the time of the Puryear revival. Calhoun was the first preacher in the church of Christ that Doran had seen who held a doctor's degree. As a matter of fact, he had seen few college teachers in the rural region where he lived in Graves County, Kentucky. Doran was fascinated that Calhoun had earned a Ph.D. from Harvard. Doran mustered enough courage one day to ask, "Brother Calhoun, what was the subject of your doctoral dissertation?" To which Calhoun replied, "Why son if I were to tell you, you would not untertand." Doran says that he wishes that Calhoun had told him that he may have understood, and he knows now that he does.

He conducted meetings until his passing; however, the number of engagements outside Nashville were limited due to his work with the Central church and radio ministry. It was on January 1, 1928, that Calhoun took over the full-time radio ministry of Central. Such times as Calhoun would be away, E. H. Ijams, an elder, preached in his stead. Calhoun gave up his work with the Belmont church on October 27, 1931, due to his increasing load of preaching for the Central church of Christ. From this time until his passing, Calhoun worked full-time for the Central church as the pulpit and as radio minister.

The Crowning Years **169**

Adron and Mignon Doran

Hall Laurie Calhoun

Mary Ettah Calhoun

A late honor came and the full circle was completed when Calhoun was brought on the faculty of David Lipscomb College to teach advanced Bible courses in Old Testament History and Old Testament Law. He taught at Lipscomb during the school year 1934–35. His name appeared in the college catalog for the year 1935–36, but he died before the fall semester began.

Indeed, the years between 1926 and 1935 were eventful and in the main rewarding years for Calhoun. He no longer played key roles in helping to make policy decisions for the brotherhood, nor is there any indication that he desired to do so. Calhoun attracted little attention outside of Nashville and his radio ministry. The Christian Church wrote him off their list and did not refer to him again except in isolated cases of adverse criticism. In recent years, graduate theses and one doctoral dissertation, address Calhoun, concentrating mainly on his role in the 1917 controversy and that usually with critical commentary.

Stephen J. Corey, a strong and militant advocate of the liberal position of the Disciples of Christ traced briefly the course of Calhoun's life after the 1917 Lexington controversy and his return to Tennessee in 1925. Corey wrote:

> This is no doubt really where Dr. Calhoun belonged. The rest of his life until his death in 1935, was spent in strongly advocating the principles, theology, and program of the group now nationally known as churches of Christ, which is opposed to the use of instrumental music in worship and to missionary societies. He held a number of evangelistic meetings in West Tennessee among rural churches and succeeded in turning most of them to the non-cooperative churches of Christ.[10]

Corey's statement written a year after Calhoun's death gives evidence that Corey knew little of Calhoun's role among the churches of Christ in the last years of his life. Not even Calhoun was certain "where he belonged." His return to Tennessee in the spring of 1925, after his departure from the Christian Church, raised about as many questions about Calhoun as were answered. It would not be amiss to say that some of the responses given by Calhoun to questions put to him were only half answered at their best as he tried to explain his newly found positions on church doctrine. It will be recalled that Calhoun cautiously came to a settled agreement with Hardeman on a number of issues before he was willing to leave the Christian Church.

Calhoun's real reasons for leaving the Christian Church were seriously questioned by some leaders in the churches of Christ. Had it not been for a few reputable leaders such as M. C. Kurfees and F. W. Smith who gave Calhoun their full endorsement, it is highly unlikely that he would have experienced as easy an acceptance as he did within the fellowship of the churches of Christ. Hardeman, whose acquaintance with Calhoun went back twenty-eight years, took the initial steps that brought about Calhoun's departure from the fold of the Christian Church. And Hardeman made the move only after receiving the fullest assurance from Kurfees and Smith of Calhoun's dependability.

It was typical of H. Leo Boles, then President of David Lipscomb College, to deliver what amounted to be an ultimatum to Calhoun requiring him to fully explain himself: "Will you teach that instrumental music in the worship and human societies for the spread of the Gospel is unscriptural?" Calhoun readily responded in the affirmative.

Calhoun may have thought that the rank and file of the churches of Christ would receive him with open arms. This did not happen very quickly. Calhoun was invited to appear on the Abilene Christian College Lectureship for the year 1928. Batsell Baxter was then president of the College. Only preachers known for their "scriptural soundness" and established reputations were invited to participate in the lectureship. Not even a small tolerance was allowed for a questionable position of a brother. When Calhoun's name appeared on the published program as the principal speaker, considerable discussion accompanied the announcement. The fact was well known that Calhoun had only recently severed his relations with the Christian Church. However, some brethren were still not convinced that he was free from "suspicion of liberal or digressive tendencies." Anticipating a large attendance, Baxter sought to escape the confines of a small auditorium by arranging a temporary seating in the gymnasium to seat two thousand and to accommodate an overflow audience. To insure Calhoun's acceptance by the brethren for the occasion, Baxter secured the letter for publication which Calhoun had written to Hardeman in which Calhoun took the uncompromising position against instrumental music and missionary societies in the church. The published letter and Calhoun's acceptance of the invitation to be on the lectureship accomplished its purpose as Calhoun was invited to return in 1929 to again serve as the principal speaker.[11]

About nine years were left for Calhoun to live after he came to Nashville in the spring of 1926. His prolonged illness during that summer cast dark shadows across an uncertain future. There were dramatic changes. What can and should be said in summing up the final years of Calhoun in a church fellowship he had abandoned at the turn of the century? He could not have imagined the unparalleled opportunities that were just ahead for him. Radio was then coming of age and a brand new era of communications was beginning to emerge. A preacher's voice could be carried into remote places even beyond the borders of the nation. Calhoun was one of the nation's first radio preachers, and he proved himself to be a master of the medium.

Only a part of Calhoun's time was devoted to his radio ministry. Calhoun learned the day by day work of a preacher. Trained in the College of the Bible and the divinity schools of the Ivy League, Calhoun understood and performed his church duties with the Belmont and Central churches to the admiration and satisfaction of all. Mary Ettah Calhoun possessed a splendid education. She taught in Georgia Robertson College, Bethany College, and later in David Lipscomb College. She knew every facet of a preacher's work and the role of a preacher's wife. She was a constant helpmeet to her husband and went with him to homes or places where the presence of a wife was in order. As Calhoun grew older, Mary Ettah became increasingly supportive of her husband seeking to lighten his load due to his advancing years and a chronic heart problem.

Calhoun was never more busy than he was in his last years and he was happy in his work. He was reaching the normal retirement years when he entered upon some of the most productive years of his life. It stands to reason that his return to Lexington from Cambridge in 1904 was filled with great hope and expectations for a commanding role in the Christian Church. Calhoun was then surrounded by his family and numerous friends in both Lexington and Bethany. There seemed to be no limit for opportunities that lay ahead for Calhoun with his talents and accomplishments in those years. However, this was not to be. But successes of such a kind, crowned the efforts of Calhoun in his last years to do what he could do best—teach and preach to audiences in vast numbers.

Calhoun was suddenly struck down. A heart condition had troubled him for years. Despite this, his days were constantly filled with endless duties thrust upon him by his multiple church activities. Calhoun suffered a heart attack early Wednesday morning on September 4, 1935. He conducted his last regular noonday service September 3, over WLAC on Tuesday. His condition worsened throughout the day of his first attack. The fatal attack came later on the same day, September 4, and his death occurred at 9:00 p.m. The news of Calhoun's death was carried over the radio and by the newspapers the following day.

Calhoun's funeral was conducted in the War Memorial Building in Nashville on Saturday, September 7. This was the only facility in Nashville capable of accommodating a huge crowd. His funeral was attended by the largest audience ever assembled in Nashville for such an occasion. The speakers who took part in the service were John T. Hinds, G. R. Bethurum, Dr. J. S. Ward, E. H. Ijams, S. H. Hall, and J. S. Batey. Calhoun was buried in Woodlawn Memorial Park in Nashville.

After the death of her husband, Mary Ettah continued to live in Nashville. She taught the Speech Arts course in David Lipscomb College from 1936 through 1942. Her students were the "preaching boys" whom she taught the art of correct pronunciation and enunciation. She lived in Elam Hall (boys' dormitory) as long as she taught in the college. She rented her Belmont home to her daughter, Margaret Lee, and her husband, but sold her home sometime afterwards. When her teaching days were finished, she continued to live in Nashville. She visited among her children and friends. She lived the last two years of her life with her oldest daughter, Mary Ettah Crowder, in Cincinnati, Ohio. Mary Ettah Calhoun died October 30, 1953, at the age of eighty-two. Her funeral services were conducted by Batsell Barrett Baxter and J. P. Sanders on November 2, and she was buried in Woodlawn Memorial Park by the grave of her beloved husband.

Orvel Calhoun Crowder wrote of the relationship between Hall Laurie and Mary Ettah Calhoun:

> His wife was the only person who was really 'close' to him, and much that passed between them was unspoken. He was enormously dependent on her extraordinary feminine strength and sensitivity. She, of course, adored him. Though the force of his personality deeply marked his children, none of them seem to have understood him, with the exception perhaps of his son, John who brought him through his breakdown.[12]

And so ended the earthly sojourn of two remarkable people. Calhoun's life was an open book filled with puzzles, riddles, and contradictions that somehow seem to defy any final explication. Each person interested in the meaning of the life of Hall Laurie Calhoun must be left to his own thoughts and judgments in the matter with the certainty that no single interpretation answers all of the questions.

As in the case of such men who greatly influenced the lives of people who came under their influence, there is no end to the Calhoun repertory of personal memoirs. Two stories set forth the great influence that Calhoun had on the personal lives of people who saw and heard him in the pulpit and listened to him over the radio. Calhoun conducted a meeting in Mt. Juliet, Tennessee. Mr. and Mrs. C. L. Garner of Madison, Tennessee, attended that meeting in July of 1927. They were planning their wedding for that fall. Garner was then preaching for a congregation in Shreveport, Louisiana, which had just notified him that his contract had been terminated. Their wedding plans had already been announced. C. J. had no money and no prospect for a job. They attended one of Calhoun's services at Mt. Juliet and he preached his best known sermon, "The Much Neglected Command," taken from the words of Jesus, "Be Not Anxious." Sarah Garner said that she and C. J. met Calhoun after the service and said to him, "Thank you Brother Calhoun for your encouragement." They left the meeting house hand in hand and made their plans to be married on schedule. Through the help of R. V. Cawthon, Sarah's father, C. J. secured a position immediately with the Old Hickory, Tennessee church of Christ, and preached there for eleven years.

There would be no way to calculate the impact of Calhoun's radio preaching to a vast audience over several years. The radio sermons of Calhoun converted Mr. and Mrs. L. O. Gholsen of Daviess County, Kentucky, during the winter of 1934. They lived on a farm outside Owensboro, Kentucky. The winter of 1934 was cold and snowy, and they followed daily the sermons of Calhoun with growing interest. They did not know of a church of Christ or a gospel preacher who would baptize them. In the spring they found a church of Christ meeting in a rented hall in Owensboro, Kentucky. Their preacher was Harvey W. Riggs who baptized them. Their son, Clayton Gholsen, is an elder in the Madison, Tennessee, church of Christ.

11

The Aftermath

The Battle Ended, but the War Raged On,
The Firing Ceased, but the Roaring Remained

The design of this chapter is to show what happened to the Christian Church as a result of the controversy which raged in the College of the Bible through the summer of 1917. Many thought that the "Battle of the Book" would end when the Board of Trustees exonerated the accused. However, this was mere wishful thinking upon the part of the liberals in the Christian Church. It should be noted that the leaders among the churches of Christ paid little attention to what they considered to be a "family fuss" among the Disciples who had thought to advance the principles of the Restoration movement by introducing instrumental music in worship and by affiliating with the missionary society.

There were three notable exceptions: M. C. Kurfees, an alumnus of the College of the Bible, called to the attention of the *Advocate* readers in the June 7 and 28, 1917, issues of the journal the problems besetting the College of the Bible. Calhoun's statement was printed verbatim from the *Standard* wherein Calhoun alleged that the exoneration of the accused president and faculty by the Board of Trustees was a farce. Mark Collis' statement in which the Board of Trustees exonerated Crossfield, Fortune, Bower, and Snoddy was also printed verbatim.

Kurfees concluded his appraisal of the Lexington debacle in an article appearing August 29, 1917, in the *Advocate* with the comment: "let the final and supreme authority in the case rise up Hercules-like, and not stop till the modern "Augean stable" is cleansed of the last vestige of German rationalism." John T. Hinds, a class mate of Calhoun in the College of the Bible, also directed attention in the *Firm Foundation* in the June 26, 1917, issue to the disturbance in Lexington. Hinds noted that McGarvey gave the last years of his life combatting destructive criticism. Hinds also noted McGarvey's inconsistency in disapproving the use of the organ in worship, and at the same time supporting the society organization.

A. B. Barrett quoted verbatim an article of J. B. Briney from the *Standard,* in which Briney severely castigated Crossfield and his faculty, who were "cuckoo-like, occupying nests feathered by others, drawing good salaries and teaching doctrines that the builders would not have tolerated a moment." Barrett concluded with his own indictment of the principles on both sides of the fuss: "But it only goes to show whose chickens have come home to roost." This appeared in the *Firm Foundation* in September of 1917.

President Crossfield and his faculty appointees did everything in their power to play down the charges filed against them by Calhoun, and to claim complete victory in the decision of the Board of Trustees. W. C. Bower's endeavors to minimize the situation claiming that the trouble, in the first place, arose out of conflicts within Calhoun. Bower charged that Calhoun had reached an impasse growing out of his Yale and Harvard graduate study:

> As a result of his exposure to liberal religious thought against the background of his fundamentalist upbringing and college education (under McGarvey), there developed in him a deep intellectual and emotional conflict. The result was a split personality, in which intelligence reached out toward a rational support system while his loyalties remained firmly attached to his conservative past.[1]

However, what had happened in 1917 at the College of the Bible and its subsequent effect on the Christian Church could not be summarily dismissed. On May 25, 1918, the term of office of Mark Collis as trustee and Chairman of the Board of Trustees of the College of the Bible expired, and he was not re-elected. Collis had served for thirty-five years as a trustee, the last twenty-five years as Chairman of the Board. However, the liberal forces had come to question and doubt the position of Collis on destructive criticism. Collis was replaced by a more liberal member and chairman. Collis countered with articles in a number of the issues of the *Christian Standard.* He said that he voted for the report of the Board on May 9, 1917, "with reservations, claiming the right to express myself if, in my judgment, the occasion should arise."

Collis did arrive at a different judgment. In the January 19, 1918, issue of the *Christian Standard,* under the heading "The Restoration Message Should Not Be Changed," Collis expressed himself regarding the liberal teaching in the College of the Bible. He wrote:

> Doubtless a weakening in the advocacy of our Scriptural plea has been brought about, in many cases, through college and university influences. A young man is anxious to equip himself as thoroughly as possible for his life-work. He seeks an institution where it is thought there is scholarship of the highest order. The institution is not in harmony with our plea. The young man soon finds that he is in an atmosphere very different from that in which he has previously moved. A change comes over him. Principles that once were held sacred by him he is now ready to surrender. The Bible has become a different book from what it was in former days. The men whom he once loved and admired are now looked upon as narrow: they have not the 'modern viewpoint'. You may hear the young brother say: "We can not expect to do our part in bringing about Christian union unless we are willing to give up some things that we have held sacred. Certainly, we must admit the unimmersed into our membership. They are Christians—some of them are better Christians than many of us. How can we exclude them from our church fellowship?' Of course, men who have imbibed such ideas as these can not be expected to preach the gospel as our fathers did—they have found a better way!

Soon thereafter, and in the years since, the Central Christian Church in Lexington and other congregations throughout the country declared themselves sympathetic with the "new liberalism". Eventually, both the Nicholasville and Providence Christian Churches drifted into the liberal ranks of the Disciples.

Another effort of great significance was made by the Christian College Bible League to call attention of the brethren to the deplorable conditions which existed at the College of the Bible. The League was formed during the annual convention of the Kentucky Missionary Society which met September 18, 1917, in Campbellsville, Kentucky. The purpose of the League as approved by a unanimous vote of those present was:

1. To recover the College of the Bible in Lexington, Kentucky, from the control of the destructive critics and to restore it to its original purpose, (and)

2. To exercise an advisory guardianship over all educational institutions having in view the preparation of young men and women for Christian work.[2]

The leaders of the Christian College Bible League were J. B. Briney and Ira M. Boswell. Both had distinguished themselves as outstanding and successful ministers of the conservative element in the Christian Church. Briney preached at Pee Wee Valley, near Louisville, and wrote a regular column for the *Christian Standard*. Boswell was serving as minister for the Georgetown Christian Church. Membership in the League was solicited all over the United States and the organizers boasted of 100,000 members. The League failed in its effort to stay the tide of liberalism at the College of the Bible, or to wrest its control from the Crossfield Administration.

However, R. A. Long, who had promised $1,000,000 to the "Men and Millions Movement," in which Transylvania University was a recipient, appeared before the Kansas City Convention and attacked the university administration for the reputation it had established by being a haven for destructive criticism. Long had conferred with Mark Collis before making his speech regarding the situation in Lexington. Because of the oppositions of such men, contributions to the College of the Bible dropped drastically. Graduates of the seminary found it difficult to secure pulpits. Stevenson called the League "a highly efficient wrecking crew." The League continued with effectiveness through 1921.[3]

The liberals who remained in control of the College of the Bible did and said everything they could to discredit the League. The October 1918 issue of the *Quarterly Bulletin* published by the College of the Bible made every effort to place the leadership of the League in a bad light. The college spokesman reported that "forty-odd persons, who had been privately invited to come together, organized the League at a late hour after the evening session of the State Convention." The author of the report called the League "self constituted, responsible to nobody, sans state and status and Bolsheviki!"[4] However, the League gained far more support among the conservatives than the liberals were willing to admit. Chapters were formed ranging from Lexington to California and into New England.

A completely new and different set up for Christian education was inaugurated by the conservatives in 1923. This came the year after the conservative Christian Church mounted its concerted campaign to discredit the liberals during the convening of the Pittsburg Congress when a "no holds barred" fight was directed against the open membership policy. The Christian Bible League had influenced enough of the members and leaders of the Christian Church that by 1923 plans were underway to establish the McGarvey Bible College in Louisville, Kentucky. The intent was to provide a "sound ministry" for "faithful" congregations. Henry J. Lutz was appointed president and Ralph L. Records and R. C. Foster were members of the faculty. Some eighty students were enrolled at the opening of the College in the fall of 1923. Without knowledge of the plans of those who began the McGarvey Bible College, a group in Cincinnati moved to established the Cincinnati Bible Institute which opened its doors in the fall of 1923 with the support of the Clark Fund headed by James DeForest Murch. John W. Tyndale was chosen president of the Institute assisted by Murch and L. G. Tomlinson. Over one hundred students enrolled for the opening session. This dramatic development will be detailed in the next chapter.[5]

The College of the Bible failed to recover its favored status after 1917. In 1921, Richard H. Crossfield resigned the presidency of Transylvania University and the College of the Bible. His resignation precipitated a move on the part of the conservatives to influence the Board of Trustees to select a president who would return the university and the College of the Bible to the "Old Paths" of McGarvey, Grubbs, and Graham. A congress was held December 7, 1920, in Lexington, Kentucky, and a committee of twelve was appointed to confer with the authorities of the College of the Bible concerning the interests of that institution.

The committee decided to send a petition to the preachers of the Christian Church in Kentucky to ascertain their opinions "as to what should be done to remedy present conditions." The chairman of the committee was Frank M. Tinder, minister of the North Middletown (Kentucky) Christian Church. Tinder sent out communications dated March 9, 1921, soliciting responses. Forty eight cards were returned with such comments:

> "Thank God! He has had the honesty at last to resign."
> R. H. Dodson, Brooksville

> "Entire faculty should resign and re-organize the College."
> John T. Brown, Louisville

"A complete re-organization with a new president and teachers who believe the Bible."

W. G. Wells, Jasper, Alabama

Mark Collis signed the card giving his approval. One minister of Poplar Plains, Kentucky, recommended the return of H. L. Calhoun.[6]

What effect this survey and the results had on the Board of Trustees is not known. After the interim presidency of Thomas B. Macartney, Jr., the Board of Trustees moved to elect on March 4, 1922, Andrew D. Harmon president of Transylvania University and the College of the Bible. Harmon was of the liberal persuasion and served in a stormy atmosphere as president until April 27, 1928. One fact was clear. The College of the Bible was lost to the liberals. This was a staggering blow to the conservatives, and they were unwilling to become reconciled to the fact. The College of the Bible was the oldest of the Disciples' colleges engaged solely in ministerial training. The College of the Bible did not drift into liberalism. It was propelled in that direction first by R. H. Crossfield, and later by others of similar persuasion.

The last vestige of the College of the Bible organized in 1865 was stripped away when on September 10, 1963, the board voted to change the name of the College of the Bible to Lexington Theological Seminary. The seminary has since kept pace with the ever changing trends and positions in modern theology. That Stephen J. Corey, Dwight E. Stevenson, and other leading spokesmen in the seminary have had little to say that is complimentary of Calhoun is discovered in their lingering chagrin that it was Calhoun who caught the liberals "red handed" and "off guard" in the 1917 controversy. This compelled a reassessment of the strategy of the liberals and forced them to deny or to admit to the allegations leveled at them by the conservatives.

No fact is clearer in Restoration history than that the subtle "villain" surprised in 1917 on the staircase proved to be none other than that of destructive criticism. This was McGarvey's label for higher criticism, and he had in mind the Graf-Wellhausen Documentary Hypothesis of the Old Testament. Karl H. Graf and Julius Wellhausen formulated the Documentary Hypothesis of the Old Testament between 1865 and 1885. They were eminent German biblical scholars who formulated the major tenets of the new theology. For this reason, the *Standard* labeled the theology of Crossfield and associates as "made in Germany". German "kultur" meant all that was hateful to Americans during the course of World War I. The corollaries of the new theology, which had been adopted by the Harvard and Yale Divinity Schools, denied the divine inspiration and infallibility of the Bible. Dean Francis Greenwood Peabody had been instrumental in the adoption of the new theology in Harvard around 1880.[7] McGarvey understood the implications of the new theology and sought to ward off its incursion into the ranks of the Disciples.

The Campbell Institute was another direct spin off of the influence of the intellectual climate in the new theology. The Campbell Institute had been under sustained attack by the conservatives since its founding in 1896 during the National Convention in Springfield, Illinois. The Institute was tied in with the University of Chicago which served as its incubator. The new theology gained a foothold in the university which had begun operations in 1892. The university boasted a graduate divinity school of the highest rank. All denominations were invited to establish "Houses" for their students in order to take advantage of the splendid facilities of the university. The Disciples took immediate advantage of the offer and forthwith established the Disciples Divinity House. Herbet L. Willett was selected as its dean. Willett was an avowed liberal fashioned in the mold of the new theology and did not seek to disguise the fact.

The Campbell Institute restricted its members to college graduates. A program with a three fold purpose was adopted to encourage a scholarly spirit, to inspire contributions to literature and thoughts of the Disciples, and to promote spiritual unity. The conservative leaders in the Christian Church were convinced that the organization was the development of a new liberal strategy to capture the schools and agencies of the Disciples. Garrison and DeGroot said the obvious: "Through this fellowship there flowed much of the vital substance nourishing the growing edge of the Disciples."[8]

The Campbell Institute came under harsh attack during the 1917 Lexington impasse through an editorial in the *Christian Standard* which charged that the Institute had "split churches, wrecked colleges, shattered the faith of young people whose lives were dedicated to the ministry, deprecates the work of our missionary societies, and kept the brotherhood in a state of ferment."[9]

Calhoun played a significant supporting role in the attacks

which the conservatives were mounting in 1922 against the powerful liberal element in the Christian Church. Calhoun's last major participation in an assault upon the liberal Disciples came in 1922 over the practice of open membership. The new controversy was of old vintage which once again addressed the questionable actions of the missionary society. The American Christian Missionary Society had been an aggravation in the Christian Church since its founding in 1849. A. W. Fortune wrote the ACMS did not have a single missionary in the field twenty five years after its founding.[10]

The Foreign Christian Missionary Society was founded in 1875 to succeed partially where the ACMS had failed. Other woes beset the FCMS and put it under attack by the conservatives. The distrust for the "old" was transferred to the "new". The FCMS came under direct attack in 1908 for the endorsement of the policy of open membership in the China mission field with the appointment of Guy W. Sarvis a protege of William Scribner Ames, an ardent and unabashed exponent of the new theology and the practice of open membership. This account will be resumed at another place.

Seemingly bearing no direct relationship to the 1917 controversy, the International Convention of the Disciples was organized in 1917.[11] This caused no concern at the time since it was thought a new organization with broader powers would solve old problems. The Disciples accomodation of conventions had long been a way of life with them on both the state and national levels. The International Convention was deemed to be an improvement over the National Convention for conducting the affairs of the Disciples. It is obvious that the liberal disciples were aware of the parliamentary advantage of a decision making body operating on all levels. The International Convention soon proved that it was cut from the same old cloth and fashioned from the same old pattern which had created the FCMS and the Campbell Institute.

Two years later, the liberal Disciples organized the United Christian Missionary Society. The UCMS was opposed almost from the day of its creation in 1919. The newly created society cojoined the American Christian Missionary Society, Christian Woman's Board of Missions, National Benevolent Association (orphan homes, et al), Board of Ministerial Relief, and Board of Christian Extension.[9] The fact is the UCMS became the compliant right arm of the International Convention. The UCMS began operations in 1920. And soon thereafter, the old charge resurfaced that open membership was being practiced in foreign missions, especially in China. In late 1921, John T. Brown, as a member of the Board of Managers of the UCMS, visited the foreign missions in the orient to determine the truth of the matter. He confirmed the suspicions of the conservatives that open membership was indeed a wide spread practice in the China mission. The *Christian Standard* gave the widest circulation to the report.[12] The "fat was in the fire again." Just as the Ben F. Battenfield letter had triggered a "chain reaction" among the Disciples in 1917, so did the Brown report in 1922. This time the controversy grew and expanded. Memories of Lexington in 1917 and lessons learned were recalled and not forgotten.

From 1922 through 1925, the Disciples were locked in a bitter struggle over the allegation that open membership was indeed a practice in foreign missions. The *Standard* mounted a campaign against the UCMS reminiscent of the 1917 trouble. The charges directed against the UCMS were bitter and caustic, and they continued intermittently from 1922 until the meeting of the International Convention in 1926 in Memphis. Following the John T. Brown report, the UCMS had dispatched its own committee to make an on the spot investigation.

The storm flags were out and flying when the International Convention met in 1926 in Memphis. The committee which had been dispatched to the orient to investigate the charge that open membership was being practiced especially in China reported that no instance of the practice of open membership in the foreign missions was uncovered. The International Convention meeting in Memphis received and endorsed the report by a bare majority. The conservatives were outraged, and they were done with the UCMS.[14]

Before leaving Memphis, the conservatives called a post-convention meeting for November 12, 1926, to set up a Committee on Future Action. The committee decided to issue a call for a "North American Christian Convention" to meet the following year October 12–16, 1927, in Indianapolis. The first North American Christian Convention met in October 1927 as planned. The first meeting was not, in the usual sense, a Disciples convention and was not meant to be. There were no resolutions, no business sessions, no official or conventional machinery, and there was no bitterness, protesting, and wrangling.

Arrangements were made for conferences of elders and deacons, on finances, women's work, and other matters of general church interest. There were worship periods and lecture sessions. This first meeting of the North American Christian Convention climaxed in a great communion service. The NACC has since met annually, with few exception, having upwards of ten thousand people in attendance ranging from family groups, church fellowships, ministers, educators, and other church leaders.[15]

Restoration historians are in general agreement that the Disciples came to a "parting of the way" during the 1926 Memphis International Convention. Tucker and McAllister observed that the Disciples remained in "shouting distance" of each other until the convening in 1927 of the first North American Christian Convention. This was the time period when the Disciples moved inexorably toward two separate fellowships. Alfred T. DeGroot chose to call the dissenting conservatives "Church of Christ Number Two".[16]

The bitterness and wrangling of the Disciples was steadily building between 1921 and 1926 over the actions of the UCMS. This is best expressed by Edwin R. Errett, who was defending the missionary society at the time Calhoun left Bethany in 1925. However, Errett wrote the following words in 1924:

> I was not bitterly opposed to the United Society at its inception. Having, however, seen its workings, I detest it, I hate it. I would rather see every dollar of its vested interest lost than to have it continue as the one big agency of our people.[17]

This declaration of Errett amounted then to the sounding of the death knell for the defense of the missionary society by the conservatives. The UCMS was placed under ban then and the opposition mounted. The gap between the conservatives and progressives widened over the next twenty years. Suddenly the full force of the conservatives was directed in 1946 against the International Convention.

There are other schismatic developments crucial to an understanding of Disciple history which remain to be examined. The stakes were high! It was a question of control. Who would occupy the chief positions of leadership in the Christian Church—the conservatives or liberals? The liberals had manned the convention floors and controlled the missionary societies and agencies of the Disciples at will. That would soon dramatically change to the dismay of the progressives. After the 1926 Memphis Convention, the conservatives were destined to prevail against the opposition. The overwhelming success of the 1927 North American Christian Convention provided the conservatives with the confidence that they were on the right road and headed in the right direction.

The conservatives began closing their ranks after the 1926 Memphis Convention to the persistent intrusions of the liberal Disciples. The "progressives," as the liberals chose to call themselves, mounted their own strategies to hold on to that considerable segment of the Disciples who favored their religious views and to win the support of others who were still undecided.

There are a few dates in the history of the Restoration movement which take precedence over the others. The inevitable division of the Disciples was set in motion in the 1926 Memphis International Convention and with the convening in 1927 of the North American Convention. Just ten years later, an editorial was published in the *Christian Standard* which precipitated the second major split of the Disciples in this century. At the time, it seemed to be just another thunderous assault of the conservatives against the practices of the progressives. On August 17, 1946, the *Christian Standard* published a proclamation titled the "Committee of One Thousand Present Their Protest to the International Convention." Nothing was left to the imagination with such verbal charges directed against the International Convention as: "The International Convention is determined and set to carry with them into ecclesiasticism all whom they can dominate"; and "The great mass of brethren . . . are refusing to be a pawn in any political worldly machine, be it Roman Catholic or Protestant." The conservatives were set for a "show down" fight which made the 1917 controversy pale in comparison.

The following two pages in the *Standard* were emblazoned with large black headlines running horizontally across pages facing each other. The first headline was one inch in height, with six-sub-headlines decreasing in print size. The headline, "An Open Letter," leaped out at the reader, which leveled the unvarnished charge of infidelity against the International Convention. Such harsh statements as "Your false representative authority," and "Your attacks against the Bible peculiarly abhorrent to our churches." All of this amounted to a call for a wholesale withdrawal of the Conservatives from the ranks of the liberals.[18] The separation of the churches of Christ from the Disciples in 1906 was accomplished quietly and without fanfare. This was not the case between the liberals and the progressives who quarreled openly and bitterly for the next ten years.

In less than a year after the appearance of the "Open Letter," a devastating editorial appeared in the June 7, 1947, issue of the *Standard* with the clarion call "Stand Up and Be Counted."[19] Previously, the names of hundreds of ministers and churches had been carried in the *Standard* protesting the actions of the UCMS and the International Convention. This time the editor proposed an "Honor Roll of the Faithful" to be run as a feature which printed both names of ministers and congregations. All churches and ministers were requested to send a card or letter stating their opposition to belonging to a denominational machine. The announcement ended with the statement: "Brethren have been demanding a listing separate from the 'Disciples' yearbook. Here it is. It is not a yearbook, of course." A veritable flood of cards and letters poured into the office of the *Standard*. The progressives were put on short notice. The successes of the conservatives were winners, and the progressives were not left in doubt of the fact. Today at the annual meetings of the North American Christian Convention, the progressives come with hat in hand and take a quiet place among the wary Independents.

Dwight E. Stevenson made a correct appraisal of this master stroke of the conservatives that would bring a jarring halt to the domination of the progressives over the Christian Church brotherhood. Stevenson uttered the "dooms day" statement which marked the end of progressive domination:

> Forces of fundamentalist reaction pulled away. Future historians may well settle upon the date June 7, 1947, as the date of decisive separation; for it was then that the *Christian Standard* published its front page editorial, 'Stand Up and Be Counted'. Thereafter, through September 6, 1947, the *Standard* published lists of churches and ministers in its weekly "Honor Roll of the Faithful". Within a few years it became evident to all that separation was complete.[20]

A major schismatic move was initiated by the progressives to counter the burgeoning successes of the conservatives. The "hand writing was on the wall"; and the progressives needed no Daniel to interpret. The conservatives had been circumvented and defeated at will, and the progressives calculated to continue doing so. The progressives began maneuvers to bring about a complete new organizational structure to the Disciples of Christ in order to salvage their vested interest in the Restoration movement. This new move came to light in the mid 1950's. A Committee on Brotherhood Organization met in the summer of 1957 in the Disciples House at Chicago. The committee was chaired by Wilbur H. Cramblett. The committee inaugurated moves which eventually after a decade led to the first self-acknowledged denominational church to emerge from the Restoration movement.

The progressives set up various committees and conferences over a ten year period which eventually led to the restructure of the Disciples of Christ. The International Convention met in October 1960, and adopted the plans for restructure to proceed.[21] As plans for restructuring moved ahead, opposition was mounting. The conservatives clearly understood the strategy of the progressives. An unidentified disciple at this time mailed to all the Christian Churches, listed in the *Yearbook,* two documents in the form of open letters, which were titled "Freedom or Restructure" and "The Truth About Restructure." The documents were widely circulated and calculated to create the suspicion that once restructure was complete then the local churches would lose their congregational autonomy and the ownership of their church property. Later it was learned that James DeForest Murch was the author and that B. D. Phillips paid for the printing and distribution of the pamphlets.[22] The call this time was not to "stand up and be counted," but "to pull out before it is too late!"

The plan for restructure was brought to fruition by the unanimous approval in 1968 of the Provisional Design by the International Convention Meeting in Kansas City. Immediately, hundreds of Christian Churches called for their names to be removed from the *Yearbook*. Numerous congregations withdrew over the next three years. In the *Yearbook of American Churches,* the three distinct fellowships which emerged in the Restoration movement are separately listed: Churches of Christ (1906), the (Independent) Christian Church and the Churches of Christ (1971), and the Christian Church (Disciples of Christ), 1971.[23] The Disciples of Christ church has since operated in much the same fashion as her sister denominations. The Disciples maintain that their primary objective is to bring the ideal of Christian unity to Christian believers of all persuasions.

The question is now raised again and for the last time in this book. Where does Hall Laurie Calhoun fit into the history of the Restoration movement? No other notable Disciple touched more bases and mirrored the facets of the Restoration movement to the same extent as Calhoun. The myopic view of Calhoun by both the Independents and the Disciples, as seen from the backdrop of the 1917 controversy, examines partially and imperfectly a talented and many splendored churchman. Stevenson described the day, March 17, 1917, that the Battenfield letter went out as the day that "lightning struck." Another writer called it an "earthquake," and who would say it was not so in Disciple history. What appeared to be rift, at the time, has since ruptured into a major "fault line" that time has not bridged.

Perhaps the best way to bring the meaning of the 1917 controversy into a sharp time focus would be to examine the present status of the Independent Christian Church and the ultra-liberal Disciples of Christ. What was said in 1917 and in 1922 about destructive criticism and the endorsement of open membership is no longer being repeated. The Disciples accept contemporary liberal theology and the practice of open fellowship as a matter of church policy. The Independents devoted more than forty years (1926–1968) attacking the UCMS and the International Convention of the Christian Church for its calculated control of the Disciples of Christ.

Today the churches of Christ, the Independent Christian Churches, and the Disciples of Christ form three unique and distinct fellowships with no religious ties to each other. They share only a common heritage in the Restoration movement which emerged from the united efforts of Barton W. Stone, Alexander Campbell, and their associates. Since 1968, the Independent Christian Churches have severed all ties and share no religious affiliations of any kind with the Disciples of Christ.

The churches of Christ, which achieved a separate identification in the United Religious Census of 1906, have no formal religious contacts whatsoever with the Disciples of Christ and very few with the Independents. The members of the churches of Christ regard both groups as erring brethren who are engaged in unscriptural practices. The churches of Christ have remained constant in their commitment to the keynote of the Restoration movement "to speak or remain silent as the Scriptures dictate."

The Independents have abandoned the endorsement of the missionary society for reasons already stated. They have clung to the organ since the latter part of the nineteenth century and continue to do so without remorse. Both fellowships share in a common alienation from the Disciples of Christ, but otherwise share little in common. Since their break with the Disciples of Christ, the Independents jealously guard the autonomy of the local church. There are no societies, boards, agencies, or executive committees exercising control or authority over the local churches. There are organizations, such as boards of trustees, which manage their schools and benevolent institutions. There are organizations similar to the North American Christian Convention, which provide open forums for discussion and direction of church affairs. The Independents boast, without justification, that they are the *bona fide* inheritors and custodians of Restoration principles and traditions.

The churches of Christ find it difficult to distinguish between the Independents and the Disciples and hold both in common distrust for deserting the Restoration plea. To the outsider looking in, the Independents and the Disciples are much like the divorced couple who have never accepted their separation yet there is no prospect for reconciliation. The Independents are no more likely to give up the organ for the sake of Christian unity than the Disciples are to abandon modern theology. The churches of Christ are not apt to accept either.

No indepth study has been made of the relationship among three separate fellowships to establish and clarify the facts as to why they really exist. This is not surprising since the last division of the Christian Church has taken place less than twenty years ago. Major attempts have been made in past years to bring about unity between the conservative element in the Christian Church and the churches of Christ. More than forty years ago, and before the division in the ranks of the Christian Church, H. Leo Boles stated in a unity meeting in Indianapolis that it was well known what caused the division in 1906 between the Christian Church and churches of Christ and what it would take to bring about unity at the present time. The Indianapolis meeting in 1939 led by Claude E. Witty, self appointed representative of the churches of Christ, and James DeForest Murch, self-appointed representative of the Christian Church, and the one that followed in Lexington, Kentucky, in 1940 were of little, if any avail. The Disciples of Christ, on the other hand, have moved away from the traditions and conventions of the Restoration movement; nevertheless, their roots are in the Stone-Campbell movement. Most other similarities stop at this place. An article appeared in the

May/June 1984 issue of the *Saturday Evening Post* titled "Disciples of Christ Going Their Way." And this is what the Disciples are now doing. The article notes that three U.S. Presidents are counted as members of the Disciples of Christ—James A. Garfield, Lyndon B. Johnson, and Ronald Reagan.

The article contains an interesting truism that "few if any take the Christian unity ideal as seriously as Disciples." Ecumenical unity is their big calling card because they encourage interdenominational cooperative religious activities. This most engaging spirit of the Disciples is summed up by Kenneth L. Teegarden, who relates that a Methodist friend once said to him: "You Disciples really keep my hopes for Christian unity alive. You haven't really united with anyone in your whole history, yet you keep on insisting the church is one. You never seem to become disillusioned about the possibilities for church union."

The Disciples of Christ are presently considering a merger with the United Church of Christ. (The United Church of Christ is named after the merger of groups who remained aloof from the Stone-Campbell Movement). The Disciples of Christ and the United Church of Christ began discussions in 1977 about a possible merger. After two years, they were still far apart; and in 1979, the next seven years were set up for further discussion with plans to continue to see each other and to hold joint religious ventures in the meantime.[24] Discussions are presently underway among those who are proposing to unite the Christian Church (Disciples of Christ) with various other denominations.

There is one other note that carries us back to 1917 and to the Central Christian Church in Lexington, an honored historical church of the Disciples. An announcement recently carried in their church bulletin, the "Chimes," states that a young married couple united with the Central Christian Church by transfer. One came from the Methodist Church and the other from the Catholic Church. Such is the practice of a latest denomination—the Disciples of Christ. Words fail us now if we tried to say more. However, there is no evidence that the Independents are willing to give up the organ for the sake of unity.

A postscript is added to this chapter to qualify any supposition that the College of the Bible controversy in 1917 created an organizational split in the ranks of the Disciples. However, the fight in the College of the Bible did prove to open the gate to the mounting dissension in the Christian Church over particular points of disagreement such as the practice of open membership, distrust for the missionary society, and a growing tolerance among liberals for destructive criticism.

The Battenfield letter made a startling revelation that the College of the Bible was under the control of a liberal president and faculty committed to the tenets of higher criticism. But it was Calhoun's candid statement that precipitated the 1917 furor through the pages of the *Christian Standard* with the full support of Editor George P. Rutledge and Russell Errett.

It is unthinkable that the results would have been anything less than a major uproar. This was so because the *Standard* had power to make it happen. These were the shots fired on "the Lexington Green" that started a theological revolution in the ranks of the Disciples which lasted fifty years (until 1968) when the Independents and progressives parted company. It is also unthinkable that the history of the Restoration movement centered in Disciple history could be accurately told apart from the contribution of Hall Laurie Calhoun who mirrored every facet of Disciple history and traveled down every road of the Christian Church from 1888 to 1935.

12

The Full Turn of the Circle

Almost fifty years have passed since the death of Hall Laurie Calhoun. Church historians have said little of Calhoun's niche in Restoration history. To redress this calculated neglect is long overdue. This chapter proposes to unravel the tangled skein of Calhoun's involvement in Disciple history from 1888 on. To chronicle Calhoun's early years presents no major problems up until the year of John W. McGarvey's death.

The first matter which we address is that of higher criticism and its relationship to the policy of open membership which had troubled the Disciples for decades. An early contributing cause for the first major dissension in the Christian Church over open membership surfaced in 1908 after the appointment of Guy W. Sarvis as a missionary to China. Subsequent controversies were all influenced, in one way or another, by the new theology. The Disciples, who were widely known for their Restoration plea of "speaking where the Bible speaks," were oddly the first to embrace the tenets of higher criticism.

With more than eighty years gone by since the endorsement of higher criticism by some of the Disciples, Calhoun's role in combating higher criticism can be viewed with more objectivity. McGarvey wrote continually in the *Christian Standard* attacking the tenets of destructive criticism. An interesting fact to note is that Calhoun wrote only two articles before 1917 exposing higher criticism. Both articles were published in the *Standard*. It is also of interest that Calhoun did not choose to continue McGarvey's department of "Biblical Criticism" in the *Standard*. Orvel Calhoun Crowder provides his assessment of his grandfather's thinking on higher criticism. He said that the reason for Calhoun's refusal to write a series of articles in McGarvey's department was because he could not "honestly give McGarvey the kind of attack on biblical criticism that would have satisfied the fundamentalist mind."

Calhoun first addressed the subject of higher criticism in an article printed July 18, 1908, in the *Standard* captioned "Is the Young Man Safe?" He cautioned that young men who were studying in the great universities of the North and East would be highly vulnerable to the teaching of sophisticated and skilled professors who documented their lectures with logic and science. Calhoun wrote: "I have no sympathy with that view which would keep our young men from such schools. Neither would I have them so indoctrinated in our peculiar views as to prejudice them against the fullest and freest investigation." He further stated, however, that "I believe the plea for which we stand is divine." Calhoun expressed confidence that a young man of average intelligence could be so well taught and grounded in the faith that he could go out and meet the "Goliaths" of higher criticism.

Calhoun wrote a second article on destructive criticism in 1909 which was also published in the *Standard*. This was the first and only time that he addressed the Wellhausen Documentary Hypothesis of the Old Testament. He reviewed Dr. Hinckley G. Mitchell's commentary on the book of Genesis contained in a series of commentaries edited by Shailer Matthews under the general title of *The Bible For Home and School*. Dr. Mitchell adopted the Documentary Hypothesis setting forth the concepts of the "Jahvistic, Eloistic, and Priestly documents." Calhoun ended his review of Genesis with an unqualified disapproval of Mitchell's commentary.[1]

We now move ahead two years beyond the 1917 Lexington controversy to a new battlefront which the conservatives opened soon after the United Christian Missionary Society had begun functioning in 1920. The long standing controversy over open membership had again surfaced; and this time around, it would not go away. The trip of John T. Brown in 1921 into the foreign missions in the orient substantiated the charge of the conservatives that open membership was being taught and practiced. The Pittsburg Congress of March 21–23, 1922, provided the open forum for the second major debate among the Disciples in a five year period.[2]

General Z. T. Sweeney addressed the Pittsburg Congress on March 23 during the last session. He charged that open membership among the churches established by the missionaries was indeed an accepted practice especially in the China mission field. The liberal Disciples declined to attack the veracity of General Sweeney, but chose instead to deliver a tirade against the Brown report. This was circulated in a statement by the Executive Committee of the UCMS.[3] The document was similar in spirit to the 1917 articles published in the *Quarterly Bulletin* of the College of the Bible designed to compromise H. L. Calhoun. The document by the Executive Committee proposed to correct misleading statements of Brown's report in order to counter the force of the substance of the Brown report and even to question his personal judgement. The attack was as harsh as the 1917 personal attack on the "Harvard graduate" who dared to expose the fact that destructive criticism was taught in the College of the Bible.[4] What could have been a more legitimate revelation than for Calhoun to state the facts of what was taking place in 1917 in the College of the Bible? Why should John T. Brown have been attacked in a similar fashion in 1922 for providing factual information about the China mission? But such was the case!

One of the major addresses of the Pittsburg Congress was delivered by Calhoun himself titled "What Destructive Criticism Destroys." An editorial followed in the *Standard* which commended Calhoun's address saying that it was "one of the great contributions to the success of that history making assembly." The editorial went on to say that had the Pittsburg Congress accomplished nothing more than the sending forth of Calhoun's message, "it would have been entirely worth it." Calhoun's address was published in an issue of the *Standard*. He defended biblical criticism as the scientific study of the Bible which holds to the divine authority and the infallible truth of the Bible. On the other hand, Calhoun described destructive criticism as discounting the divine inspiration and authority of the Bible.[5]

Calhoun did not address the subject of destructive criticism in the same way that McGarvey did. He exposed the corallaries of destructive criticism as faith destroying, espcially to young men training for the ministry. Calhoun was convinced that he understood what he was talking about, and he thought that he could best describe the dangers inherent in the new theology. On the other hand, he had little to say about the substance and message of the new theology in print and what made it so dangerous. He addressed in one more article the problem of higher criticism before leaving the Christian Church.

His last article was titled "Bible College Teaching the Bible," which appeared in the October 28, 1922, issue of the *Standard*. In this article, Calhoun did not directly address destructive criticism, but it is obvious that he had it in mind. He emphasized that the Bible should be taught scientifically with more than syllabi in hand. He insisted that philosophy and theology could not be substituted for the teaching of the Bible. He perhaps had in mind the captious criticism of the student contentions that Calhoun was fastened to the "question and answer" method of the McGarvey *Syllabi*.

Calhoun's name appeared at the end of 1922 in the *Christian Standard* with a promise which never materialized. The question has been raised about the fact that Calhoun did not carry on McGarvey's department in Biblical Criticism. The announcement was made December 23, 1922, that Calhoun would begin such a department on Biblical Criticism. One fact is outstanding that Calhoun was still held in the highest esteem in 1922 by the conservatives:

> Early in the year, Prof. Hall Laurie Calhoun will open this department as a regular 'Standard' feature. Bro. Calhoun needs no introduction to our readers. He is a dear friend to 1000's of them. His years of Bible study and teaching, his graduate work at both Yale and Harvard, his experience as preacher and evangelist, have fitted him ideally for this important work. In simple popular style, but with a true scholar's love of truth, he will strengthen the faith of Christians—old and young—in the Book of books.

We may only guess that the reason that the articles were not forthcoming may have been because of the priority of the big fuss growing out of John T. Brown's report on the foreign missions.

What conclusions can be drawn about Calhoun's personal beliefs on the eve of his leaving the Christian Church? Only one other article came from Calhoun which was published July 21, 1923, in the *Standard* which may shed some light on the answer. He wrote of the 1923 Bethany College Spring Commencement. His last words about the college were congenial and complimentary. There was no indication in this article that Calhoun was displeased with conditions and circumstances in Bethany College. President Cloyd Goodnight delivered the baccalaureate sermon on Sunday morning June 10. In the afternoon, a concert of sacred music was presented by the College Band on the campus. Calhoun concluded: "A more enjoyable meeting than this was never held by Bethany alumni." In less than a year, Calhoun began corresponding with N. B. Hardeman anticipating severing all ties with both Bethany College and the Christian Church. We may only conjecture that after 1923, Calhoun began to leave off trying to change among the Disciples what could not be changed. Knowing the thinking of Wilbur Cramblett, the driving force behind Bethany College, and the theology of John Barclay, minister of the Bethany Memorial Christian Church, who was a disciple of Harry Emerson Fosdick, Calhoun would not stay in Bethany and he had no other place to go among the Disciples.

The second skein to unravel in Calhoun's role among the Disciples was his support of the missionary society. His thinking on the missionary society was indeed ambiguous and inconsistent. In the 1904 Newbern trial deposition, Calhoun testified saying: "I do not understand the fundamental teachings of the Christian Church to make missionary societies a test of fellowship." Calhoun made a curious statement relating to his support of the missionary society testifying: "I have never in my life given one cent through a missionary society, nor have I ever by word or act encouraged one."

This was said in view of the fact that he knew full well that he had supported in 1902 the Christian Woman's Board of Missions. It will be remembered that Calhoun wrote from Cambridge the "New England Letter" which was published in the *Christian-Evangelist*. He wrote of a farewell reception given in the St. James Christian Church for four persons who were going as foreign missionaries under the auspices of the Christian Woman's Board of Missions. A voluntary offering of $38.78 was presented to the missionaries who were being sent to India by the well wishers as a token of their love and personal interest. We may assume that the Calhoun family made a personal contribution at the time. He wrote that this was the first group of missionaries to sail from Boston. Calhoun commented that no single event in the history of the work of the Christian Church in New England had done so much to stir up enthusiasm in missions.

That H. L. Calhoun participated in the Tennessee Missionary Society after his return to Conyersville in 1893 is a matter of record. After his return to Lexington in 1904 from Cambridge, Calhoun fully endorsed and participated in official capacities in the Kentucky Society until he moved to Bethany in 1917. His interest in and support of the missionary society obviously had not changed over the years. During the Pittsburg Convention, he indirectly addressed the problem of open membership in the foreign missions. A major article by Calhoun was published July 29, 1922, in the *Standard,* titled "Should Distinctive Tenets of Disciples of Christ Be Taught on Foreign Fields?" He thought that such should be. This article had been delivered first as an address on April 20, 1922, which Calhoun made to the Disciples Congress in Columbus, Ohio.

One fact is outstanding in the address. Calhoun assumed the right of the missionary society to exist in principle as an aid and expedient. His address then marked out three distinct groups contained in the Disciples fellowship. The first group included the conservative membership of the Christian Church with whom Calhoun was identified. Calhoun described the second group whom he labeled as modernists who accepted the new theology. To accept the practice of open membership he pointed out presented no problem to them. A third group took the position that any Christian belief was superior to heathenism. This group maintained that unity based on the law of love should necessarily take precedence over Disciples doctrine in foreign missions. Calhoun stood firm in the first position and discounted the second and third positions as contradictory and unacceptable.

Three years later, however, Calhoun specifically condemned the missionary society and the use of the organ in worship. Edwin R. Errett, in spite of his bitter condemnation of the UCMS, accepted the concept of the organ and society, but not its abuse. And the 1925 editorial comment faulted Calhoun for leaving the Christian Church while admitting there was much wrong with the missionary society. Calhoun was charged with leaving one distinct fellowship to join another equally distinct group.

The third skein of Calhoun's religion to be examined was his thinking about instrumental music. His long standing approval of the organ in the meeting house was not abandoned until 1925. The attempt will be made at this place to capsule the instrumental music controversy from 1850 to the turn of the century when churches began to divide over the organ in order to provide a background for Calhoun's position. Alexander Campbell disapproved of the playing of instruments of music in worship writing that "to all spiritual minded people such aids would be as a cowbell in a concert."[6] Moses E. Lard harshly condemned the placing of an organ in a church writing that when an organ was placed in a church house that would be "the day on which it reaches the first station on the road to apostasy."[7] The first instrument of music to be placed in a meeting house was in the Park Avenue Christian Church no later than the middle 1850's in New York. In the second case, L. L. Pinkerton introduced a melodeon in 1859 in the Midway, Kentucky, Christian Church.[8] Pinkerton said he was the first to do so.

The music question was surfacing about 1860. Isaac Errett addressed the subject first in an article in the *Millennial Harbinger* in October, 1861, titled "Church Music." Errett was writing on the broader subject of church music. He correctly observed that the New Testament knows nothing of choir singing or instrumental music. Errett made another statement that the New Testament "knows as little of congregational singing as of choir singing." What Errett said in this statement has no substantial scriptural or historical merit. Errett argued that the innovations of choirs and instruments will not be checked by captious criticism. Errett's advice was for training the church in good vocal music. "The church is entitled to good music."[9]

John W. McGarvey was the first to call for an open and candid discussion on the use of instrumental music in worship. McGarvey opposed the organ based on the silence of the Scriptures. McGarvey contended that instrumental music was used by the Israelites. Moses and the Israelites sang their song of deliverance from Egypt accompanied by timbrels (Exodus 15:20,21). David commanded the use of instruments in temple worship (Psalms 150). The New Testament, on the other hand, is silent on the subject in both example and commandment. A. S. Hayden sought to discount McGarvey's arguments. The matter was far from being settled at the time.[10]

Errett stated the case for the use of instrumental music in worship in articles published in 1870 in the *Christian Standard*. Errett accomplished this, not through logic based upon scripture, but through plausibility. Errett left the impression that he was writing impassionately. He wanted it understood he did not advocate the organ to please the human ear, but he advocated its use as a leader and guide to the voices of the congregation. Errett defended the placing of an organ in the meeting house if it met the unanimous approval of the members. Errett then made another sudden turn. He counseled against using the organ for the sake of harmony. Nevertheless, Errett is charged with dividing the church.

The essence of Errett's reasoning which led to the adoption of the organ goes something like this: if it is right to sing and play a religious song in the parlor, why is it wrong to do so in church. Why is it right to do so in the Sunday school downstairs and wrong when the organ is played in worship upstairs. Through the acceptance of this kind of specious logic, the organ was literally moved from the parlor to the church all over the country.[11]

In 1870, Isaac Errett took John W. McGarvey to task for making this statement: "It is impossible to find a plainer case of an innovation in the evil sense of the term, than is presented in the use of instrumental music in worship." It is obvious that Calhoun understood McGarvey's position on the organ; however, he adopted Errett's position that the organ was just an aid to worship in the same sense as a tuning fork and a song book. The UCMS had turned itself into a sectarian body exercising a control over the Christian Church short of tyranny. Calhoun eventually categorized the instrument of music as a companion to the missionary society since both had troubled the church and caused internal dissension. He said that instrumental music had corrupted the worship.

The question may be legitimately raised in regard to David Lipscomb's thinking on the presence of instrumental music in the church as it relates to Calhoun. To be sure, Lipscomb followed with intense interest the exchanges between McGarvey, Hayden, Errett, and others. The statement has been made that Lipscomb remained silent on the music issue until 1878. As a matter of fact, this statement is without foundation because Lipscomb addressed the organ question in response to a letter written to him dated August 6, 1873, from a brother in Murray, Kentucky, who wanted Lipscomb's thinking on using the organ in Sunday school and church services.

Lipscomb made a clear and highly significant statement. He wrote: "This question has been discussed extensively in other of our periodicals. We had hoped the discussion there would suffice." Lipscomb concluded the sum of the whole matter by saying:

> Prayer and praise, thanksgiving, singing and making melody in the heart unto the Lord are acts of worship ordained of God. But no authority do we find for the organ. How can man worship God in the name of Christ where Christ's name is nowhere mentioned in connection wih the organ. It is no appointment of God. It is no part of the law. There can be no obedience to it. It frequently prevents singing and becomes a substitute for it. It there subverts an appointment with God.[12]

Lipscomb wrote in the same article that he did not think anyone had claimed authority from the Scriptures to use the organ in worship. He had never done so. He took an uncompromising stand in opposition to the missionary society in 1866 and he never faltered. And he did the same in regard to the organ after he had listened to his brethren and read what they had said. To Lipscomb, the organ had no place in the worship. McGarvey tolerated the organ and preached in churches that practiced the use of instrumental music until the year of his death. Lipscomb never did, no not ever. Lipscomb preached for the non-organ church in Union City, Tennessee, while Calhoun was preaching for the organ church there.

Calhoun had an article printed on March 19, 1931, which appeared in the *Gospel Advocate* fifty-eight years after Lipscomb's denunciation of the organ, and Calhoun used in his article the identical Scriptural reasoning of Lipscomb. The article was titled "Worship—Singing and Prayer." Calhoun had indeed turned the full circle from "non-organ church" to "organ church" and back again to "non-organ church." Thirty-five years previously he had refused the request of Lipscomb and Harding to write such an article taking a stand against those who used the organ in worship. Calhoun did not use a single argument in defense of his position that was customarily used in music debates. He made no references to the Old Testament use of musical instruments in worship, or the claim that the word *psallo* authorized the use of the instrument in Christian worship. He uses Paul's explicit statements that psalms, hymns, and spiritual songs are to be sung in worship and the melody is to be made in the heart. Calhoun implies in his article that if the Holy Spirit had intended the use of instrumental music in worship, the Scriptures would have said so. Calhoun was severely scriptural and thorough in his presentation and left the matter strictly on that score. David Lipscomb would have been pleased to have been serving as editor of the *Gospel Advocate* when Calhoun's article was printed in 1931.

We return to 1917 to travel briefly down a track which was laid by Calhoun's critics and lasted but little longer than the "Toonerville trolley." The student supporters of Calhoun in the College of the Bible controversy were described as a small coterie of trouble makers. Much was made of the support of President R. H. Crossfield and his faculty by a majority of the students of Transylvania and the College of the Bible. As a matter of fact, the supporters of Hall Laurie Calhoun were worthy, mature and competent allies who later distinguished themselves admirably in high positions in the Christian Church. If the leadership of the Independent Christian Church would show disposition to take time and remember, they could learn that their excellent program of religious education at the present time, at every level, has been a direct spin off of the Lexington debacle.

Three of the principles in the 1917 dispute were Ralph L. Records, Irvin T. Green, and Peyton H. Canary. What happened after 1917 in their lives? The truth is that each enjoyed a distinguished career within the conservative Christian Church. Peyton H. Canary was humiliated with a curt letter of dismissal from Transylvania University by President Crossfield which has been cited earlier. Canary lived a worthy and fruitful life dedicated to the cause of the Conservative Christian Church. He was first enrolled in Transylvania University in 1914 and entered Bethany College in September 1917, and graduated from Bethany College in 1918. Canary earned the Master of Science degree in Education in 1930, and the Ph.D. in 1934 in English and Psychology from Indiana University. He served as head of the English Department in Central Normal College in Danville, Ohio. He was Staff and Feature writer for the *Christian Standard*. Canary served as Treasurer for the North American Christian Convention, and served also as a member of its Executive Committee. He eventually was department head of the Comparative Religion Department in the Cincinnati Bible Seminary. Canary preached on a regular basis for Christian Churches from 1914 on. His whole life was marked by dedicated service to the Christian Church.[13]

Irving T. Green went in September 1917 to Bethany College. He earned the Master of Arts and the Bachelor of Divinity degrees both in Bethany College. He later attended Yale University. And in 1921, Green was appointed Professor of New Testament and Biblical Doctrine in Bethany College. Ralph L. Records (1883–1965) was a true yoke-fellow as he joined hands with Calhoun in the 1917 expose. Records was a graduate of the College of the Bible, Transylvania University, and pursued graduate studies in Kentucky University and the University of Chicago. In 1913, he became the Head of the Chemistry Department in Transylvania University. He resigned his position in protest against the Report of the Board of Trustees of the College of the Bible exonerating the accused liberal faculty charged with teaching destructive criticism in their classes. We have been unable to find out anything about what happened to Ben F. Battenfield after the 1917 school year. It will be recalled that at the height of the 1917 controversy that it was rumored a new seminary would be started in Lexington, Kentucky, with Calhoun as its head.[14]

However, the McGarvey Bible College was established instead in 1923, in Louisville, Kentucky. J. B. Briney, Ira Boswell, and Ralph L. Records were moving forces behind the founding of the McGarvey Bible College. And at about the same time the Cincinnati Bible Institute was founded and began operating. Neither knew of the plans of the other. The Cincinnati Bible Institute was headed by John W. Tyndall. Negotiations were begun and completed for merging the two schools which resulted in the organization of the Cincinnati Bible Seminary which started operations in 1924, and developed into the largest ministerial training school in the Christian Church.

Ralph L. Records was appointed president of the Cincinnati Bible Seminary in 1926 and served the institution for twenty-four years. Many obstacles including the "Great Depression" years were surmounted by the Seminary. The Cincinnati Bible Seminary has developed into an imposing citadel of strength for the Independent Christian Church.[15] Every college and university of higher education then in existence under the control of the Christian Church was lost to the liberal Disciples of Christ in 1917 as later events proved. This proved to be a boon to the conservative element in the Christian Church. The conservatives have since founded a network of Bible schools and colleges which stretch across the nation and beyond. Milligan College in Johnson City, Tennessee, is one of the regionally accredited colleges of higher education operated by members of the Christian Church. In addition to the Cincinnati Bible Seminary, they have two other distinguished seminaries. The seminaries are also regionally accredited.

A fourth skein in Calhoun's career demands a disentanglement from the biased unfair charges leveled at Calhoun during the College of the Bible trouble. The investigations proposed to determine if destructive criticism were actually being taught. W. C. Bower mounted his personal attack against Calhoun during the course of the investigation, and he continued to address Calhoun's role in the so called "heresy trial" until near the end of his active life. Bower was the person who coined the phrase to describe the proceedings of the Board of Trustees as a "heresy trial". A companion phrase to the "heresy trial," which came later, was that the whole controversy revolved around the question of academic freedom.

In 1962, Bower described what he considered to be the concepts of the "conservatives" and the "liberals" during the 1917 time period. The Disciples movement according to Bower was separating into two distinct groups even then. He depicted the liberals in their "plea for union among all Christian believers." The "proposed restoration of the New Testament church" was declared to be the mission of the conservatives. Bower identified himself with the progressive group which continued to hold for the plea for Christian unity. According to Bower, the reactionary group, with which he identified Calhoun, placed its primary emphasis upon restoration of the New Testament order of faith and practice. Bower wrote: "The two trends were contained within the Disciple movement until the 1920's. The result was growing tension within the brotherhood with continuous vituperative attacks upon the progressives to the extent that local and national conventions were scenes of strife, bitterness, and a struggle to seize control of the machinery of organizations led by the *Christian Standard*."

Bower then stated quite accurately that: "The dissension reached a crisis in 1917 in an attack upon the College of the Bible led by Dean H. L. Calhoun and a group of twelve students and sponsored by the *Christian Standard*." Bower divulges an interesting fact that he, R. H. Crossfield, A. W. Fortune, and E. E. Snoddy were elders in the Central Christian Church. Bower roundly assailed the "Independents" identifying Mark Collis, pastor of the Broadway Christian Church as a leader among the dissenters. Bower disallowed the nomenclature of "Independents" since he maintained that these churches engaged in cooperative mission and charitable efforts. Bower states one of the major contentions which we have set forth in this biography of Hall Laurie Calhoun:

> The division thus created has affected the entire brotherhood. Numerous churches have defected from the mainstream of Disciples history. Factions have risen in others, and those splinter groups have become the nuclei of new noncooperative churches.[16]

Bower drew a line separating the "progressive" Central Church with thirteen sympathetic cooperating Christian Churches in the Lexington area as opposed by the "Independent" Broadway Christian Church in Lexington whose petition was supported by a covey of "Independent" churches.

Bower applauded the success of the "progressives" upon the

withdrawal of the "Independents" saying the "Disciples have pursued their life and work in harmony of spirit and unanimity of purpose. Gone are the days of dissension and bitterness that frustrated all attempts at constructive cooperative effort." These words were published six years before the Disciples of Christ restructured their fellowship and issued their official list of churches in the *Yearbook of American Christian Churches*. Some fifteen years later since the "restructure" was accomplished, the "peace and tranquility" of the Disciple of Christ movement is as elusive as ever. Their plea for "union" rather than "restoration" divided the disciples and continues to do so.

The odd thing about the whole matter is the fact that Bower should have named Hall L. Calhoun as the leading nemesis of the liberal disciples. As a matter of fact, John T. Brown was attacked more often and over a longer period of time than Calhoun through documents sent out by the "progressives" to counter Brown's influence. The *Christian Standard* sustained "headlined" accusations for decades directed at the "progressives" that would make the 1917 expose look like a side show. The *Standard* featured accusations against the UCMS that went on for more than thirty years. Why was Calhoun made the "scape goat" by the progressives? One fact is clear that Calhoun stood "head and shoulders" above his peers in academics and evangelism. The answer is clear that Calhoun and the *Standard* forced the liberals out into the open in 1917. The charge of a "heresy trial" by Bower was a well calculated ploy. The controversy centered on the accusation that "destructive criticism" was being taught in the College of the Bible. This was understood by the entire Disciple brotherhood.

The "progressives," in the name of Christian liberty and academic freedom, embraced the latest findings of higher criticism. The conservatives were described, on the other hand, as reactionaries who were intent on going back to restore the primitive New Testament church. It is ironic that both groups justified their religious stances in past history. Shall Charles Darwin's *Origin of the Species* be the beginning point of Christian unity, or the gospel of Jesus Christ and the church he founded be the ultimate model. The "progressives" claimed the first with qualification, and the conservatives the latter.

The criticisms leveled against Calhoun by Bower in 1917 continued until Bower's declining years. The account of the controversy was always the same. He continued to portray "the heresy trial and the description of its setting in a room in Morrison Hall." Bower understood better than anyone else the real significance of the 1917 matter. He wrote: "As a result of the long controversy, the progressives and the conservatives were drawn into opposing positions. Individuals and churches aligned themselves on one side or the other." The actual separation between the two groups took place in 1946 and 1947 when the *Standard* called for disciples and churches everywhere to "stand up and be counted".

Bower seemed to have been obsessed with his feelings of disapproval for Calhoun, and he let few opportunities pass without saying so. The denunciations of Hall L. Calhoun by Bower are especially revealing, not so much of Calhoun, but of Bower, himself. Crossfield, Fortune, and Snoddy said little outside of what was published in the *Quarterly Bulletin* of the College of the Bible, and they all shied away from attacking Calhoun. Fortune's account of the 1917 controversy was restrained and almost apologetic, and he declined to deliver direct and vicious criticism against Calhoun.

W. C. Bower no doubt strove to deliver a well balanced evaluation of Calhoun. However, he could not resist the temptation to become personal in his attacks. We turn first to some of his remarks, which more or less, were intended to compromise Calhoun. Bower's most often appraisal of Calhoun was that he possessed a "split personality." While Bower criticized Calhoun on one hand, he blessed him on the other. Of the 1917 controversy, Bower wrote: "The unhappy role of Dean Calhoun in this episode calls for understanding rather than condemnation, tragic as it proves to be. First, of all, he was a disappointed man. His hopes to succeed President McGarvey had been dashed when the board elected Dr. Crossfield." Bower was indeed correct in this appraisal of Calhoun. Calhoun did become an unhappy man. Why should he not have been disappointed? This anxiety within him becomes obvious, not only because he did not permanently succeed McGarvey, but also because of the loss of the College of the Bible to the "progressives."

In view of such statements, Bower wrote: "I cherish no bitterness toward him. I think he was a victim of circumstances and the unwilling tool of sinister outside agencies that took advantage of his personal conflicts." Bower finally praised Calhoun with a double tongue and double-edged words when he wrote: "With his genial personality, his ability, and his training, he might well have become an outstanding leader of the original dynamic pleas for the union of Christians rather than of the legalistic, literalistic and obstructionist Restoration phase of the Disciples movement."

As late as June 1, 1960, Bower delivered an address to the faculty and students of the Lexington Theological Seminary on the "great controversy of 1917." Bower came up simultaneously with an open palm of praise and a back hand of criticism in which he was still echoing the old refrain. Bower described Calhoun as one of "the most gracious men personally I have known." But he then follows with his favored diatribe that Calhoun suffered a "split personality." A factual observation which we make in this place is that no other contemporary of Calhoun, early or late in life, made a similar observation either among the "Independents" or the "Progressives." Bower did not attempt to disguise the fact that after the 1917 controversy had ended in victory for the progressives that he was even then a liberal shaped in the theology of higher criticism. He never failed to portray Calhoun in the mold of the opponents of efforts to bring the church into the twentieth century.

The Lexington *Leader* on July 26, 1982, carried a feature obituary at the time of the passing of William Clayton Bower. Sixty-five years after the 1917 Lexington "earthquake," the *Leader* commented: "Bower considered himself a liberal, but not a radical on religious matters, and in 1917, his beliefs on evolution put him at the center of a landmark heresy case that was brought before the College of the Bible Board of Trustees." Dr. Glyn Burke, minister of the Central Christian Church, preached Bower's funeral. He used as his text, "Know ye not that a great man is fallen in Israel?" Adron Doran was among the fifty or more who attended the funeral. William Clayton Bower enjoyed a long distinguished career among the Disciples in the College of the Bible, the University of Chicago, and the University of Kentucky.

Other Disciple historians present Calhoun in a wholly objective and scholarly fashion. Tucker and McAllister have done this in their comprehensive study of the Restoration movement titled *A Journey in Faith*. The authors evidence a dispassionate approach to Calhoun's role in the "battle of the Book" which they refer to as the most influential seminary of the Disciples at that time. The authors declare that indeed Calhoun was being groomed by McGarvey for the presidency of the College of the

Bible. The authors accepted Dean Francis G. Peabody's appraisal that it "had been a wonder" how Calhoun could complete two years of study under George Foot Moore and still retain his "orthodoxy." They wrote that Calhoun labored to preserve the College of the Bible as a bastion of orthodoxy, but that his liberal associates frustrated his efforts.

There is another side of this coin. The conservatives of the Christian Church saw Calhoun in an entirely different light. He was not castigated unduly by them for leaving their ranks in 1925, nor have they written unfavorably about him until this day. James DeForest Murch, author of *Christians Only,* played a major role in separating the "conservatives" from the "progressives" as the "restructure" of the Disciples entered its final stages. Murch did not gloss over the fact that the take-over of the College of the Bible was a deliberately calculated ploy which succeeded:

> It is small wonder that at the death of McGarvey (1911) and others of 'the old school' at Lexington, the liberals moved in for 'the kill'. At all odds the faculties had to be cleared of this threat to "progress". Hall L. Calhoun, a Ph.D. from Harvard, had been tagged by McGarvey to succeed him as president of the College of the Bible. Other conservatives were being prepared in schools of comparable and unquestioned scholarship, to carry on the tradition of sound Biblical training. Dr. A. W. Fortune and certain liberals on the board had other ideas. Almost immediately R. H. Crossfield, a liberal, was chosen president not only of the College of the Bible but of Transylvania College as well. Calhoun was made dean of the seminary in 1912 and proceeded to do the best he could to maintain orthodox Biblical standards. But the inexorable liberal purge was on.[17]

This statement made in 1952 was a later installment of the 1917 controversy, and it is part of a tale that is still unfolding.

There is no reasonable way to end the Calhoun story. We have endeavored to see Calhoun in the early and late years of his life. Calhoun traveled a few rough stretches in his life before 1917. He was complimented by John R. Williams in his youth; He became the protege of John W. McGarvey after he entered the College of the Bible in Lexington in 1888. David Lipscomb and James A. Harding were aware of his splendid talents as a preacher and prospective teacher. His unpleasant, though not altogether unprofitable, exchanges with M. C. Kurfees in 1900 constitute a short term matter. Kurfees was instrumental in bringing Hardeman and Calhoun together for a conference in 1924. The deep friendship between F. W. Smith and Calhoun lasted from their student days together in the College of the Bible until the passing of Smith.

Aside from the handful of critics with "personal axes to grind," Calhoun is best viewed from the side of the conservatives in the Christian Church who made common cause with Calhoun and have not to this day sought to discredit him in any way. Of course, he was accepted by the churches of Christ, with but a few reservations, when he separated from the Christian Church in 1925.

An editorial in the *Christian Standard* in April of 1916 paid Calhoun some very high compliments. A series of brief personality sketches were being printed in the *Christian Standard*. Calhoun neglected to provide to the journal personal data for his own biography. The feature editorial, nevertheless, was printed which stated in part: "Hall Laurie Calhoun is the well beloved and highly esteemed dean of the college of the Bible in Lexington. It is a high honor to follow in the steps of John W. McGarvey, but Calhoun bears the mantle of the great teacher with genuine dignity and modesty."

Calhoun was described as a favorite teacher by his students. His schedule called for him to be up at 4:30 each morning studying until class time, teaching all week, preaching on Sundays, and holding meetings during vacation periods. And the further statement is made that "with his good wife and his well ordered family about him, he feeds his strong, rich life, and spends its strength daily in his chosen calling as teacher and preacher."[18]

The *Christian Standard* published another editorial with deep regret in 1925, regarding Calhoun's statement which he made on leaving the Christian Church. Calhoun was lauded by the editor with the highest commendation:

> Whether or not one fully agrees with Prof. H. L. Calhoun in all his statements, or his actions, no one acquainted with his deep sincerity and high motives can entertain anything but an abiding respect for him. Few, in these latter days, have rendered such distinguished services in preserving the simple and pure faith of the New Testament as has Professor Calhoun. His years of faithful and consecrated teaching of the Bible as God's holy word have made of him an outstanding character among those who seek to restore the

New Testament organization, its teachings, ordinances, and its life. We are, therefore, assured that the readers of the following statement from him will give to it a most sympathetic consideration.[19]

The editorial was written in response to Calhoun's published statement "Why I Left". This was made public prior to his going to Freed-Hardeman College. The editor seems to lament the fact that the Christian Church had lost such a great man in their ranks. "All who know Professor Calhoun will wonder why he found it necessary to publish such a statement." Calhoun's position was supported: "Those with whom he has been laboring, and among whom he has wrought such great achievements, will agree with practically all his statement."

The editorial blamed the churches of Christ for refusing to fellowship the Christian Church which adopted the organ and the missionary society on the grounds of denying the liberty and freedom to the churches who chose to use them. The statement is made in the editorial that shows clearly the problems suffered in the Christian Church: "That many grave abuses have arisen, both from the use of the organ and also the missionary society, no one even casually informed on conditions would think for a moment of denying." What was then said amounts to confession: "with Professor Calhoun our hearts have ached over the evil and insidious abuses that are clothed under the cloak of 'Christian liberty'."

In view of the mounting hostility at this very time directed against the United Christian Missionary Society and the harsh language of Edwin R. Errett condemning the UCMS, there is another puzzling statement about Calhoun: "When he makes either of those a test of fellowship, then he is, in our humble judgement, violating the spirit of the New Testament Church." The editorial concludes with the statement: "This, we know, Professor Calhoun would not intentionally do." At this place, we introduce our editorial comment. In 1946, the conservatives were done with the liberals; and in 1947, they called for the faithful to "Stand Up and Be Counted." When the "Independents" called for the United Christian Missionary Society to go, the organ should have been sent close behind for similar, if not identical, reasons that caused in 1906 the separation of the churches of Christ from the Disciples.

Epilogue

IN 1926, Ralph Lafayette Records became President of the Cincinnatti Bible Seminary. The McGarvey Bible College had merged with the Seminary two years before. Records, who was Chairman of the Chemistry Department at Transylvania University, had been associated with Calhoun in the 1917 controversy at the College of the Bible and later as a member of the Graduate School of Religion in Bethany until 1919. There is no indication that Calhoun made any effort to persuade Records, Irvin T. Green, and Peyton H. Canary, who were co-laborers with him at Lexington and Bethany, to join him in his decision to leave Bethany College and the Christian Church. Calhoun seemed to have gone his own way in 1925 while his former colleagues retained their status among the conservative Disciples.

On June 9, 1927, certainly at the invitation of President Records, Calhoun went to the Cincinnati Bible Seminary to deliver the spring commencement address. The occasion presented a rather unusual situation for both Calhoun and Records. They had fought the "Battle of the Book" against the "destructive critics" together in 1917, and had lost decisively to the liberals. Calhoun had become identified with the churches of Christ in Nashville while Records had remained with the conservative element in the Christian Church which had supported Calhoun in his efforts to wrest the College of the Bible from those who supported the new theology. Orvel Crowder stated that Calhoun and Records remained close personal friends and carried on a personal correspondence. Crowder said that he had talked on several occasions with Records about his grandfather.

Calhoun reached the last major turning point of his life in the spring of 1926. Orvel Crowder described his grandfather's state of mind in 1926 in that critical juncture in his life that "he began to experience a sense of failure to what had happened at the schools where he worked." Calhoun passed in just one year from the shadows of a desperate illness into one of the happiest periods of his life that lasted until his death. In the spring of 1927, he delivered the baccalaureate sermon for the graduating class of David Lipscomb College. Leon McQuiddy engaged Calhoun to write the *Teacher's Quarterly*. He was preaching to overflow audiences in the Belmont church of Christ, and preaching over radio station WLAC. He also addressed the graduating class of the Cincinnati Bible Seminary. And so it may be said that Calhoun failed in a time of his greatest successes and succeeded after what must have seemed to him the most crushing failures life could thrust upon a person. This biography seeks to accord Hall Laurie Calhoun his deserved niche in the disciples "Hall of Fame"; and whatever that may be, we are not presumptuous to know or say.

Calhoun's speaking engagement at the Cincinnati Bible Seminary did not go unnoticed by members of the churches of Christ as was expected. The testy editor of the *Christian Leader*, F. L. Rowe jumped right on his subject:

> Brother Hall L. Calhoun of Nashville delivered the commencement address last Wednesday evening to the Cincinnati Bible Seminary students at Westminister Church on Price Hill. We are told the address was according to the Book and calculated to make a lasting impression on the student body.[1]

Rowe commented that the *Advocate* would publish the lengthy address which it did in four installments.

F. W. Smith came to Calhoun's defense without mincing words in his reply to Rowe, which was printed July 7, 1927, in the *Advocate*. Calhoun had not gone to Cincinnati without giving careful consideration to the matter. Smith, Calhoun, and their associates were convinced that the move would do no harm and possibly could do some good.

Rowe stated that he had been reliably informed that representative brethren in Nashville would attend the North American Christian Convention meeting which met for the first time October 1927 in Indianapolis. Smith discounted the rumor that a brother would represent a Nashville church of Christ or the *Advocate* with the remark that no congregation in Nashville would think of sending one.

Rowe did not fault Calhoun for making the address; however, he assailed Calhoun and those associated with him on the *Advocate* staff for thinking any profit would result from the venture. Going on the assumption that Nashville brethren would attend the NACC, as Rowe had been misinformed, his comments are pertinent to the perennial revival of dialogues between the Independents and churches of Christ leaders calculated to bring unity between the Independent Christian Church and the churches of Christ:

> It will be the purpose of these representatives from the South to plead with the Convention people at Indianapolis to give up their unscriptural practices, such as the organ, the society, and any other inner wheels, and to go back to the Old Jerusalem plan. Knowing the history of similar efforts and recalling as we do lengthy discussions held by representative brethren in both bodies, it is our prediction that nothing whatever will be accomplished.

Rowe also addressed the impact that he thought the address would have on the student body of the Seminary and attached no expectation for any positive results:

> The writer is fairly well acquainted with the student body of the Bible Seminary and has talked with a number of them . . . They are not discussing the organ and it will not be drawn into their movement, neither will they consent to the elimination of the Missionary Society . . .

Rowe had been fifty percent correct in his prediction to date, The conservatives have abandoned the missionary society, but they cling with fanatical devotion to the organ. Restoration history records that numerous churches were troubled and divided in the wake of the ongoing passage of the Independents over the organ and the missionary society. Christian Churches have forced church splits over the issues over the years without remorse.

Aside from the exchange of words between Smith and Rowe, what was it that Calhoun had to say in the Cincinnati address which made it especially significant? Smith assured Rowe that the address was "according to the Book," and that Calhoun's Nashville brethren had urged him to make the address which was well received and calculated to do good; however, after the passage of forty years, the Independents and churches of Christ are still far apart. One salient fact in the address is clear that Calhoun strove to show that the Scriptures provide the only secure ground for Christian unity. Calhoun made a play on certain words in his address to illustrate his train of thought which he intended for clarification.

Calhoun candidly recognized the cleavage existing between the Christian Church and the churches of Christ which is today as deep as ever. The liberal Disciples are not considered here because the Independents and the churches of Christ share only a common historical heritage with the liberal Disciples. The liberal Disciples "sowed the wind" and are presently "reaping the whirlwind." The Christian Church (Disciples of Christ) has suffered a steady declining membership over the past twenty-five years. Their present confirmed membership is 770,227. And they are sad about the fact, and many of them are angry and feel betrayed. However, their leaders continue to march to the sound of the organ. Human societies form an integral part of their denomination. Their preachers and leaders endorse liberal theology couched in secular ideologies of the most recent intellectual positions in sociology, psychology, the natural sciences, and modern theology.

Calhoun made a play on "our" equals "yours" plus "mine" in the Cincinnati speech. He was inferring that the "you" and "yours" described that group in the Christian Church which supported the *Christian Standard,* and was indentified with the Cincinnati Bible Seminary. On the other hand, the "I" and "mine" signified that large constituency of the church of Christ which was identified with the *Gospel Advocate* and David Lipscomb College. He singled out David Lipscomb College from the other colleges operated by members of the churches of Christ for a recognizable reference. Calhoun sought to erase those distinctions between the two fellowships by referring to "our religion." He means by this the Christian religion as set forth in the Scriptures. He then presented a series of statements (not a creedal formula) which had long been a part of Restoration sermons and writings.[2] Calhoun addressed the scriptural principles of the Christian faith: We believe that the Bible reveals to the alien sinner the law of pardon; that the Bible reveals to the Christian the law of life; that the Bible represents to us the church of Christ as built by him on Peter's confession; that the church, and not some humanly devised society, must make known the manifold wisdom of God; that the Bible makes known the church whose head is Christ; that the church, which makes known the five acts of worship, enjoins singing and excludes the mechanical instruments in worship; that the Bible reveals the law of love; that the Bible presents the great motive leading us to forsake sin; that the Bible prophesies the future to the eternal light of an endless day; that the Bible reveals to us the coming of the Son of man, the resurrection and the final judgment; that the Bible reveals to us the home that Jesus has gone to prepare.[3]

He repeated almost word for word the Cincinnati address in a lecture which he later delivered at the Abilene Christian College Lectureship (1928 and 1929). Calhoun, in writing of "our religion," meant the biblical Christian religion which "grows and restores itself as a tree that has flourished for thousands of years." However, he erred in implying that the Christian Church shared large common ground with the church of Christ in his designation of "our religion." The two fellowships were then distinct and separate churches and had been since 1906.

Certainly a curious part of Calhoun's Cincinnati address is in its conclusion. He invoked memories of three eminent Restoration leaders, John W. McGarvey, Isaac Errett, and David Lipscomb, and committed an irreconcilable error by placing them in identical categories. First, he complimented McGarvey with words written by the eminent Greek scholar, Dr. Joseph Henry Thayer, who said that McGarvey possessed "the most thorough knowledge of the English Bible of any living man: a man who wrote the most splendid commentary of the Book of Acts that has ever been written." Calhoun described the "saintly McGarvey" as one who has defended the church of Christ from destructive criticism.

Calhoun then eulogized Isaac Errett as one who "by his pleasing personality, trenchant pen, and his powerful preaching did more to popularize and propagate the plea of the Disciples than any other man of his generation—the matchless Isaac Errett." It is significant to note that during the Newbern, Tennessee, church trial that Calhoun had testified that the Disciples spoke of Isaac Errett as being "the finest man and if we wanted to send a man or representative among people who knew nothing of us to give them a correct and clear conception of what we really stand for perhaps the best man we could send." It has been brought out in another place in this biography that McGarvey and Errett held polarized positions on instruments of music played in worship. Whereas Errett defended the use of the organ in worship, McGarvey tolerated the playing of the organ in worship to preserve unity and liberty in the fellowship.

Calhoun lastly commended Lipscomb with superlative praise:

> Take another man, who, by his firm stand for the alone-sufficiency and all-sufficiency of the word of God as our rule of faith and practice, did more to preserve our plea from modern ecclesiasticism represented by organized missions, from the fad of federation and from the formalization of Christian worship through the introduction of mechanical instruments of music where the sound was too often substituted for sense and the motive that prompted the singing of the hired chorus was too often greenback rather than the grace of God in the heart—than perhaps any other man.[4]

Calhoun in summation stated: "It is another fact that nowhere among the churches of Christ are there people found who believe that mechanical instruments of music or humanly organized societies are matters of faith, or that either one or both must be used in order to have the Christian religion in its perfection." Calhoun closed his address with an earnest plea for Christian unity. Calhoun had now retreated in the late years of his life from the dogmatic assertion that he made in his deposition in the Newbern church trial that it would be just as wrong to divide a church by opposing the playing of the organ during worship as it would be to endorse the playing of the organ in the worship. Both McGarvey and Calhoun would not accept the fact that in most cases that it was indeed the use of the organ that caused church splits.

There is little, if anything, that Calhoun said in his address in the Westminster Church on Price Hill which could not have been accepted by Records and his conservative brethren. Today some Independent Christian Churches choose not to use the organ as a matter of preference. Calhoun seemingly was unaware of the inconsistencies and contradictions when he placed the three Restoration giants in the same fellowship in his Seminary address: "neither of the three men whom we have mentioned believed that either humanly devised missionary societies or mechanical instruments of music were any part of the inspired service and worship of God, nor was either a matter of faith."

As a matter of fact, Errett disapproved of the organ only if its presence caused a disturbance in the church. Errett maintained that a church which harmoniously chose to adopt the organ in the worship could do so without violating any scriptural commandment or precedent. McGarvey contended that to divide a church over the presence of an organ in the meeting house was a worse evil than its presence. We are unable, even in the case of the beloved John W. McGarvey, to escape the "old saw" that "two wrongs never make a right." Errett and McGarvey endorsed the missionary society and promoted the society with great zeal. David Lipscomb condemned, without equivocation, both the human society and the organ as alien to the Scriptures. Calhoun seemed to have been making an effort to convince students in the Cincinnati Bible Seminary that the three men were in complete agreement among themselves and with the likes of Records and Calhoun. And in personal application, this may have very well been the case with Calhoun.

Unwittingly Calhoun set his own trap by representing himself as being for "everybody some" and for "everything a little" while at the same time claiming to be a "man of the Book." As a matter of fact, Calhoun's position on the organ and the missionary society exactly matched that of Isaac Errett. And to Errett's pleasing plausibility, Calhoun presented his own implausible "unanswerable argument" which is convincing only to those who wish to be convinced by it.

That Calhoun placed David Lipscomb, Isaac Errett and John W. McGarvey in the same religious body in his Cincinnati address is clearly unacceptable. Lipscomb eventually had ceased to address Errett on points of christian doctrine through the *Advocate* when he became convinced it was useless to do so. Calhoun also had a short memory in his eulogies of McGarvey and Lipscomb. Lipscomb had confronted both McGarvey and Calhoun in 1904 in Lexington when they gave their depositions in the Newbern church trial. Lipscomb deplored the lawsuit at the outset and strove to avoid the legal encounter. He urged the Newbern church members, who objected to the organ, to give up the church property in lieu of going to law. Lipscomb made a special overture to G. N. Tillman, an elder of the Vine Street Christian Church and a prominent Nashville attorney, to join with him to bring the disputants together to work out an amicable settlement to forestall the lawsuit. Tillman, who represented the "organ crowd" and while deprecating the church scandal, said that he favored a legal decision to determine the property rights in the case. Lipscomb failed to bring the two groups together since they were bent on having their day in court.

The testimony of McGarvey and Calhoun in the Newbern lawsuit was patently self contradictory. Both objected to instruments of music being made a part of Christian worship. Both deplored dividing a church over the issue. However, here the both of them were lending their voices to a bitterly fought lawsuit over the property right of a church. Neither McGarvey nor Calhoun held membership in an "organ church" at the time.

The court decision in favor of the "organ group" in the Newbern trial was a sore disappointment to Lipscomb. In answer to a question put to Lipscomb by P. R. Slater how Lipscomb could justify his personal presence in court, Lipscomb replied it was the duty of the Christian to tell the truth as the Apostle Paul did when he was called before the Jewish Sanhedrin and Caesar's tribunal. Lipscomb kept the *Advocate* readers informed of the history and course of the lawsuit, the settlement, and his thinking on the matter.[5]

For David Lipscomb, the Newbern church "take-over" was one more betrayal of the Restoration plea by Christian Church leaders. This is reflected in a statement that Lipscomb made in the *Advocate* printed March 2, 1905, about a month before Judge Cooper's decision in the Newbern lawsuit. In the article, Lipscomb addressed J. B. Briney who had been a principal witness in the Newbern case. With no direct reference to the lawsuit, Lipscomb wrote about Briney that "over twenty years ago he convinced me that he was not a fair and just man." And Lipscomb went on to say in connection with Briney: "I published that he and Calhoun said they would worship with the burning of incense or auricular confession as practiced by the Roman Catholic Church if they were not required to do anything they believed was wrong." We must say, however, this statement attributed to Briney and Calhoun was hardly more than an exaggerated hyperbole calculated to illustrate a religious position. The statement actually throws no additional light on Calhoun's thinking. When Lipscomb was once persuaded that a respondent sought a personal victory at the cost of truth, he would no longer dignify that person by addressing him in the *Advocate*. However, the record shows that Lipscomb questioned the judgment of Calhoun between 1896 and 1900, but not his honesty.

There is no evidence that Lipscomb and Calhoun had other personal exchanges after the 1900 unpleasantries arising over Calhoun's "unanswerable argument" defense of instrumental music. We pause to wonder what must have been running through the mind of the aged Lipscomb as he listened to Dr. Hall

Laurie Calhoun, lately of Harvard University, testify in the Newbern lawsuit. He was perhaps lamenting that such a talented person was now lost to the "organ and society" Christian Church with all the implications.

Though he did not say so, the Newbern lawsuit confirmed Lipscomb's belief that division in the ranks of the disciples had become an established fact. The church split in 1903 in Henderson, Tennessee, over the organ was a local matter and created limited attention. The Newbern trial was another matter. The leaders of the church of Christ and Christian Church were in direct confrontation. Indeed John W. McGarvey, the *Christian Standard,* and the College of the Bible were on one side; and David Lipscomb, the *Gospel Advocate,* and the Nashville Bible School stood on the other side. The Christian Church won a lawsuit in 1905 and a church building, but a part of the price was the loss of the local church. Churches of Christ were put on immediate notice that the Christian Church valued the organ more than Christian unity.

David Lipscomb never called for a separation of the church of Christ from the Christian Church, but the division did occur in a totally unexpected fashion. The Nashville *American* published a correspondence between David Lipscomb and S. D. N. North. North was the Director of the Bureau of the United States Religious Census. North wrote Lipscomb to determine, if indeed, the church of Christ and the Christian Church formed two distinct and separate religious bodies. Lipscomb's response certified that the church of Christ and the Christian did indeed form two distinct and separate religious bodies. The action taken by Lipscomb and his associates resulted in separate listings for the two churches in the U. S. Religious Census for 1906.[6] Although, the religious census was not published until 1910. The disciples neglected to recognize the government action then and have had little to say about it since. Strange indeed is the fact that as Calhoun spoke in Cincinnati in the spring of 1927, the Christian Church even then was on the verge of another division in its ranks. This time, however, the fight centered around the UCMS and the International Convention. This story has been told in another place.

In spite of Calhoun's indecision regarding the organ, he was not troubled by the issue until near the end of his life. When he began preaching for the Providence Christian Church in Jessamine County, Kentucky, in 1907, the organ had not been introduced. In 1910, a group in the Providence Church, who favored the organ, canvassed the membership with a petition to obtain favorable signatures. Mrs. Alama Browning, still living in Lexington, recalls the Sunday the organ was voted into the Providence Christian Church. Her father, George Downing, was then an elder in the Providence Christian Church. Her mother, who was a Baptist, voted for the organ. One elder, William Marrs, who was scheduled to preside at the Lord's Table that Sunday morning, instead took the floor to oppose the organ and then walked out of the building in protest. Margaret Marrs, a retired Lexington school teacher and granddaughter of William Marrs, related the occasion. Marrs and his family probably worshipped with the Chestnut Street Christian Church where McGarvey had gone in 1903. Mrs. Browning, then nineteen years old, was the only person in the congregation who could play the organ and the first to do so in the Providence Christian Church. Mrs. Browning remembers that Calhoun neither publicly nor privately objected to the introduction of the organ into the Providence church then or thereafter.

Calhoun did not accept any further invitations to address any similar groups in the Christian Church after the 1927 Cincinnati address. Orvel Crowder, in a letter dated January 4, 1985, wrote that Records had, on several occasions, extended invitations to Calhoun to deliver lectures in the Cincinnati Bible Seminary. He sought to persuade Calhoun to join him on the faculty of the Seminary following Calhoun's departure from Henderson and his resulting illness in the spring of 1926. Calhoun invariably replied that without the approval of the church of Christ leaders in Nashville it was not expedient for him to do so. Calhoun by then had learned the "time delayed" lesson that David Lipscomb and James A. Harding had tried to teach him in 1896 that he would be leaving a wrong impression by going among the Disciples for speaking engagements. Calhoun never seemed to understand the incorrigible stand of the Christian Church on "expedient innovations," nor have some interested leaders in the churches of Christ since. And with the emergence of each new "unity movement" such as the Murch-Witty effort in the late 1930's and early 1940's, each has died away in the din of battle. Such is apt to happen to the 1984, so named, "Joplin Summit" meeting.

Calhoun did not preach in the vicinities where he had previously preached for the Christian Church. It could be that he was not invited. However, Calhoun did preach for the Murray,

Kentucky, church of Christ on the subject of evolution where he had preached in 1894 for the "organ church." Alonzo Williams, a well known and highly respected preacher for the church of Christ, was preaching for the Murray church of Christ at this last visit of Calhoun to preach in Murray.

F. L. Rowe's criticism of Calhoun was not an isolated incident. Calhoun began his radio ministry with the Central church of Christ in January 1928. James A. Allen, editor of the *Gospel Advocate* at the time, wrote a severe criticism against Calhoun in the *Advocate*. Allen had been invited to speak over radio station WLAC which was canceled. He was prepared to deliver a rebuttal sermon in response to a sermon which Dr. James I. Vance, minister of the Nashville First Presbyterian Church, had preached on baptism over radio station WSM.[7] Dr. Vance had made no reference to the Central Church radio ministry. Personal letters were exchanged over the matter heretofore undivulged. N. B. Hardeman and M. C. Kurfees both wrote letters to Allen concerning the controversy between Allen and Calhoun. Allen complained in a letter addressed to Calhoun that A. M. Burton had shown prejudice against him by circulating a letter of criticism directed against Allen, which some unidentified person had written to Burton. Kurfees thought it had been ill advised, in the first place, for Allen to have written the announcement for the *Advocate* readers.[8]

Allen published a later announcement in the *Advocate* stating that "Brother Hall L. Calhoun has repeated the invitation to me to preach in the pulpit of the Central church of Christ in this city, with the distinct understanding that barring offensive personalities, I am free to preach anything I believe Jesus wants me to preach."[9] Allen voiced his approval of Calhoun's judgment in the matter which brought an end to the unpleasant situation. Calhoun found a growing support among distinguished church leaders such as A. M. Burton. No other adverse comments directed against Calhoun appeared thereafter in the *Advocate,* or in any other publication of the churches of Christ. And Calhoun was completely ignored by the Disciples after he abandoned their ranks.

The observation was made at another place in this biography that Hall Laurie Calhoun grew up as a very private and complex person which personality he carried with him all his life. We seem to know where Calhoun stood on scriptural matters, but we are never exactly certain. He never issued a single disclaimer to his "unanswerable argument" in defense of the use of instruments of music in worship or the missionary society. Calhoun held membership in "organ churches" for most of his adult life and preached for them without qualm of conscience until the last nine years of his life. Calhoun seemed to be saying in the end that a tree is known by the fruit it bears and that the organ and missionary society had been allowed through human error to become corrupting influences in the church by improper use and mismanagement.

And now for a final word to the reader who has been exposed to verifiable facts of the earthly sojourn of Hall Laurie Calhoun. Most of what is known about Calhoun is accessible through the religious periodicals cited in this book. And the living memories of Calhoun, by those who knew him in life, are as diverse as if he had lived his life in widely separated places among different people in the world at different times. No one person ever witnessed Calhoun evolve in any one place or in one particular era so as to be able to say "I know the man." His life spanned the post Stone-Campbell period which recorded the radical separation of the Christian Church twice in twenty years. Calhoun's role in the Christian Church may be compared to the "flawed hero" in a Greek tragedy who perished in the splendor of his ideas not shared by others.

The authors began this study in a search of the real Hall Laurie Calhoun, and they are reasonably confident that they have succeeded in good measure. And we leave Calhoun an omnibus of paradoxes, enigmas, complexities, and self-contradictions, over whom the reader now is at liberty to ponder.

ENDNOTES

CHAPTER ONE: American Calhouns

1. Hall Laurie Calhoun, *Personal Family Genealogy,* in possession of Hall Calhoun Crowder, written by Hall Laurie Calhoun.

2. Hall Laurie Calhoun, *Our Family History in Seven Chapters,* "Scottish and Irish," Cleveland, Tennessee, 1929.

3. *Family History,* "Early American," and "Tennessean Ancient," Cleveland, Tennessee, 1929.

4. *Personal Family Genealogy.*

5. *Family History,* Chapter VI, "Tennessean Medieval," Cleveland, Tennessee, 1929.

6. *Personal Family Genealogy,* ibid.

7. Goodspeed, "Henry County," *History of Tennessee* (Nashville: The Goodspeed Publishing Company., 1887), p. 829; W. O. Inman, Henry County Historian, letter dated November 17, 1981.

8. *Family History,* Chapter V, "Tennessean Medieval," Cleveland, Tennessee, May 10, 1929.

9. GA, 1930, p. 102.

10. *Personal Family Genealogy,* ibid.

11. W. T. Shelton, printed newspaper copy of the obituary of James C. Calhoun. Source is not identified. In possession of Margaret Lee Calhoun Seely.

12. Hall Laurie Calhoun, *My Life in Seven Chapters,* Chapter One, written for the information of his wife also to be preserved for his descendants, Cleveland, Tennessee, 1929.

13. *Ibid,* Chapter Three, "Man."

14. Samuel Cole Williams, *Beginnings of West Tennessee* (Johnson City, Tennessee: Watagua Press, 1930), p. 187.

15. GA, 1930, p. 75.

16. GA, 1903, p. 76.

17. GA, 1930, p. 102.

18. *Ibid.*

19. GA, 1887, p. 693.

20. GA, 1930, p. 102.

21. Mary Ettah Crowder, *Personal Memoirs* in possession of Hall Crowder Calhoun.

22. GA, 1899, p. 698.

23. Fred I. Hatler, Sr., Information from city and church records, and tombstone epitaphs in a letter dated September 6, 1981, Martin, Tennessee.

CHAPTER TWO: Heritage and Education of Hall Laurie Calhoun

1. William E. Tucker and Lester G. McAllister, *Journey in Faith* (St. Louis: the Bethany Press), p. 49.

2. Winfred Ernest Garrison and Alfred T. DeGroot, *The Disciples of Christ: A History* (St. Louis: The Bethany Press, 1948), pp. 72, 73.

3. Charles William Dabney, *Universal Education in the South,* 2 vols. (Chapel Hill: University of North Carolina Press, 1936), vol. 1, pp. 47–50.

Endnotes **225**

4. Barksdale Hamlett, *History of Education in Kentucky,* Frankfort, Kentucky: Department of Education, 1914, pp. 3, 24, 27.

5. *Beginnings of West Tennessee,* pp. 174–177.

6. Goodspeed, *ibid.*, pp. 814–830.

7. Contained in letter July 13, 1981, written by W. O. Inman, Historian of Henry County, Tennessee.

8. The Mayfield *Monitor,* Mayfield, Kentucky, 1877.

9. Contained in a letter dated October 7, 1981, written by Rebel C. Forrester, Historian of Obion County, Tennessee.

10. *Kentucky University Alumni Book,* p. 50.

11. Information provided by Dorothea Eloise Calhoun Elder.

12. W. O. Inman letter, dated July 13, 1981. See above.

13. Personal Memoirs of Mary Ettah Calhoun Crowder.

14. Dwight E. Stevenson, *Lexington Theological Seminary* (St. Louis: The Bethany Press, 1964), pp. 11–21.

15. Stevenson, p. 380.

16. W. C. Morro, *Brother McGarvey* (St. Louis: The Bethany Press, 1940), p. 113.

17. Dwight E. Stevenson, *The Bacon College Story* (Lexington, Kentucky: The College of the Bible, 1962), p. 7.

18. *Ibid.*, pp. 27–30.

19. *Ibid.*, p. 30.

20. *Ibid.*, pp. 44–49.

21. Morro, pp. 116–117.

22. Morro, pp. 118–126.

23. *Lexington Theological Seminary,* pp. 60–72.

24. Biographical data written by Hall Laurie Calhoun in a group of

poems titled "My Wife's Life in Seven Chapters," Cleveland, Tennessee, 1929.

CHAPTER THREE: The Progress of a Preacher

1. GA, 1887, p. 693.

2. GA, June 6, 1888, p. 15.

3. GA, 1935, p. 996.

4. Morro, p. 222.

5. GA, 1894, p. 383.

6. GA, 1894, p. 550.

7. GA, 1894, p. 630.

8. Paducah *Daily News,* March 28, 1895; Fred Newman, *The Story of Paducah* (Paducah, Kentucky: Young Printing Company, 1927, 1980), pp. 204, 205.

9. GA, 1896, p. 461

10. GA, 1896, p. 440.

11. GA, 1897, p. 616.

12. GA, 1897, p. 760.

13. GA, 1897, p. 776.

14. GA, 1898, p. 752.

15. GA, 1899, p. 709.

16. GA, 1900, p. 293.

CHAPTER FOUR: Georgia Robertson Christian College

.. J. M. Powell and Mary Nelle Powers, *N.B.H.* (Nashville, Tennessee: *Gospel Advocate* Company, 1964) pp. 131, 132.

2. New College, Calhoun dedication sermon, GA, 1897, p. 760.

3. Georgia Robertson Christian College Catalog (1900–01).

4. *Ibid.*

5. GA, 1901, pp. 706–708, 712.

6. *Ibid.*

7. Newbern, Tennessee, Trial Depositions, see chapter six.

8. GA, 1900, p. 760.

9. GA, 1903, p. 113.

10. GA, 1903, p. 53.

11. GA, 1903, p. 53.

12. GA, 1903, p. 15.

13. GA, 1903, pp. 81, 82.

14. GA, 1903, p. 77.

15. A letter by Hall L. Calhoun to John W. McGarvey, August 10, 1901. See Edward Ormand Hale, *A Man in Controversy Hall Laurie Calhoun*, B.D. Thesis, Lexington Theological Seminary, 1978, for personal letters written to John W. McGarvey and Mark Collis.

16. A letter by Hall L. Calhoun to Mark Collis, August 15, 1901.

CHAPTER FIVE: Hall of Ivy

1. *Journey in Faith*, p. 371.

2. A letter by Hall L. Calhoun to John W. McGarvey, November 16, 1901.

3. Haskell B. Curry, "Memoirs of S. S. Curry," *Today's Speech*, VII, No. 4 (November, 1959), pp. 7ff.

4. *Lexington Theological Seminary*, p. 123.

5. *Addresses* delivered at the observance of the 100th Anniversary of the Establishment of the Harvard Divinity School, Cambridge,

Massachusetts, October 5, 1916 (Cambridge: Harvard University, 1917).

6. George Foot Moore, *Encyclopedia Judaica,* vol. 12, (1971), p. 294; *Dictionary of American Biography,* pp. 124-126.

7. CS, 1903, pp. 1076- 1101.

8. Memoirs of Mary Ettah Crowder.

9. Marie Louise Baldwin: *Notable American Women 1607-1950, A Biographical Dictionary,* Edward T. Jones, et al (Belknap Press of Harvard University, 1971), pp. 86-88.

10. Personal Memoirs of Mary Ettah Crowder.

CHAPTER SIX: From Professor to President

1. *The Crimson,* 1904, Kentucky University, vol. VI, June, 1904.

2. *The Autobiography of J. W. McGarvey,* (Lexington, Kentucky: The College of the Bible, 1960), pp. 17, 18.

3. Newbern, Tennessee Trial Depositions, April 1903-January 1905, Compiled and Arranged for Library Use by H. Leo Boles, Shelved in the Gospel Advocate office, Nashville, Tennessee.

4. CS, 1905, p. 905; CE, 1905, p. 544.

5. Morro, pp. 240, 241.

6. *Lexington Theological Seminary,* pp. 137, 138.

7. George W. Bushnell, *The Development of the College of the Bible Through Controversy* (unpublished B.D. Thesis, The College of the Bible, 1934), p. 43.

8. *Lexington Theological Seminary,* pp. 140-149.

9. *Ibid.*, p. 151.

10. Personal Diary of Hall Laurie Calhoun; *History of Providence Christian Church,* (Lexington, Kentucky: Providence Christian Church, 1980).

11. Hall L. Calhoun, "New England Letter," *The Christian-Evangelist* (October 2, 1902), p. 689.

12. From Reports of Kentucky. *Christian Missionary Convention*, participations of Hall Laurie Calhoun listed for 1914, 1915, 1917, 1918.

13. Winfred E. Garrison, *Christian Unity and Disciples of Christ* (St. Louis: The Bethany Press, 1955), p. 114.

14. *Addresses* delivered at the Observance of the 100th Anniversary.

CHAPTER SEVEN: A Firestorm in the Bluegrass

1. CS, 1917, pp. 764, 765, 769. The controversy within the College of the Bible was introduced to the Christian Church constituency on March 31, 1917, in the *Christian Standard* and is noted in the face of the chapter unless otherwise indicated.

2. Responses to the allegations made in the *Christian Standard* were printed in the official publication of the College of the Bible, the *Quarterly Bulletin*. Responses to allegations made against President R. H. Crossfield, Professor E. E. Snoddy, Professor A. W. Fortune, and Professor George Henry appeared in the issues of the bulletin for May 1917, August 1917, January 1918, February 1918, and April 1918. The *Christian Evangelist* favored the accused and documentation appears in the face of the chapter with a citation from the *Christian Century*. M. C. Kurfees informed the readers of the *Gospel Advocate* during the course of the proceedings in 1917, pp. 547, 618, 622, 766. Dwight E. Stevenson, *Lexington Theological Seminary* (St. Louis, Missouri: The Bethany Press, 1964), pp. 165–207; this is the only complete chronological presentation of the 1917 controversy in the College of the Bible.

3. CS, *Ibid.*, p. 765.

4. *Ibid.*

5. *Ibid.*, p. 793

6. *Christian Century,* 1917, pp. 6, 7.

7. W. C. Bower, *Through the Years* (Lexington, Kentucky: Transylvania College, 1954), pp. 36-44.

8. See the "Controversy File" on the 1917 College of the Bible proceedings, Transylvania College Library.

9. Stevenson, *Lexington Theological Seminary* pp. 187, 199.

CHAPTER EIGHT: On Campbell's Mountain

1. *Lexington Theological Seminary,* pp. 168–200.

2. CS, 1917, p. 1708.

3. W. K. Woolery, *Bethany Years: The Founding of Old Bethany* (Huntington, West Virginia: Standard Printing and Publishing Company, 1941), pp. 204–206.

4. CS, 1917, p. 1116.

5. CS, 1917, p. 1368.

6. Minutes of the Board of Trustees for Bethany College (1917–1925). The location of the documentation will follow the dates for the respective meeting written into the Minutes.

7. Woolery, pp. 191, 192.

8. CS, 1902, p. 1267.

9. CS, 1917, p. 185.

10. *Lexington Theological Seminary,* p. 140.

11. Woolery, pp. 211–214.

12. CS, 1919, p. 1053.

13. Board Minutes of Bethany College. See above.

14. *Ibid.*

CHAPTER NINE: Home Again in Tennessee

1. Minutes of the Board of Trustees of Bethany College (1917–1925). See above.

2. Personal Memoirs of Mary Ettah Calhoun.

3. John Barclay, *What Ought To Be Can Be* (St. Louis: Bethany Press, 1966), pp. 11–13.

4. The named and dated correspondence between Hall Laurie Calhoun and N. B. Hardeman referred to in this chapter is located in the personal Hardeman-Calhoun file in possession of Mary Nelle Hardeman Powers, Memphis, Tennessee.

5. Freed-Hardeman College Bulletin, April 1925.

6. GA, 1925, p. 99.

7. References to the *Gospel Advocate* dated in the chapter are not repeated unless otherwise noted.

8. Freed-Hardeman College Bulletin. See above.

9. GA, 1925, p. 439.

10. CS, 1925, p. 506; *Christian-Evangelist*, 1925, p. 246.

11. *The Tennessee Christian,* June, 1926, pp. 2, 3, 6.

12. CS, 1870, p. 252.

13. Calhoun-Hardeman correspondence. See above.

14. Unpublished article of N. B. Hardeman titled, "H. L. Calhoun and Freed-Hardeman College," and initialed by N. B. H., in possession of Mary Nelle Hardeman Powers. See above.

CHAPTER TEN: The Crowning Years

1. Hardeman-Calhoun Correspondence file. See above.

2. GA, 1926, p. 591.

3. Herman Norton, *Tennessee Christians* (Nashville, Tennessee: Reed and Company), 1971, pp. 290. ff.

4. Personal information provided by Dorothea Eloise Calhoun Elder.

5. GA, 1926, pp. 1185, 1241; GA, 1927; p. 9.

6. Lacy Huffman Elrod, *A Study of a Downtown Church*, George Peabody College for Teachers, M.A. Thesis, June 19, 1931, Nashville, Tennessee, pp. 1–140.

7. GA, 1928, p. 892.

8. *Babbler,* college newspaper, David Lipscomb College, June 27, 1927, p. 1.

9. GA, 1927, p. 940.

10. Stephen J. Corey, *Fifty Years of Attack and Controversy* (St. Louis: Christian Board of Education, 1953), pp. 53, 54.

11. William S. Banowsky, *The Mirror of a Movement* (Dallas: Christian Publishing Company, 1965), pp. 68, 79, 81.

12. Orvel Calhoun Crowder, personal letter, dated April 9, 1983.

CHAPTER ELEVEN: The Aftermath

1. Bower, *Through the Years,* p. 39.

2. CS, 1917, p. 1526.

3. CS, 1917, p. 1406.

4. "Christian College Bible League," The College of the Bible (*Quarterly Bulletin,* X (No. 2), December, 1917.

5. James DeForest Murch, *Christians Only* (Cincinnati: Standard Publishing Company), pp. 244, 255.

6. "Controversy File," Transylvania University Library.

7. George Hunton Williams, *The Harvard Divinity School* (Boston: The Beacon Press, 1954), pp. 168ff.

8. *The Disciples of Christ: A History,* p. 381.

9. CS, 1917, p. 1406.

10. Alonzo Willard Fortune, *The Disciples in Kentucky* (The Convention of Christian Churches in Kentucky, 1932). p. 355.

11. *Journey in Faith,* pp. 341, 342.

12. *Ibid.,* pp. 344ff.

13. CS, 1922, pp. 109–120.

14. *Journey in Faith,* p. 382.

15. Murch, p. 256, 257.

16. William E. Tucker, *J. H. Garrison and Disciples of Christ* (St. Louis: The Bethany Press, 1964), p. 212.

17. *The Bible Banner,* August, 1939, p. 6.

18. CS, 1946, pp. 561, 562.

19. CS, 1947, pp. 402, 451.

20. *Lexington Theological Seminary,* p. 292.

21. *Journey in Faith,* p. 421.

22. *Ibid.,* p. 444.

23. *Ibid.,* pp. 446, 447.

24. Keith E. Clark, "Next Year: A Decision on Unity," *The Disciple,* March, 1984, pp. 18, 19.

CHAPTER TWELVE: The Full Turn of the Circle

1. CS, 1909, pp. 2233, 2246.

2. CS, pp. 3277, 3278; 3412, 3413.

3. CS, 1922, pp. 109–120; 199, 200.

4. *Christian Century,* 1917, p. 6.

5. CS, 1922, pp. 3455, 3456.

6. MH, IV, vol. 1, 1861, pp. 581, 582.

7. *Lard's Quarterly,* March, 1864, p. 332.

8. Arthur V. Murrell, *The Effects of Exclusivism in the Separation of the Churches of Christ,* Dissertation for the degree of Doctor of Philosophy, Graduate School of Vanderbilt University, May, 1972, p. 92.

9. *Ibid.*

10. MH, 1864, pp. 510–514; MH, 1865, pp. 38, 88, 115, 182, 186.

11. CS, 1870, pp. 130, 140, 148.

12. GA, 1873, pp. 854–856.

13. P. H. Canary, transcript, Transylvania University, September 20, 1917; Bethany College alumni data.

14. *Lexington Theological Seminary,* pp. 198, 199.

15. "An Appreciation of the Life of Ralph Records," *The Founder and Builder,* Voice of the Louisville Bible College, June, 1983.

16. William Clayton Bower, *Central Christians Church: Lexington, Kentucky* (St. Louis: 1962), p. 43.

17. *Through the Years,* pp. 38–43.

18. Murch, p. 241.

19. CS, 1916, p. 1047.

20. CS, 1925, pp. 506, 507.

EPILOGUE:

1. GA, 1927, pp. 636, 637.

2. *Ibid.,* pp. 628, 629.

3. *Ibid.,* pp. 651, 652.

4. *Ibid.,* pp. 733, 736.

5. *Ibid.,* 1904, p. 772; *Ibid.,* 1905, p. 153; pp. 312, 313; pp. 408, 409; pp. 440, 441; p. 456; pp. 472, 473; p. 489; pp. 568, 569; p. 601; p. 648; p. 680.

6. *Ibid.*, 1907, p. 457.

7. *Ibid.*, 1928, p. 869.

8. M. C. Kurfees in a personal letter to H. L. Calhoun dated Louisville, Kentucky, November 10, 1928.

9. GA, 1928, p. 1041.

Bibliography

BOOKS
  I. Religious Journals Used Multiple Times with Explanation of Abbreviation Used.
    Bible Banner—No abbreviation used
    Christian Century—No abbreviation used
    Christian Standard—CS
    Firm Foundation—No abbreviation used
    Gospel Advocate—GA
    Millennial Harbinger—No abbreviation used

  II. Personal Memoirs, Letters, Records, and Conversations of the Hall Laurie Calhoun Family.
    Calhoun, Hall Laurie:
      Personal Family Genealogy of the Calhoun Family.
      Our Family History in Seven Chapters: "Scottish"; "Early American"; "Tennessean Ancient"; "Tennessean Medival." Cleveland, Tennessee, 1929.
      My Life in Seven Chapters: "Boy"; "Man"; "Lover"; "Husband"; "Father"; "Friend." Cleveland, Tennessee, 1929.
      My Wife's Life in Seven Chapters: "A Picture"; "First Sight"; "Engagement"; "Wedding"; "Wife." Cleveland, Tennessee, 1929.
      Records of Ministerial Work: Nicholasville Christian Church (1904–1906); Providence Christian Church (1907–1917); Belmont church of Christ and Central church of Christ, (1927–1933).
    Conversation with Dorothea Eloise Calhoun Elder, Nashville, Tennessee.

Conversation with Margaret Lee Calhoun Seely, Nashville, Tennessee.

Crowder, Orvel Calhoun:
Personal letters dated Enid, Oklahoma: April 9, 1983; April 22, 1983; October 14, 1983; December 7, 1984; "Hall Laurie Calhoun—A Memoir."

Personal Family Memoirs of Mary Ettah Stacey Calhoun.

Personal Family Memoirs of Mary Ettah Calhoun Crowder.

III. BOOKS

Addresses Delivered at the Observance of the 100th Anniversary of the Establishment of the Harvard Divinity School. Cambridge: Harvard University, 1917.

Banowsky, William S. *The Mirror of A Movement.* Dallas, Texas: Christian Publishing Company, 1964.

Barclay, John. *What Ought To Be Can Be.* Saint Louis: Bethany Press, 1954.

Bower, William Clayton. *Central Christian Church,* Lexington, Kentucky. Saint Louis: The Bethany Press, 1962.
Through The Years. Lexington, Kentucky: Transylvania College, 1954.

Corey, Stephen J. *Fifty Years of Attack and Controversy.* Saint Louis: Christian Board of Education, 1953.

Dabney, Charles William. *Universal Education in the South,* 2 vols. Chapel Hill: University of North Carolina Press,

Fortune, Alonzo Willard. The *Disciples in Kentucky.* The Convention of Christian Churches in Kentucky, 1932.

Garrison, Winfred E. *Christian Unity and the Disciples of Christ.* Saint Louis: Bethany Press, 1948.

Goodspeed. "Henry County." *History of Tennessee.* Nashville: The Goodspeed Publishing Company, 1887.

Hamlett, Barksdale. *History of Education in Kentucky.* Frankfort, Kentucky: Department of Education, 1914.

McGarvey, John William. *The Autobiography of J. W. McGarvey.* The College of the Bible, 1960.

Morro, W. C. *Brother McGarvey.* Saint Louis: The Bethany Press, 1940.

Murch, James De Forest. *Christians Only:* Cincinnati: Standard Publishing Company, 1962.

Newman, Fred. *The Story of Paducah.* Paducah, Kentucky: Young Printing Company, 1927.

Norton, Herman. *Tennessee Christians.* Nashville, Tennessee: Reed and Company, 1971.

Powell, J. M., and Mary Nelle Hardeman Powers. N.B.H., Nashville, Tennessee: Gospel Advocate Company, 1964.

Stevenson, Dwight E. *The Bacon College Story*. Lexington, Kentucky: The College of the Bible, 1962.
Lexington Theological Seminary. Saint Louis: The Bethany Press, 1964.
Tucker, William E. *J. H. Garrison and Disciples of Christ*. Saint Louis: The Bethany Press, 1964.
Tucker, William E., and Lester G. McAllister. *Journey in Faith*. Saint Louis: The Bethany Press, 1975.
Williams, George Hunston. *The Harvard Divinity School*. Boston Beacon Press, 1954.
Williams, Samuel Cole. *Beginnings of West Tennessee*. Johnson City, Tennessee: Watagua Press, 1930.
Woolery, W. K. *Bethany Years: The Founding of Old Bethany*. Huntington, West Virginia: The Standard Printing and Publishing Company, 1941.
Wright, John D. Jr., *Trasylvania: Tutor to the West*. Lexington: University Press of Kentucky, 1975.

IV. Journals, Magazines, and Printed Materials
Clark, Keith. "Next Year: A Decision on Unity." *The Disciple,* (March, 1984), 18, 19.
College of the *Bible Quarterly* Bulletin, 8, No. 2. (May, 1917); 8, Vol. 4 (August, 1917); 10, No. 2. (December, 1917); 9, No. 2 (January, 1918); No. 2. (February, 1918, A supplement; 10, No. 1 (October, 1918).
Crimson, 1904.
Curry, Haskell B. "Memoirs of S. S. Curry," *Today's Speech,* VII, No. 4 (November, 1959), 7, 8.
Dictionary of American Biography. Ed. Dumas Malone, New York: Charles Scribner's & Sons, 1934, pp. 124–126.
Encyclopedia Judaica, 1971, III, 294.
History of the Providence Christian Church. Lexington, Kentucky, 1980.
Kentucky University Alumnus Book.
Notable American Women (1607–1950), A Biographical Dictionary, Eds. Edward T. Jones, et al. Belknap Press of Harvard University, 1971. pp. 86, 88.
Reports of the Kentucky Christian Missionary Society, 1914, 1915, 1917, 1918.
Tennessee Christian.

V. Unpublished Manuscripts and Other Records
"Board Minutes of the Board of Trustees (1917–1925)." Bethany College, Bethany, West Virginia.
Bushnell, George W. *The Development of the College of Bi-*

ble Through Controversy. Unpublished B.D. Thesis: The College of the Bible, 1934.

Elrod, Lacy Huffman. *A Study of a Downtown Church*. Unpublished M.A. Thesis: George Peabody College for Teachers, 1931.

Hale, Edward Ormond. *A Man in Controversy*. Unpublished B.D. Thesis: Lexington Theological Seminary, 1978.

Hardeman, N. B. "H. L. Calhoun and Freed-Hardeman College." N. B. Hardeman Personal Files, in possession of Mary Nelle Hardeman Powers, Memphis, Tennessee.

"Longer Cathechism on the Attack on the College of the Bible." Controversy File. Lexington, Kentucky, Transylvania College Library.

Murrell, Arthur V. *The Effects of Exclusivism in the Separation of the Churches of Christ*. Dissertation for Degree of the Doctor of Philosophy. Graduate School of Vanderbilt University, 1972.

Tennessee, Church Trial, April, 1903 to January, 1905. Compiled and Arranged for Library Use by H. Leo Boles. Gospel Advocate Office, Nashville, Tennessee.

VI. Newspapers

Babbler. David Lipscomb College Student Newspaper, June 27, 1927.

Mayfield *Monitor,* Mayfield, Kentucky, 1877.

Paducah, Kentucky, *Daily News,* March 28, 1895.

Shelton, W. T. "Obituary." Printed Newspaper Copy not identified in the Possession of Margaret Lee Calhoun Seely, Nashville, Tennessee.

Index

Abilene Christian College, 171
Agassiz Grammar School, 84
Allen, James A., 221
American Christian Missionary Society, 182
Associate Presidents (Freed-Hardeman College), 139, 147, 153
The Authorship of the Book of Deuteronomy, 80, 82, 83
Bacon College, 40
Baldwin, Maria Louise, 84
Barclay, John, 138, 139, 197
Barrett, A. B., 176
Battenfield, Benjamin F., 103, 105, 117, 123
Belmont church of Christ, 163
Bethany College, 124-130, 135
Bethurum, George R., 156, 162
"Biblical Criticism," 193-196
Blood River church of Christ, 30
Boswell, Ira M., 160
Bower, William Clayton, 96, 205-207
Bowman, John Bryan, 40-42
Brigance, L. L., 147
Briney, J. B., 109, 119, 120
Broadway Christian Church, 49
Brother McGarvey, 43, 88
Brown, H. A. (Gus), 49
Brown, John T., 95, 183
Browning, Mrs. Alma Downing, 89
Buffalo Seminary, 40, 128
Burton, A. M., 154

Calhoun, Hall Laurie, 26-29
Calhoun, (John Hall, Martha L., Agnes T., James Caldwell, Hall Laurie, Pleasant Hope), 26
Calhoun, John, 53
Calhoun, John Samuel, 24
Calhoun, John Shelton, 24, 31, 32, 37
Calhoun, Martha Louisa, 30, 32
Calhoun, Mary Ettah, 53
Calhoun, Nancy Seely, 24
Campbell Institute, 119, 181
"camp meetings," 27
Canary, Peyton H., 109, 110, 118, 120
Cane Ridge revival, 39
Cornelison, Peral Mae, 111, 118, 119
Central church of Christ, 164, 165, 167
Cherry, Lafayette, 44
Christian Century, 111
Christian Church, Henderson, Tennessee, 69-72
Christian College Bible League, 177, 178
Christian-Evangelist, 99
Christian Woman's Board of Missions, 99, 182
Church of Christ, 188-190
Cincinnati Bible Institute, 179
Cincinnati Bible Seminary, 211-215
College of the Bible, 37, 39-42, 47, 48, 72, 73, 91-93, 180
Collis, Mark, 47, 73, 107, 176, 177
Colquhoun, Sir John, 23

Committee of One Thousand Present Their Protest to the International Convention, 185
Conyersville, 25
Conyersville church of Christ, 48
Conyersville Male and Female Academy, 35, 36, 45
Cramblett, T. E., 124, 130, 133
Cramblett, Wilbur H., 138, 187
Crimson Rambler, 110
Crossfield, Richard Henry, 94, 95, 96
Crossfield's circular letter, 105, 107
Crowder, Orvel Calhoun, 173
Culchone (Colquhoun), 23
Curry, Samuel Silas, 77,78, 87
Daughtery, Leonard, 51
David Lipscomb College, 170
DEAN CALHOUN APEALS TO THE BROTHERHOOD, 116-21
"destructive criticism," 81, 83, 203-206
Disciples Divinity House, 181
Doran, Adron, 169
Elam, E. A., 50
Errett, Edwin R., 184
Errett, Isaac, 215
Errett, Russell, 107
Fairhurst, Alfred, 47, 115
Fanning, Tolbert, 97
Foreign Christian Missionary Society, 182
Fortune, Alonzo Willard, 95
Fosdick, Harry Emerson, 139
Franklin, Tennessee, church of Christ, 56, 57
Freed, Arvey Glenn, 57
Freed-Hardeman College, 65, 76, 141-150, 153-156
Georgia Robertson Christian College, 46, 58, 59, 62-64
Goodnight, Cloyd, 133,134, 138
Graham, Robert, 42, 47
Graf-Wellhausen Documentary Hypothesis of the Old Testament, 180, 181
Green, Irving Taylor, 114, 118, 131, 202
Grubbs, Isaiah Boone, 41
Hall, Martha Louisa, 24, 32
Hall, S. H., 161
Hardeman, Nicholas Brodie, 62, 63, 141
Harding, James A., 48, 49
Harmon, Andrew D., 180
Harvard Divinity School, 78-85

Harvard Divinity School Address, 78-80
Harvard University Centennial anniversary, 101, 102
Henderson, Tennessee, Christian Church, 62, 69-72
Hemry, G. W., 120
"heresy trial," 112-116
Hinds, John T., 175, 176
"Independent" Christian Church, 188-190
(Independent) Christian Church and Church of Christ; Christian Church (Disciples of Christ); churches of Christ, 187-89
International Convention of Disciples, 182, 183
International Sunday School Association, 100, 101
Kentucky Christian Missionary Society, 99, 100
Kentucky University, 37, 40, 41
Kurfees, M. C., 65, 144, 146
Lappin, S. S., 95, 131
Lard, Moses Easterly, 42
Lard's Quarterly, 47
Lexington Theological Seminary, 180
Lipscomb, David, 65, 67
Loos, Charles, 47
Martin, T. Q., 149
Marx, Edwin, 111
Mayfield Seminary, 31, 35
McDougle, Ernest Clifton, 50, 71
McGarvey Bible College, 179
McGarvey, John William, 37, 39
McGarvey, John W. Jr., 88
McQuiddy, J. C., 56, 58, 62
Milligan, Robert, 41
"missionary Society," 56
Moore, George Foot, 79
Morrison Hall, 113
Morro, William Charles, 43, 93
Murch, James DeForest, 189, 208
Myhr, A. I., 59
Nashville Bible School, 54-56
National Teachers' Normal and Business College, 63, 75
Newbern, Tennessee, "Church Trial," 54, 89-91, 217-219
New College, 57, 63
"New England Letter," 197
Nicholasville Christian Church, 97

North American Christian Convention, 183, 184
Notes For Memoirs, 88
"Open Letter," 186
"open membership," 182, 183
"organ," 50, 65-67, 199-201
Peabody, Francis Greenwood, 78, 208
Phillips, B. D., 187
Phillips, T. W., 129
Providence Christian Church, 50, 97
Records, Ralph L., 116, 117, 131, 203, 211
The Remains of the Old Latin Translation of Leviticus, 85
Reserve Officers Training Corps, 132, 133
"restructure" of the Disciples of Christ, 187
Robertson, J. F., 63
Russell Street church of Christ, 161, 162
Rutledge, George P., 107
School of Religion (Bethany College), 124, 125, 127, 131, 133, 134
Shaw, Knowles, 62
Sheffer, W. H., 55, 58
Shelton, Martha (Mattie), 48
Shelton, W. T., 25, 29, 36
Smith, E. P., 147
Smith, F. W., 145, 146
Smith, G. Dallas, 71
Snoddy, Elmer Ellsworth, 96
"split personality," 176
Srygley, F. D., 62
Stacey, Huldah Peyton, 43

Stacey, John Cockerel, 43
Stacey, Mary Ettah, 43-45
"Stand Up and Be Counted," 186
St. John, A. A., 70
Student Army Training Corps, 132
Teacher's Quarterly, 166
Tennessee Christian, 151
Tennessee Missionary Society, 197, 198
Tenth Street Christian Church, 31, 53
Transylvanian, 110
Transylvania Seminary, 33, 40
Transylvania University, 94
"unanswerable argument," 65
Union City High School, 36
United Christian Missionary Society, 182, 183
United States Religious Census for 1906, 219
Vawter, C. R. L., 107
Watkins, Maurine Dallas, 110, 118
West Point Academy, 36, 37
West Tennessee Christian College, 63
"What Lies Behind the Camouflage," 121
"Why I Did It?", 151
Willett, Herbert L., 119
Williams Fellow, 101
Williams, John R., 30, 31, 48
Witty, Claude E., 189
Yale Divinity School, 76-78
Yearbook of American Churches, 187
Yellow Fever Cemetery, 32